Also by Leonard Downie Jr.

*Justice Denied: The Case for Reform of the Courts*

*Mortgage on America: The Real Cost of Real Estate Speculation*

*The New Muckrakers: An Inside Look at America's Investigative Reporters*

Also by Robert G. Kaiser

*Cold Winter, Cold War*

*Russia: The People and the Power*

*Great American Dreams: A Portrait of the Way We Are* (with Jon Lowell)

*Russia from the Inside* (with Hannah Jopling)

*Why Gorbachev Happened: His Triumphs, His Failure and His Fall*

# THE NEWS
# ABOUT
# THE NEWS

# THE NEWS
# ABOUT
# THE NEWS

*American Journalism in Peril*

Leonard Downie Jr.
*and* Robert G. Kaiser

*Alfred A. Knopf · New York · 2002*

THIS IS A BORZOI BOOK
PUBLISHED BY ALFRED A. KNOPF

www.aaknopf.com

Knopf, Borzoi Books and the colophon are registered
trademarks of Random House, Inc.

Library of Congress Cataloging-in-Publication Data
Downie, Leonard.
The news about the news : American journalism in peril / by
Leonard Downie Jr. and Robert G. Kaiser. — 1st ed.
p.   cm.
Includes bibliographical references and index.
ISBN 0-375-40874-6 (alk. paper)
1. Journalism—United States. 2. Journalists—United States—
Interviews. I. Kaiser, Robert G., [date]. II. Title.
PN4855 .D64 2002
071'.3—dc21        2001037735

Manufactured in the United States of America
Published March 1, 2002
Second Printing, March 2002

*For Don, Ben and all
our colleagues at
the* Washington Post


*And in memory of
Katharine M. Graham
(1917–2001)*

# Contents

# THE NEWS
# ABOUT
# THE NEWS

# Chapter One

# NEWS MATTERS

The story is a legend now, but it really did happen. Early in the morning of June 17, 1972, inside the headquarters of the Democratic National Committee in Washington's Watergate office building, police arrested five men wearing business suits and rubber surgical gloves and carrying cameras and sophisticated bugging devices. The *Washington Post* assigned a longhaired newsroom roustabout named Carl Bernstein and one of the paper's newest reporters, Bob Woodward, to report the story. Over the next two years they unraveled a tangled conspiracy of political spying and dirty tricks, wiretaps, break-ins, secret funds and a criminal cover-up—all orchestrated by President Richard Nixon's White House.

For a long time the *Post* was the only news organization to take Watergate seriously. The Washington establishment brushed the story off, and Nixon's allies put pressure on the *Post* to drop it. But after months of Woodward and Bernstein's revelatory stories, government investigators and then the Congress joined the pursuit. Impeachment proceedings began, and on August 9, 1974, Nixon became the first president of the United States ever to resign his office. Watergate became an example for the ages, a classic case when journalism made a difference.

Good journalism does not often topple a president, but it frequently changes the lives of citizens, both grand and ordinary.

When Robert Hopkins telephoned *Washington Post* columnist Courtland Milloy, he was sixty-five years old, a diabetic on kidney dialysis three times a week and the desperate father of three young children, ages four, five and six. Their mother had abandoned the family soon after the birth of the youngest child and shortly before Hopkins's illnesses had been discovered. When Milloy met the Hopkins family, they were squatters in an abandoned apartment complex in a run-down Washington neighborhood. The children charmed Milloy, as did Hopkins's determination to hold his family together, get his kids off to school and find them something to eat. They were surviving on $566 a month in social security benefits.

"Robert Hopkins says he hopes I can help," Milloy wrote in the *Post*. "With his health deteriorating and his children's needs skyrocketing, he reluctantly places his case before the court of last resort."

After Milloy's column appeared, Hopkins received $10,000 in donations from readers. A widow with a comfortable house invited Hopkins and his children to move in with her. Other readers offered to take the Hopkins children to restaurants and amusement parks, to mentor and tutor them, to buy them clothes. In a second column, Milloy described Hopkins opening letters containing checks and offers of help: " 'Who are these people?' [Hopkins] asked, tears of amazement in his eyes. 'Are they real?' "

Good journalism holds communities together in times of crisis, providing the information and the images that constitute shared experience. When disaster strikes, the news media give readers and viewers something to hold on to—facts, but also explanation and discussion that can help people deal with the unexpected. So on September 11, 2001, and for some time after, Americans remained glued to their televisions, turned in record numbers to online news sites and bought millions of extra copies of their newspapers to help absorb and cope with the horrors of shocking terrorist attacks on the United States. In the weeks that followed, good reporting allowed Americans to participate vicariously in the investigations of the terrorists and the government's planning for retaliation. Journalists could educate Americans about Islamic extremists, the history of Afghanistan, the difficulty of defending the United States against resourceful and suicidal terrorists, and much more. Journalism defined the events of September 11 and their aftermath. In those circumstances the importance of journalism was obvious, and much discussed.

Whether widely noticed or not, good journalism makes a difference somewhere every day. Communities are improved by aggressive, thorough coverage of important, if everyday, subjects like education, transportation, housing, work and recreation, government services and public safety. Exposure of incompetence and corruption in government can change misbegotten policies, save taxpayers money and end the careers of misbehaving public officials. Revelations of unethical business practices can save consumers money or their health. Exploration of the growing reach of computer databases can protect privacy. Disclosure of environmental, health, food and product dangers can save lives. Examination of the ways society cares for the poor, homeless, imprisoned, abused, mentally ill and retarded can give voice to the voiceless. News matters.

In 1999 the *Chicago Tribune* documented the experiences of scores of men sentenced to death in Illinois who had been beaten by police into confessing crimes, had been represented at trial by incompetent attorneys or had been convicted on questionable evidence. Soon after the newspaper published its findings, the governor of Illinois suspended all executions.

Houston television station KHOU began reporting in February 2000 that Ford Explorers equipped with certain kinds of Firestone tires had been involved in dozens of fatal highway accidents. Its reports led to nationwide news coverage, federal investigations and the recall of millions of tires, undoubtedly saving many lives.

The *Star-Ledger* in Newark, investigating the 1998 shooting of four men by New Jersey state police, used the newspaper's lawyers to force the state to disclose records that showed state police had targeted black motorists by using racial profiling. The paper's stories drew national attention to the police practice of drawing up the profiles of "typical" criminals based on race and stopping random suspects based on such profiles. This reporting helped create a national political issue and led to action by both the state and federal governments to reduce the use of profiling.

Salt Lake City television station KIVX and the city's two daily newspapers, the *Salt Lake Tribune* and the *Deseret News,* uncovered corruption in the bidding process that had won the 2002 winter Olympic games for Salt Lake City. The city's Olympics promoters had showered gifts and financial favors on members of the International Olympic Committee and their relatives. This news mushroomed into the biggest scandal in the history of the Olympics and led to changes in bidding for future games. It also shook the pillars of the Salt Lake City community.

The *Oregonian* newspaper in Portland found that many of the 140,954 holders of disabled parking permits in Oregon were not disabled at all but had obtained their permits fraudulently. By using a computer to compare the state's permit records with Social Security Administration data, the newspaper discovered that holders of 13,412 disabled parking permits were dead; able-bodied relatives were renewing and using the dead people's permits to park free at meters. State officials promised a crackdown on abusers and changes in procedures for issuing and renewing permits.

The *Miami Herald* exposed pervasive voter fraud in the 1997 Miami mayoral election. Campaign workers for the mayor and other candidates registered nonresidents at phony addresses in the city, validated absentee ballots for people living outside Miami, punched other voters' absentee ballots without their permission and paid $10 each to poor and homeless people to persuade them to vote. The election result was subsequently overturned in court.

The *Philadelphia Inquirer* revealed in 1998 that police had manipulated their crime records to make the city appear safer than it was in widely publicized FBI statistics. The police erased some crimes from their records entirely, and downgraded robberies, burglaries, car break-ins, stabbings and assaults to minor offenses like "threats," "lost property," "vandalism," "hospital cases" and "disturbances," which are not included in the FBI's accounting of serious crimes. The *Inquirer* reported later that Philadelphia police had also failed to investigate thousands of sexual-assault complaints, rejecting many of them as "unfounded" and hiding others in file drawers. Official investigations and reforms of police procedures followed.

Little Rock's *Arkansas Democrat-Gazette* brought to light beatings, sexual assaults and other mistreatment of delinquent children in a state detention center and wilderness camps in 1998. A year later, the *Baltimore Sun* reported that guards were brutally beating teenagers in Maryland's state boot camps for delinquents. Investigations, resignations and camp closings followed in both states.

Good journalism—in a newspaper or magazine, on television, radio or the Internet—enriches Americans by giving them both useful information for their daily lives and a sense of participation in the wider world. Good journalism makes possible the cooperation among citizens that is critical to a civilized society. Citizens cannot function together as a community unless they share a common body of information about their surroundings, their neighbors, their governing bodies, their sports teams, even their weather. Those are all the stuff of the news. The best journalism digs into it, makes sense of it and makes it accessible to everyone.

Bad journalism—failing to report important news, or reporting news shallowly, inaccurately or unfairly—can leave people dangerously uninformed. The news media failed to report adequately on the overextended and corrupt savings and loan industry before it collapsed and cost depositors and taxpayers billions of dollars during the 1980s. The press failed to discover and expose the tobacco industry's cover-up of evidence of the addictive and cancer-causing effects of smoking and its clandestine marketing of cigarettes to young people until plaintiffs' lawyers discovered both in the course of liability lawsuits during the 1990s. At a time when nearly half of eligible Americans don't vote, the news media have steadily reduced their coverage of government and elections, leaving citizens vulnerable to negative and misleading political advertising that fills the airwaves instead, enriching television and radio stations during election campaigns. Although Americans are more globally connected than ever, most news media steadily and substantially reduced their coverage of foreign news during the last years of the twentieth century, depriving Americans of the opportunity to follow the world around them. This fact was widely discussed after the terrorist attacks of September 2001, when foreign stories suddenly became fashionable again.

Bad journalism can misinform. Television newscasts and many newspapers routinely overemphasize crime news, so Americans continue to fear that crime is getting worse when it has actually been decreasing for years. Journalists eager to attribute the deadly bombing of the Oklahoma City federal building in 1995 or the catastrophic explosion of TWA Flight 800 over Long Island to Islamic terrorists misled Americans before they knew that the real culprits were Timothy McVeigh and an exploding fuel tank on the Boeing 747. Glowing, uncritical coverage of new technology companies in the late 1990s encouraged many Americans to sink their savings into speculative stocks and mutual funds that soon crashed, collectively costing them billions of dollars.

Much bad journalism is just lazy and superficial. Local television stations lard their newscasts with dramatic video fragments of relatively inconsequential but sensational fires and auto accidents. Broadcast and cable networks devote news time to mindless chat and debate. Newspapers fill columns with fluffy trivia and rewrites of press releases and the police blotter.

Bad news judgment is commonplace. "If it bleeds, it leads" is a self-mocking slogan among local television journalists, but also an accurate description of the reflex of television news directors to make gory crime stories the first news items on the 11 o'clock news. The celebrity divorce, the police raid on a massage parlor, the opening of a county fair—all too often, it doesn't have to be new, or factual, or interesting, or important to be labeled "news."

Journalists have a special role in preserving one of America's greatest assets, our culture of accountability. Americans expect their leaders to behave responsibly, and usually take remedial action when they don't. This is an important reason why American society works better than many others. Accountability is a crucial aspect of our national ideology, which was based on the rejection of tyranny, defined by the founders as the unjust use of power. Americans in positions of power generally assume that someday they may have to account for how they have used their power. This is especially true for those who hold power in our government "of the people, by the people, for the people," but for others as well. Corporate officers hold power over companies and their customers. Foundation officers hold power over the distribution of vast sums of money. Those with power in film studios, television networks, book publishers and recording companies shape our popular culture. American society is diverse and decentralized; countless citizens exercise some power over the lives of other citizens.

Accountability is an important check on that power. Our politicians know that informed voters can throw them out of office; corporate CEOs recognize the authority of their boards of directors and the influence of their stockholders; a cop taking bribes knows he doesn't want to get caught. Good journalism is a principal source of the information necessary to make such accountability meaningful. Anyone tempted to abuse power looks over his or her shoulder to see if someone else is watching. Ideally, there should be a reporter in the rearview mirror.

Solemn obligations are far from the only justification for good journalism. The journalist's ability to connect readers or viewers to the comedy and tragedy that surrounds us all makes life richer and more rewarding. One of the rewards of being alive is watching the world change. During our nearly four decades in journalism we've seen amazing changes that have redefined the American experience: the creation of a middle-class majority in the United States; economic and cultural globalization; the celebrification of just about everything; the power of America's youth culture to infect the country and the world; the emergence of women, African Americans and gay people; and great migrations from Latin America and Asia; the long and frustrating struggle with terrorism. Journalism described all of this, though not always as quickly or thoroughly as it could have. Any attentive American could keep up with this changing world by following the news. Good journalism gives every one of us the opportunity to be real citizens of our own time.

Human beings are instinctively curious, and journalism relieves curiosity. The real workings of big-time sports, the backstage gossip from the worlds of movies and television, the personalities and company histories behind the names listed on the New York Stock Exchange, new cures and old remedies for every kind of ailment, the condition of our environment, details of community and neighborhood life—virtually the entire range of human curiosities is covered by good journalism. So it should matter to Americans that the news is at risk today. In an information age, when good journalism should be flourishing everywhere, it isn't.

Tantalizingly, the best journalism in America is better than it has ever been. This was demonstrated dramatically in the traumatic days that followed the terrorist attacks in September 2001, when the best newspapers published extraordinary editions filled with detailed reporting, emotion and explanation. Today's finest reporters are better educated and more professional than their forebears; many are recognized experts in their fields. They are more inclined to dig deeper, better able to challenge conventional wisdom and more likely to report authoritatively on important subjects of all kinds—business, finance, education, religion, health, sports. The news business, once populated mostly by white men, has been transformed by an influx of women and people of color. These journalists have helped expand the definition of news to include more of the realities of life in an increasingly diverse nation. And the best journalism—much of it produced by a small number of newspapers—now reaches more Americans than ever on the newspapers' Internet sites and through their relationships with, and influence on, the best news programs on television and radio.

That's the good news. But bad news is more typical. Too much of what has been offered as news in recent years has been untrustworthy, irresponsible, misleading or incomplete. Sometimes, good journalists with the best intentions fall short of their aspirations or make mistakes. But the most alarming weaknesses of the news media have been systemic, and they have seriously undermined good journalism. Too many of those who own and lead the nation's news media have cynically underestimated or ignored America's need for good journalism, and evaded their responsibility to provide it.

Most newspapers have shrunk their reporting staffs, along with the space they devote to news, to increase their owners' profits. Most owners and publishers have forced their editors to focus more on the bottom line than on good journalism. Papers have tried to attract readers and advertisers with light features and stories that please advertisers—shopping is a favorite—and by de-emphasizing serious reporting on business, government, the country and the world.

If most newspapers have done poorly, local television stations have been worse. Typically, local stations provide little real news, no matter how many hours they devote to "news" programs. Their reporting staffs are dramatically smaller than even the staffs of shrunken newspapers in the same cities. The television stations have attracted viewers—and the advertising that rewards their owners with extraordinary profits—with the melodrama, violence and entertainment of "action news" formulas, the frivolity of "happy talk" among their anchors and the technological gimmicks of computer graphics and "live" remote broadcasting.

The national television networks have trimmed their reporting staffs and closed foreign reporting bureaus to cut their owners' costs. They have tried to attract viewers by diluting their expensive newscasts with lifestyle, celebrity and entertainment features, and by filling their low-budget, high-profit, prime-time "newsmagazines" with sensational sex, crime and court stories.

All-news cable television channels and radio stations—to which the networks have ceded much of the routine coverage of serious national and foreign news—fill many of their hours as cheaply as possible with repetitive, bare-bones news summaries and talk shows that present biased opinions and argument as though they were news.

In the nineties, one of television's greatest strengths, the ability to provide real-time, continuous coverage of important events as they are unfolding, was repeatedly squandered on "wall-to-wall" blanket coverage of less important but emotionally charged events, usually crime and tragedy. This coverage was frequently marred by misleading reporting and talking-head analysis that distorted the facts, meaning and importance of events like school shootings or freak accidents, projecting sideshows into the center ring of national life.

Much of what has happened to news has been the by-product of broader economic, technological, demographic and social changes in the country. Most newspapers, television networks and local television and radio stations now belong to giant, publicly owned corporations far removed from the communities they serve. They face the unrelenting quarterly profit pressures from Wall Street now typical of American capitalism. Media owners are accustomed to profit margins that would be impossible in most traditional industries. For General Motors, a profit margin of 5 percent of total revenue would mark a very good year, but the Tribune Company of Chicago, which owns newspapers and television stations located all across the country, wants a 30 percent margin. Many local television stations expect to keep 50 percent of their revenue as profit.

Protecting such high profits can easily undermine the notion that journalism is a public service.

New technology and the increasing diversity of American society have fragmented the news media and their audiences. Multiplying cable television channels and Internet sites made some form of news available everywhere, all the time, increasing the competition to be first with the most enticing story while loosening traditional standards of confirmation, accuracy, taste and fairness. The proliferation of news outlets has shrunk the audience of each one and weakened the commercial domination of individual newspapers and television stations and networks, so their owners and managers have been wary of increasing their investment in news coverage or risking unpopular journalism.

Many in the news business became convinced that in an era of unparalleled prosperity and security, Americans would rather be entertained than informed. The consequences of this attitude are obvious on every television news show, and in too many newspapers. The temptation to push serious news aside in favor of glitz and melodrama has too often been irresistible. A national infatuation with celebrities, both encouraged and exploited by news media, has had a profound influence on journalism. It has also tempted too many journalists to try to become celebrities themselves.

More change is coming rapidly. Digital and satellite technology will allow an explosion in the number of television and radio signals that consumers can receive through the air, and will give local television stations the opportunity to offer multiple channels where now they provide one. The expansion of the country's network of fiber-optic cable will bring nearly infinite capacity to transmit sound, pictures and words by landlines into America's homes. Soon millions of consumers will combine television, Internet and telephone service in a single box. Advances in wireless communications are putting cordless Internet-connected computers into briefcases, handbags, pockets and mobile phones. Already, the Internet mixes print, photo, audio and video news coverage into multimedia packages on many Web news sites.

These developments guarantee further strain on the businesses of most news-media owners, threatening their exceptional profitability and their budgets for news coverage. Free news on the Internet is already competing with newsstand sales and paid subscriptions for newspapers and magazines. The audience for television news is splintering among over-the-air broadcasting, cable and the Internet. Advertising revenue—which pays most of the costs and provides most of the profits for all news organizations—is sloshing around these media unpredictably, destabilizing their business models.

So many of the pressures affecting the news business at the end of the twentieth century undermined the best journalism. Nevertheless, when terrorist attacks on New York and Washington produced the biggest news story in years, the networks, local television stations, newspapers and other news media all knew how to respond. They rose to the occasion, giving the country some of the best, and most helpful, journalism Americans had seen in a long time.

This juxtaposition of the bad and the good suggests that the time is right to take a look at the news business. How the news has changed, and why, and what could and should happen in the future are the subjects of this book. Using our own experiences and interviews with dozens of others who produce the news for newspapers, television, radio and the Internet, we'll try to show you why the news is what it is. We want to share with you an insiders' perspective on the news business, and thus to demystify it.

We have three goals: to explain why good journalism is so important, to increase the knowledge of consumers of news about how the news business works and to encourage public support for the best journalism. Consumers who understand and demand the best are more likely to get what they want.

But we'll try not to preach. We want to bring the news business alive by taking you inside newspapers, television networks, local stations and Internet news sites to explain how the news is gathered and reported. We'll explore the values at work in news organizations, and how they are changing. You will meet the nightly news anchors of the three major television networks and hear from the editors of many of the nation's newspapers. You will see what happens in the control rooms of television stations as they assemble their newscasts. You will see what is happening with and to news on the Internet. You will watch investigative reporters working on the most difficult and important kind of journalism. We'll give you opportunities to second-guess the decisions of news executives confronting delicate decisions about what to publish.

The two of us look at the news business from a privileged perch. The only employer either of us has ever had is the *Washington Post*. Eugene Meyer, one of the most successful investors of his generation and a dollar-a-year public servant under presidents from Wilson to Truman, bought the *Post* at a bankruptcy auction in 1933, for $825,000. He wrote a friend soon after buying the paper: "My only interest is to make a contribution to better knowledge and better thinking. If I could not feel an ability to rise above my personal interests . . . I would not have the slightest pleasure in being a publisher." For most of the next twenty-one years the *Post* lost money.

To the hard-nosed businessmen who run many of today's media companies, Meyer's attitude would seem quaint. But it has survived through three generations. Meyer's daughter, Katharine Graham, and her son, Donald Graham, have run the paper according to Meyer's founding principles, which committed the *Post* to "tell the truth as nearly as the truth can be ascertained." Meyer explicitly put the public interest ahead of his own: "In the pursuit of truth, the newspaper shall be prepared to make sacrifices of its material fortunes, if such a course be necessary for the public good," he wrote in 1934. The *Post* ran that risk when it published the Pentagon Papers and pursued the Watergate story.

We have never had the experience—common at too many other newspapers—of being ordered to compromise our news coverage to accommodate a demand for higher profits, or to pander to customers to try to increase circulation or sell more advertisements. The impediments we have faced in the pursuit of good journalism are our own limitations, not the commercial interests or political preferences of our proprietor. Profits do matter at the *Washington Post*—they pay for the increasing costs of producing good journalism—but it is news that matters most. This attitude is shared at some other newspapers, but too few.

These are the values that shaped us. We will use them to evaluate the state of the news business, which is at a crossroads. A bright future could lie ahead, but that is far from certain. How it turns out will make an enormous difference for the United States. Independent, aggressive journalism strengthens American democracy, improves the lives of its citizens, checks the abuses of powerful people, supports the weakest members of society, connects us all to one another, educates and entertains us. News matters.

# Chapter Two

# AMERICANS
# AND THEIR NEWS

As their sons and brothers fought for independence from 1775 to 1783, tens of thousands of Americans in the thirteen colonies devoured flimsy weekly newspapers to follow the progress of their revolt against the British Crown. They learned of Cornwallis's surrender to George Washington at Yorktown many days after it occurred, but they got the news. Two hundred twenty years later, virtually every American adult turned to newspapers, television, radio or the Internet to follow the horrific news from New York and Washington after terrorists flew jetliners into the World Trade Center and the Pentagon. From the beginning, disseminators of news have connected American citizens to the shared events that shaped their national experience.

News outlets have evolved with the country, through the rise of Jacksonian democracy, the Civil War, the end of slavery and the assimilation of generation after generation of immigrants to the prosecution of wars, the growth of government and industry, technological revolutions, the struggles for equal rights for women and minorities and America's changing role in the world. They continued to evolve into a multimedia era whose biggest stories included the trial of O. J. Simpson and the tribulations of Monica Lewinsky and Bill Clinton.

In part because of the advocacy reporting and pamphleteering of Ben Franklin, Tom Paine, John Peter Zenger and other colonial journalists who helped inspire the American Revolution, the country has always given a special status to journalism. Nine of the original thirteen states constitutionally guaranteed freedom of the press. The Bill of Rights then added the First Amendment to the U.S. Constitution: "Congress shall make no law . . . abridging the freedom of speech, or of the press."

In the formative years of the new republic, politicians, government officials and journalists jousted repeatedly over how far the press could go in challenging the politically powerful. Some of the same Founding Fathers who gave us the First Amendment also produced a sedition law that briefly threatened press freedom by punishing antigovernment journalism until it expired in 1801. Gradually over the next two centuries, American courts gave ever-greater protection to journalists and their work. The courts have barred government from imposing its will or prior restraint on the press, except for wartime censorship. The Supreme Court has made it difficult to punish the press after publication of hurtful or embarrassing information, absent malicious disregard for the truth. No other nation gives its journalists so much constitutional protection, and as a result, so much responsibility.

That constitutional umbrella has sheltered both the best and worst purveyors of news. Most early American newspapers were organs of political parties or other special interests that used their papers to promote their own causes and to spread scandal about their opponents. A Scottish immigrant journalist named James R. Callender became notorious for publishing allegations of financial and personal improprieties by Alexander Hamilton, and later, for printing the rumor that Thomas Jefferson had fathered several children with his slave Sally Hemings. Other early newspapers were primarily commercial publications offered to the business elite through expensive annual subscriptions. These opinionated papers, struggling to survive with relatively small readerships, unabashedly favored the interests that supported them. They indiscriminately mixed advertising with their meager news content, even presenting paid advertising as news.

In the 1830s the democratization of political and economic life associated with the presidency of Andrew Jackson, the growth of cities, the spread of public education and literacy and improved printing technology made possible the "penny press," new and lively independent daily newspapers sold on the streets for a penny apiece. The stodgy commercial papers sold for six cents a copy. The *New York Sun*, the *New York Herald* and the *Baltimore Sun* were all born as penny papers in the 1830s, followed in the next two decades by the *New York Times*, the *Washington Evening Star*, the *Chicago Tribune* and many others. The most successful penny papers sold tens of thousands of copies daily, far more than their predecessors. They were supported primarily by advertisers who wanted to reach this mass audience, rather than by annual subscription fees or subsidies from political parties or other special interests. They attracted large readerships by covering much more news than their predecessors.

"The Penny Press invented the modern concept of 'news,' " press historian Michael Schudson has written. "For the first time the American newspaper made it a regular practice to print political news, not just foreign but domestic, and not just national but local; for the first time it printed reports from the police, from the courts, from the streets, and from private households. . . . For the first time, the newspaper reflected not just commerce or politics but social life . . . not the affairs of an elite in a small trading society, but the activities of an increasingly varied, urban, and middle-class society of trade, transportation and manufacturing."

Earlier newspapers printed their editors' musings together with correspondence sent by friends, travelers or politicians and the texts of commercial and political documents, like shipping announcements or presidential addresses to Congress. The more aggressive penny papers hired their own reporters to search out news. They reported eye-opening stories about daily life—especially crime, local politics and social conditions—that the stodgier six-penny papers denounced as sensationalism. That label stuck to the populist press throughout the rest of the nineteenth century. But the penny papers' vivid coverage of real life, though often colorfully sensational or highly partisan, drew more and more readers in city after city across the growing country.

Some New York newspapers, led by James Gordon Bennett's *Herald,* Horace Greeley's *Tribune* and Henry J. Raymond's *Times,* introduced more serious news coverage of public affairs, including stories from their own reporters posted in Washington and overseas. In 1848 a group of New York newspapers formed the Associated Press to exploit telegraph communications to gather news more widely around the country for themselves and other papers who would pay to use their stories. Over time, the Associated Press developed a detached, factual style to make its stories acceptable to client newspapers that often had sharply conflicting political points of view. The newspapers themselves only slowly made their own reporting more factual and less opinionated.

Newspaper readership grew further during the Civil War, which was covered by legions of reporters. Some papers hired artists to produce illustrations of the battlefields to accompany dispatches from the front. After the war, Joseph Pulitzer and William Randolph Hearst built the first mass-circulation press empires. Theirs and other big-city newspapers grew in numbers and size with ever-more-sensational coverage of sex, violence and the scandals of high society. The biggest cities had multiple newspapers publishing numerous editions every day. Competition for readers and advertising dollars was intense. The biggest papers sold hundreds of thousands of copies a day.

These newspapers' freewheeling owners and editors curried public favor by declaring their independence from political parties, although they often had strong political biases of their own. Intellectual and political critics lambasted "press lords" like Hearst, Pulitzer, Colonel Robert R. McCormick of the *Chicago Tribune,* and Harrison Gray Otis of the *Los Angeles Times* for misusing their news columns to promote their own interests and to please advertisers. But they prospered, becoming conspicuously wealthy and powerful.

In the late nineteenth century the popular papers began to promote individual reporters and encouraged their star correspondents to write with distinctive personal styles. Adventurers like Henry Morton Stanley, who found the missing missionary David Livingstone in Africa, and Richard Harding Davis, Hearst's favorite war correspondent, became national celebrities. Other famous journalists introduced investigative reporting that exposed corrupt politicians, ruthless corporations and the deprivations of immigrants and city slum dwellers. The popular newspapers used investigative "crusades" to promote themselves as champions of the people and to build circulation. Self-restraint was not a feature of this era, and the competition among papers often pushed them from legitimate crusading into crass sensationalism, or "yellow journalism," named for a popular cartoon character, The Yellow Kid.

At the turn of the century national magazines began to publish serious investigative reporting on social conditions in a fast-industrializing country. This was the journalism President Theodore Roosevelt dubbed muckraking. Writers such as Lincoln Steffens, Upton Sinclair, Ida Tarbell, Ray Stannard Baker and David Graham Phillips—many of whom first wrote for newspapers and borrowed their subject matter from earlier newspaper crusades—forced Americans to confront corruption in both government and business, including the powerful and largely unregulated oil, railroad, banking, insurance and food-processing industries. Their revelations of monopolistic business practices, bribery, election rigging, stock manipulation, racketeering and abuse of labor and public health reached a national audience in books and popular magazines, such as the *Saturday Evening Post, Everybody's, McClure's, Ladies' Home Journal* and Hearst's *Cosmopolitan.* They helped create the political climate for Roosevelt's trust-busting, and for congressional passage of the Pure Food and Drug Act (1906), and ratification by the states of the Seventeenth Amendment to the Constitution (1913), which provided for direct popular election of the U.S. Senate.

At the same time, the first quality newspapers, led by a revitalized *New*

*York Times,* were becoming important. The better papers exploited two new journalistic devices that allowed reporters to exercise their own news judgment: the interview and the summary lead paragraph. Both created new roles for the journalist, who could show what he (virtually all were men) thought was important by the way he questioned a public figure or summarized a news event. Reporters on the better papers began to develop real expertise in the subjects they covered, and to write interpretive articles. They began to add context and explore motivation in their accounts of events of the day. Newspapers including the *Times,* the *World* and *Herald* in New York, the *Sun* in Baltimore, the *Courier-Journal* in Louisville and Pulitzer's *Post-Dispatch* in St. Louis became more reliable in their journalism. Many continued to emphasize crusading investigative reporting. The *Post-Dispatch* uncovered the biggest Washington story of the 1920s, Teapot Dome, a scandal involving the leasing of government-owned oil reserves to private interests.


In the late nineteenth century better printing presses and the railroads, which carried papers around the country, made newspapers America's first mass medium. Changing technology in the twentieth century transformed newspapers again and again. Advances in photography and newspaper printing allowed papers to publish timely photos of news events. Photographs made possible the tabloid newspapers that appealed to the multitudes of immigrants who had crowded into the cities and had difficulty reading English. In New York they had a choice of three: the *Daily News,* the *Mirror* and the *Graphic.* The tabloids emphasized crime, violence, scandal, sex and celebrities, from Prohibition mobsters and Hollywood stars to sports heroes and socialites. They sometimes fictionalized first-person versions of the juiciest stories of ordinary people caught in extraordinary circumstances: "I Know Who Killed My Brother," or, "For 36 Hours I Lived Another Woman's Love Life." One of the most notorious early tabloid exclusives was a photograph that filled the January 14, 1928, front page of the *Daily News.* Taken inside the death chamber at Sing Sing by a photographer who had strapped a camera to his ankle, it showed vividly the execution of husband killer Ruth Snyder in the electric chair.

The Roaring Twenties brought radio and talking motion pictures. Americans gathered around their living room radio consoles and flocked to the new movie palaces for entertainment. The theaters offered filmed newsreels, and the fledgling radio networks began to broadcast regular news programs. Radio gave its listeners live coverage of some of the biggest news events of the day, including the 1924 political conventions, the 1925 courtroom clash of Clarence Darrow and William Jennings Bryan at the Scopes evolution trial in Tennessee and the 1927 heavyweight fight between Jack Dempsey and Gene Tunney.

Newspapers began buying radio stations and producing on-air news programs. Although some publishers worried that radio would steal audience and advertisers, a committee of the American Newspaper Publishers Association argued in 1927 that radio reporting of news events could actually stimulate newspaper sales. And according to press historian Edwin Emery, that is just what happened for years afterward.

But competition from radio, which could report breaking news first, often as it was happening, did change newspapers. They began to publish better-informed and more interpretive reporting on politics, economics, labor relations, science, medicine and agriculture. They featured increasingly influential, nationally syndicated columnists like Walter Lippmann, Arthur Brisbane, David Lawrence and Marquis Childs, most of whom wrote from Washington.

Mass-circulation national magazines—some dating back to the mid-nineteenth century and many more founded in the first four decades of the twentieth—also published increasingly influential journalism. *Time* and *Newsweek* provided easy-to-read roundups of each week's national, foreign, business and cultural news. *Life* and *Look* pioneered photojournalism that took their readers on vivid pictorial tours of the modernizing world around them. *Fortune* specialized in business news. *The New Yorker, The Atlantic Monthly, Harper's, The Nation* and *The New Republic* combined original, in-depth reporting with literary writing and provocative analysis of important news topics. During what Northwestern University media studies professor David Abrahamson has called "the golden age of magazines," from the end of World War I until the late 1950s, they were an influential national news medium that supplemented newspapers and radio with added depth and intellectual vigor.

But if the press succeeded in developing some intellectual self-confidence, it also fell under the influence of the prevailing political and economic establishments. From the Great Depression in the 1930s through World War II and the beginning of the Cold War in the 1950s, reporters seemed to reflect establishment views more often than they exposed the failings and foibles of the powerful. They seldom challenged government news management or the press agentry of private business and the entertainment industry. Pundits like Lippmann unabashedly gave private advice to politicians, and many White House reporters considered themselves pals of the president. Much of what passed for investigative reporting relied on leaks from government agents and congressional committees investigating organized crime, corrupt labor unions and suspected Communists.

Then at the beginning of the 1950s television arrived, transforming the world of news. Suddenly Americans could see their national leaders at work in televised political conventions, press conferences and dramatic events like Vice President Richard Nixon's 1952 "Checkers speech," when he denied the improper acceptance of money, and Senator Joseph McCarthy's Red-baiting bullying in the Army-McCarthy hearings. Through interview programs, public figures became regular guests in American living rooms. The distance between the powerful and the hoi polloi shrank.

As television's technologies improved, viewers were taken to the remote scenes of big stories. They were brought right into the civil rights struggles of the late fifties and early sixties with vivid pictures of sit-ins, marches and confrontations with segregationist officials and police. In November 1963, television gave virtually every American an intimate view of the most traumatic national experience of the age, the assassination of John F. Kennedy and its aftermath, including the televised murder of his accused assassin, Lee Harvey Oswald.

The Kennedy assassination marked the beginning of a time of shattering change, and thanks to television, all Americans could participate. On television they could witness, nearly firsthand, the political assassinations, urban riots, antiwar protests and other social upheavals of the sixties and early seventies. These events divided and changed the country. They also pushed serious journalism to a new place in American life. Vividly reporting the futile war in Vietnam and the turmoil that opposition to it caused at home made the news media controversial. For the first time in the post–World War II era, some American journalists, including very prominent ones, moved away from the establishment. Lippmann, the best-known newspaper columnist in the world, became a leading critic of the Vietnam War and a symbol of this change. When, after the Tet Offensive of 1968, Walter Cronkite of CBS told his millions of viewers that victory in Vietnam seemed impossible, politicians understood that popular support for the war was evaporating.

So it was not just political tactics but a more profound sign of the times when Nixon and his vice president, Spiro Agnew, began to demonize the news media at the end of the 1960s. Agnew denounced "nattering nabobs of negativism"; Nixon put journalists at the top of his enemies list. In

1971, when the *New York Times* began publishing stories based on the Pentagon Papers, a secret history of the Vietnam War prepared in the Pentagon, Nixon decided to use the federal courts to try to restrain the *Times* and then the *Washington Post,* after the *Post* acquired a copy of the Papers. The Supreme Court resolved the ensuing confrontation in favor of the newspapers, but Nixon's assault on the press had a palpable effect.

When the Watergate break-in occurred a year later, nearly every reporter in Washington outside the *Post* (there were then about two thousand accredited Washington correspondents) ignored the story. The *Post*'s contribution to Nixon's downfall was one of the most important moments in modern journalism. With enormous assistance from Robert Redford, Dustin Hoffman and Jason Robards, who turned Bob Woodward, Carl Bernstein and Ben Bradlee into mythic heroes in director Alan Pakula's film version of Woodward and Bernstein's book, *All the President's Men,* the *Post*'s role in the Watergate affair entered American mythology.

Journalism became one of the most popular majors on American campuses. Many universities created or enlarged journalism schools and departments. Newsrooms infected by Watergate fever launched into investigative journalism with a fervor unmatched in the history of American newspapers. By the mid-1970s a majority of the Pulitzer Prizes for newspaper journalism went to investigative reporting—revelations of police and government corruption in Indianapolis, Chicago and New York, the influence of the Teamsters Union in Alaska, illegal export trading by big grain companies in the Midwest, unequal enforcement of federal tax laws and more.

The national news and opinion magazines, along with new "city magazines" like Clay Felker's *New York* and small but influential muckraking magazines like Warren Hinckle's *Ramparts* and Charles Peters's *Washington Monthly,* joined in the investigative reporting. Some of their stories presented this reporting with strongly voiced narrative writing and first-person literary license, a style born at *Esquire* magazine in the sixties that became known as "new journalism." Examples of the genre, most published in magazines, altered the sensibilities of American journalists in the sixties and seventies. *Harper's* devoted an entire issue to Norman Mailer's "The Steps of the Pentagon," a diary of his participation in anti–Vietnam War demonstrations in Washington. *Rolling Stone* published Hunter Thompson's iconoclastic and influential "Fear and Loathing" reports on the 1972 presidential campaign. *Esquire* and *New York* showcased the adventurous journalism of former newspaper reporter Tom Wolfe. Journalists at the most daring newspapers and magazines borrowed liberally from one another's reporting and writing techniques in a period of fervid creativity.

The years after Watergate were heady ones for newspaper journalists. Looking back over recent history, journalists could say they had done their duty under the First Amendment by giving the country the information it needed to cope with the civil rights era, the Vietnam War and the Watergate scandal. The *New York Times* symbolized serious journalism, but now there were new competitors trying to become distinguished newspapers, including the *Washington Post,* the *Los Angeles Times* and the *Philadelphia Inquirer.* The *Miami Herald* and *St. Petersburg Times* were feisty and aggressive. Other newspapers improved significantly, and talented young people banged on their doors looking for jobs.

Now we can see that the enthusiasm of that moment was misleading. The crusading journalism typified and inspired by the Watergate story gradually tapered off during more tranquil times. Changing news-media economics threatened the improvements in journalism. And television was consolidating its status as the first source of news for most Americans. The Roper Survey, a national opinion poll, had first found that a majority of Americans said they got their news predominantly from television in 1963, the year CBS and NBC expanded their evening news broadcasts to thirty minutes. This was an early-warning signal that the national attention span was shrinking, that a lot of citizens were satisfied by the relatively small number of brief news stories a television broadcast could give them. Newspaper readership began a long decline that has continued ever since. Metropolitan newspapers, mostly evening papers, began to fail and close, until, by the 1980s, only half a dozen American cities—New York, Los Angeles, Chicago, Boston, Denver and Seattle—had competing major daily newspapers. In most metropolitan areas, only one dominant daily survived. Each remained profitable, sometimes extraordinarily profitable, because of its monopoly on local print advertising.

Most of the surviving papers were collected into the large chains that now own more than 1,200 of the nation's 1,500 dailies. Squabbling among heirs led some newspaper-owning families to sell to the chains. Others could not resist the windfall fortunes that the chains offered on the assumption (usually correct) that they could increase a new property's profitability through more efficient, sometimes ruthless, management.

Still other family owners amassed their own chains of newspapers and turned their holdings into lucrative, publicly owned corporations.

For most of the first two centuries of American history the country's newspapers were deeply rooted local institutions. So were the first television stations, many of them owned by newspapers. Some were public-spirited, others merely provincial, but everyone in town knew who the owner was and where to find him. The growth of chain ownership transformed the nature of the newspaper and television businesses. Control shifted from the towns or cities where the papers and stations were located to distant corporate headquarters. Typically, their publishers and editors, or general managers and news directors, now shuttle from one newspaper or TV station to another as they climb the corporate ladder, never staying in any one community for more than a few years. Increasingly, their decisions about the newspapers' or stations' budgets and news coverage are shaped, if not dictated, by corporate executives at headquarters.

The three original television networks mushroomed into giant corporations, fed by the enormous revenues advertisers would pay to hawk their wares on the networks' entertainment shows and increasingly extensive news programming. As the government abandoned most regulation of broadcasting in the 1980s and 1990s, mammoth corporate owners, including the chains that owned many newspapers, gobbled up local television and radio stations. The networks themselves were all taken over by mega-corporations of which they were relatively small parts. Some of the new corporate owners of media companies then bought cable TV systems that became the pathway for television into most Americans' homes. And they launched or bought all-news cable networks and channels that offered local, national, international, financial, sports and weather news on the steadily increasing number of cable channels available in most households.

Magazines also changed. Some of the most famous titles—including *Life, Look* and the *Saturday Evening Post*—died because their mass-marketing advertisers found television a more productive medium. The weekly newsmagazines *Time, Newsweek* and *U.S. News & World Report* survived by cutting their news-gathering staffs and other expenses while putting more emphasis on coverage of popular celebrity, lifestyle, entertainment and consumer news. New magazines thrived by catering to smaller audiences for individual interests like entertainment, cars, decorating, gardening, fashion, sports, health, personal investing and technology—subjects that attracted specialized audiences that advertisers wanted to reach. Perhaps the most influential magazine journalism is now being produced by business magazines, including *Business Week, Fortune* and *Forbes,* which cover financial news authoritatively and aggressively, although they have not been immune to pressures from owners to hold down costs.

At the end of the twentieth century a new medium was born, the Internet. Here was a tool with the potential to transform the news business and, some pessimists thought, to kill off America's remaining newspapers. The World Wide Web gives anyone using a computer anywhere on earth a virtually infinite choice of sources for news and information, reliable and not. Anyone who puts a site up on the Web can be a supplier of "news." When America Online, an Internet upstart, bought Time Warner, an old-media Goliath, everyone knew that a new age had dawned.

In contrast to the individuals and families who founded most American newspapers, television stations and networks, the owners of the new media-centered conglomerates are big public companies. Most of them are monuments to the transformations that have redrawn the American corporate landscape over the last several decades. Every one of the important media corporations in modern America is a good deal bigger than it was just a few years ago. Constant growth is a favored way to satisfy Wall Street investors' demands for rising earnings, quarter by quarter. These corporations focus on maximizing short-term profits and thereby increasing their stock prices.

Several of these companies have put extraordinary arrays of "content providers" under a single corporate roof. AOL Time Warner combined the most popular pathway to the Internet with movie studios, cable news networks, book publishers and a stable of mass-circulation newsmagazines. The Walt Disney Company combined the ABC network and local television affiliates with Internet ventures and its entertainment empire of movie studios, cable networks (including ESPN and the Disney Channel), theme parks and sports teams; ABC News was in there somewhere. Viacom/CBS combined CBS and dozens of television and radio stations with movie studios, cable networks and book publishers—and CBS News. NBC News was absorbed into General Electric, one of the nation's largest and most diversified corporations, a holding company whose most profitable subsidiary is in the moneylending business. GE created partnerships with another behemoth of the computer age, Microsoft, to create the MSNBC cable news network on television and MSNBC.com on the Internet.

At best, news constituted only a small part of these empires. At worst, news seemed to become an extension of their entertainment businesses and a way to promote them. Both the networks and local TV stations devote portions of their news programs to promotional features about their parent networks' entertainment shows. The networks' own television newsmagazines feature crime and celebrity stories to compete for prime-time ratings with dramas and situation comedies. NBC decided that such "infotainment" was a better prime-time product than old-fashioned entertainment—much cheaper to produce, easy for a network to control and attractive to advertisers.

Even in the media companies for which news remained the primary product, news coverage often appeared to be a lower priority than their profit margins and stock prices. In 2001, Gannett owned ninety-nine newspapers with a combined daily circulation of nearly 8 million, and twenty-two television stations broadcasting to one-sixth of the country's TV audience. Knight Ridder had thirty-two papers with nearly 4 million circulation in cities from Miami and Philadelphia to San Jose. Newspaper editors and television news directors in such large chains have been held more accountable for controlling costs and increasing profits than for improving the quality of their journalism.

"The media world was invaded by money," explained William B. Ziff Jr., chairman of a family company that published specialty magazines like *Car & Driver* and *Popular Photography,* and later *PC Magazine* and *MacUser.* "What had been a sedate and family-oriented corner of the business world was thrown into the financial spotlight. . . . The pressure on publishing management to produce enhanced financial performance became progressively more intense. . . . Most would have been better off without it."

Pressure to increase the profits of media companies has not been an isolated phenomenon. Throughout the American economy, there is unprecedented pressure to maximize profits, putting "shareholder value" ahead of all other considerations. The corporations that own the news media are subject to all the business trends and economic demands that have reshaped American business in the 1980s and 1990s, affecting nearly every part of society. Lawyers began to divide their days into six-minute increments so they could bill a client for each 360-second slice. Doctors found the practice of medicine turned upside down by profit-conscious insurance companies and health-management organizations.

In the news business these pressures changed the nature of ownership. For generations since Ben Franklin started the *Pennsylvania Gazette,* news

organizations were mostly owned by individuals or families, who took
responsibility for them, nurtured or abused them and passed them on to
succeeding generations. Sometimes they made serious money, but often
they didn't. The Bingham family, which owned the *Louisville Courier-
Journal* and *Times* for seven decades, often tolerated minuscule or nonex-
istent profits. The Cowleses, who owned the *Des Moines Register* and
*Tribune* for eight decades, similarly survived years of meager profitability.
Eugene Meyer suffered his losses with the *Washington Post.* In all three of
those cases the owners drew pleasure from their roles as purveyors of a
public service—good journalism. The first owners of the three television
networks were also willing to sacrifice some profit for public service.
Today's new patterns of corporate ownership have fundamentally altered
the nature of news organizations by changing the incentives and rewards
that guide their proprietors. When a sharp downturn in the American
economy caused newspaper advertising revenues to plummet in 2001, for
example, newspapers' corporate owners ordered deep cuts in news staffs
and space in the papers for news to maintain large profit margins.

Ownership isn't the only important thing to change in the modern media
era. The audience is different too. Inevitably Americans have changed
with their country. In 1995, for the first time, Americans had more of their
savings in stocks and bonds than in real estate; the family home was no
longer the principal American nest egg. This seems symbolic of a broad
sociological change. Money has always driven American life, but in the
modern era wealth has been democratized. The country moved from a
working-class society to a middle-class society in the thirty years after
World War II, and in the next three decades consumption (and consumer
debt) accelerated dramatically. It takes no more than a visit to one of the
country's immense shopping malls to see what democratized wealth has
wrought in America.

For nearly fifty years after World War II, the Cold War with the Soviet
Union dominated American life, and gave a significance to news that
most Americans readily understood. But in an era of mostly peace and
prosperity, millions of American consumers turned their backs on civic
life to focus on personal development, enrichment and pleasure. In the
nineteenth and early twentieth centuries, politics was itself a source of
public entertainment, but politicians could not compete with modern
modes of entertainment: the movies, television and radio, stock-car rac-
ing, the Internet. By the nineties, many Americans had decided it wasn't

worth their time to follow events in the world around them. Surveys showed a steady decline in the number of Americans who said they enjoyed keeping up with the news a great deal—down to 45 percent of the population by 2000. Newspaper circulation gently declined through the eighties and nineties; viewership of television news dropped more precipitously.

And yet, the news retained an important place in American life. This was indisputably clear after September 11, 2001. Terrorist attacks on the United States, the biggest news story in decades, made nearly all Americans avid consumers of news. In the days following the attacks, newspapers sold millions of copies beyond their normal circulation; more Americans watched television coverage than had ever watched news on television before. Online news sites were visited by millions—more than twice as many as had ever used them previously.

In fact this was an extreme example of a phenomenon already identified in numerous studies of Americans' consumption of news. Even before the United States was attacked, three-fourths of all adult Americans watched news on television, listened to it on radio or looked at a newspaper every day, while a steadily growing number of people also looked for news on the Internet. Even before the terrorist attacks, Americans regarded news as important to their lives and crucial to a free society. But they were interested primarily in big stories, not the ordinary run of news. In surveys by the Pew Research Center for the People and the Press, a majority of Americans said they closely followed the major news events of the 1990s, including the Persian Gulf War, presidential elections, major natural disasters and mass shootings in high schools. But without a big story, most people paid less attention. In another Pew survey, 52 percent of Americans said they only follow national news when something big is happening; 63 percent said the same about international news.

Increasingly, Americans got their news in bits and bytes: on television, as they got up in the morning, ate dinner or went to bed at night; on the radio, as they drove to and from work; in newspapers, scanned hurriedly in spare moments or put off until Sunday; on the Internet, as they surfed the Web at work and home. They consumed news as headlines, weather and traffic reports, sports scores and highlights, stock quotes and school lunch menus.

And more of what people thought of as news came in popular entertainment formats—prime-time network television magazines, television and radio talk shows, celebrity magazines, gossip sites and chat rooms on the Internet—that mixed fact, rumor and opinion, and sometimes even fiction. Some of the most closely followed news stories, according to the Pew Research Center surveys in recent years, were about celebrities, especially the accidental deaths of Princess Diana and John F. Kennedy Jr., which dominated TV newsmagazines, talk shows and Internet chat for days.

Even the more serious news media adjusted to changing public appetites. A study of the three major network newscasts, the covers of *Time* and *Newsweek* and the front pages of the *New York Times* and the *Los Angeles Times* between 1977 and 1997 showed a marked shift away from government and international news to news about lifestyle, celebrity, crime and scandal. "Moreover, if one expands the definition of news media to include the universe of everything on television or the news rack, celebrity, entertainment and scandal have become a much larger percentage of what audiences get," concluded the Committee of Concerned Journalists, an organization of our colleagues formed to articulate the journalistic profession's own disquiet with trends in the eighties and nineties.

A great many Americans developed a powerful skepticism about what they heard, saw and read in the news; distrust and even hostility toward the news media became common. The signals were often mixed, however. Surveys found strong public disapproval of the media's coverage of the Monica Lewinsky–Bill Clinton scandal; many said the coverage was salacious and excessive. But when ABC broadcast an interview with Lewinsky in prime time, it drew an audience of 49 million people, bigger than any previous audience for a network news program.


But the audiences after September 11, 2001, were bigger. A genuine national crisis confirmed that Americans still want good journalism when they perceive that their own interests are at risk. Pandering to the popular appetite for scandal and celebrity had been commercially rewarding for some, but the terrorists reminded us all of the difference between pap and serious journalism.

The terrorist attacks were the second instance in less than a year of a serious story that captured the public imagination. The disputed presidential election of 2000 did the same, increasing newspaper sales and television news audiences.

Even without terrorist attacks or a hung election, there was compelling evidence that good journalism could be good business. Though many news organizations moved away from traditional journalistic standards in the eighties and nineties, the best news products continued to thrive in the marketplace. The *New York Times,* National Public Radio, the *Wall Street Journal,* the *Washington Post*—all have done well journalistically *and* financially, though the advertising recession of 2000–2001 hurt them all. The best metropolitan papers also thrived, including the *St. Petersburg Times,* the *Dallas Morning News,* the *Sacramento Bee* and the *Portland Oregonian.* Those newspapers and television news broadcasts that declined in quality—the *Miami Herald,* the *St. Louis Post-Dispatch,* CBS News—lost more of their audience than the best news media. Many of the local television stations with the best newscasts also tended to attract the most viewers (though there were exceptions).

September 11, 2001, and its aftermath demonstrated that even in news organizations with modest ambitions, owners, editors and journalists knew how to respond to an event of transcending importance. There were excesses and mistakes, of course, but the coverage was generally excellent. The television networks realized at once that they had to cancel all commercials and focus on the story. Even the most profit-conscious newspaper chains let their papers spend heavily on extra editions and expanded news coverage.

The longer-term consequences of a new war on terrorism would not be visible for years, but it seemed possible, at least, that those horrific events might rekindle a commitment to public-spirited journalism not only in the best news organizations, but in the more numerous ones that had previously skimmed lightly over the news, giving their readers and viewers the intellectual equivalent of thin soup. Of course, this could be wishful thinking. But those who own and lead this country's news media had a new opportunity to consider the appeal of revelatory, aggressive, intelligent journalism.

# Chapter Three

# NEWS THAT
# MAKES A
# DIFFERENCE

Consider this idea for a story:

A contentious, litigious and secretive organization that promises to help its members work through their psychological problems in return for substantial cash payments has been waging a kind of warfare against America's least-popular bureaucracy, the Internal Revenue Service. The organization has declared itself a religion, and wants the tax-deductible status enjoyed by America's churches. The IRS resists this idea for years, going to court to prove that the organization is a commercial enterprise, not a church. The courts agree, but the organization keeps the pressure on the IRS, even hires private detectives to harass IRS agents individually, sues them in courts all over the country and tries to influence the director of the agency personally. Then, suddenly and unexpectedly, the IRS does a complete flip-flop, abandons years of legal wrangling and grants the organization the religious status it seeks. But the agency explains nothing about how or why it changed its mind.

Sound like the raw material for a great piece of journalism? It was. Thanks to a reporter named Douglas Frantz and the editors who helped and supported him, readers of the *New York Times* could read it in memorable detail in a wonderful example of investigative journalism that ran in the *Times* in March 1997. The story recounted the strange tale of how Scientology won the tax-exempt status of a religious organization.

This was no Watergate story. Its practical consequences were negligible. The IRS never altered or explained its ruling. Millions of dollars that the IRS once said Scientology ought to pay in taxes will never be paid. But everyone who read the story—and others that followed—got an education in the operations of these two powerful and secretive institutions.

This was news that made a difference. It disclosed important information not previously known. When journalists use resourceful reporting and vivid presentation to hold the powerful accountable for their acts, they fulfill their highest purpose. They help encourage the honest and open use of power, and they help make America a fairer society.

There isn't enough accountability reporting. Much that ought to be publicly known remains secret. Countless abuses and injustices remain unexamined and uncorrected. Partly this is because too few news organizations attempt journalism of this kind. Partly it is because good accountability reporting can be excruciatingly difficult. It is usually tedious, time-consuming and exasperating for journalists, and expensive and risky for news organizations. Movies like *All the President's Men,* or *The Insider,* about a CBS News investigation of the tobacco industry, give a glimpse of what investigative reporting is like, but movies inevitably glamorize and dramatize their subject matter to make it more entertaining. No Hollywood director could do justice in a two-hour movie to the patient slogging that goes into the toughest journalistic investigations, or to the difficult decisions that must be made about pursuing them and publishing or broadcasting their results.

Frantz's investigation of the IRS and Scientology is a textbook example of how to do this kind of reporting. We'll describe it in detail to illuminate the complexity of the task, and the decision making it requires. Then we'll recount an ambitious investigation of the Washington, D.C., police department to find out why the city's cops were shooting and killing more civilians than any other department in the country—thirty-two shot and twelve killed in 1998. That investigation, by the *Washington Post,* caused the police to retrain every man and woman on the force. In 2000 just one civilian was killed by police gunfire in Washington.

Then we'll look at an embarrassing case where we failed as watchdogs. Our failure allowed Ronald Reagan and his associates to abuse their power and the Constitution of the United States in ways that would have been impossible if we had done our job properly. Finally we'll recount an internal debate inside a big news organization (our own) of a kind that is not unusual but is rarely visible to the public. The debate was provoked by a different kind of accountability reporting—an attempt to explain the personal history and character of a candidate for president. The specific dispute was whether to publish a story about a love affair that had taken place twenty-eight years earlier.

## A Risky Story

The Church of Scientology was founded in 1954 by a writer named L. Ron Hubbard. For years Scientology sought to persuade the Internal Revenue Service that it was a religion and deserved the same tax deduction given to traditional religious groups. Scientology took in hundreds of millions of dollars, and for decades the IRS insisted that it was a business, not a religion. In October 1993 the IRS reversed course and gave Scientology the tax status of a church. Just a year before the IRS reversal, the U.S. Court of Federal Claims had upheld an earlier IRS decision to deny tax-exempt status to Scientology's Church of Spiritual Technology, citing, among other things, "the commercial character of much of Scientology."

The IRS's decision, announced in 1993, was a one-day story at the time. Following its normal policy and laws protecting taxpayers' privacy, the IRS did not explain why it had changed course on Scientology. It didn't even reveal the terms of its final agreement with the newly blessed church, though it could have done that. Scientology itself has always been aggressive about protecting itself from public scrutiny, and it too disclosed very little information.

Three years later, in 1996, Doug Frantz was looking for a story to investigate. Frantz, then forty-six, was a newcomer to the *New York Times* national staff, whose editor at the time was Dean Baquet, then forty (in 2000 Baquet became managing editor of the *Los Angeles Times*). The two men were old friends; they had worked together in the 1980s at the *Chicago Tribune.* Frantz, an ordinary-looking man with close-cropped hair, and Baquet, a compactly built African American with a steady gaze and an easy manner, could be mistaken for a pair of FBI agents or police detectives. But they were ambitious journalists, eager to make a mark.

"Doug and I sat down and said, let's find something . . . that's big and that's compelling and that's risky, with an emphasis on risky," Baquet recounted four years later. "In an odd way I think newspapers have moved away from taking risks. . . . So I told him to just go take some time and scout around and come back with something."

Frantz did. A lunch with an old friend produced a tip. "He mentioned that he had heard a story about a private investigator who worked for Scientology going after some IRS officials," says Frantz. "And I thought it sounded really interesting. He sort of dropped it in passing. And so I came back and talked it over with Dean and said you know I'd like to just . . . take a few weeks and see if there is anything here. . . . The context right away was that these private investigators might have played some role in the IRS reversal over the church's tax-exempt status."

Reading "the clips"—earlier stories about the Scientology tax deduction, which these days are in electronic databases rather than the old files of paper clippings—Frantz found a mystery. "We actually had it on the front page of the *New York Times* back in October of '93, when the IRS issued its decision. But nobody had explained it in any way that I could find what really happened, I mean, why the IRS would abandon a position it had held steadfastly for twenty-five years.

"The first thing I did after [reading] the clips is the first thing I always do, just to see what documents are available. You often start out with a story that will turn out to be unprovable or unwritable, and nobody wants to go too far down that road. So I went down to the IRS library, where they have a place set aside in the reading room specifically for Scientology documents and there are about twelve linear feet of these documents there, and I spent a week going through those documents. . . . I also gathered some court opinions that had upheld the agency's denial of this [tax-exempt] status [to Scientology]."

Frantz's friend who had given him the original tip also gave him the name of a private investigator who had worked for Scientology, Michael Shomers. "I had a devil of a time tracking him down," Frantz recalled. "He was in Maryland when he worked for Scientology, but he had given up his license as a PI and he had moved out of state somewhere. I found somebody who had worked with him in Maryland, who thought he'd gone to Florida, and then, by looking through publicly available phone records, I found a couple of Michael Shomerses in Florida, and I tracked this guy down in Jacksonville."

After a couple of conversations on the phone, Frantz flew to Jacksonville to take Shomers to dinner. The private detective turned out to be an excellent source, direct and forthcoming about what he had done for the Scientologists. He said he had gathered personal information about IRS agents who might be vulnerable to pressure in 1990 and 1991, taken IRS documents from a conference the agency held in California and investigated conditions at apartment houses owned by IRS officials to see if they violated the local housing codes. He said he later developed second thoughts about the Scientologists and how they might be using the information he had acquired. Most helpful of all, he had kept documents that Frantz could use to double-check what Shomers told him.

"Corroboration is essential when dealing with any source, but particularly when you're dealing with a source who's making allegations involving both the IRS and the Church of Scientology," said Frantz. "Corroboration is better than gold."

He began meticulously to assemble a picture of Scientology's efforts to put pressure on the IRS. He had Shomers's account of efforts to find exploitable weaknesses in the lives of various IRS agents. With the help of former church officials, who spoke on the record, and participants in these efforts, Frantz established that Scientology had created and funded an organization called the National Coalition of IRS Whistle-blowers, which was active "for nearly a decade," beginning in 1984. Its greatest success was to provoke a 1989 congressional investigation of IRS enforcement activities.

Altogether Frantz spent several months looking for and talking to private investigators and others who had worked for Scientology on IRS-related matters, and then checking out their stories independently. He even found residents of apartments owned by IRS officials who confirmed that a man had visited their homes looking for housing-code violations.

Not every lead produced new facts. Frantz had difficulty tracking down another private investigator who had worked with Shomers for Scientology. When Frantz finally got him on the telephone, the investigator said he would have to check with his client and call back. He never did.

"By that time," Frantz recounted, "I'd figured out where he lived, so I drove out to his house late one afternoon out in Rockville [a Maryland suburb of Washington, D.C.], and it was a very nondescript tract house. And I went up and knocked on the door and nobody was home. So I sat out in my car for a couple of hours in front of the house waiting for him to come home. And a next-door neighbor came out and was angry that I was sitting on their street and wondered what in the hell I was doing there. I apologized and said I was waiting for [the private investigator] to come home and he said, 'Well, he's never here.' I don't know whether that's true or not, but I figured it was a long shot that I would catch him at home anyway. So I left."

A dramatic moment in Frantz's reporting came about four months into his investigation, when he felt ready to talk to officials of the Church of Scientology. This is an important step in most investigative reporting projects, when the reporter confronts his subject with questions that have arisen during the investigation. It gives the subject an opportunity to respond to the reporter's findings. For good reporters, this is important both to ensure accuracy and fairness and to demonstrate open-mindedness.

Baquet did not want Frantz to go alone to Scientology headquarters in Los Angeles, because of Scientology's reputation as a highly litigious organization, so he took along a colleague from the paper's Los Angeles bureau. Throughout the reporting project, Frantz and his editors did all they could to minimize the risk of lawsuit.

When they arrived, Frantz recounted, "We announced ourselves and were taken to a very small upper-floor conference room, fifteen by twenty [feet] at the most, with a big table surrounded by nine people. That made me realize right away—if I was ever naïve enough to think it was going to be just another interview—that it wasn't. . . . It remains the most difficult interview I've ever had."

The meeting began with a forty-five-minute attack on him, Frantz recalled, with the Scientologists and their lawyers working from a stack of his past stories. Frantz said the Scientologists had concluded he was hostile to them "before I had written a word." One Scientology lawyer, Gerard E. Feffer, a partner in the big Washington law firm of Williams and Connolly, told Frantz the questions he was asking demonstrated that he was practicing yellow journalism. Scientology officials and lawyers emphasized that the IRS decision to change course and declare Scientology a tax-exempt religion represented nothing more than the end of an unfair IRS campaign of harassment against Scientology. "To say our relations started off on the wrong foot is an understatement," Frantz recalled.

Eventually Frantz established that Scientology had indeed made extensive use of private investigators to scrutinize the IRS and its officials. In his story he quoted Feffer: "The IRS uses investigators, too." Feffer said the IRS had used its Criminal Investigation Division "to put this church under intense scrutiny for years with a mission to destroy the church." Scientology was responding in kind.

Scientology had also used the courts to pressure the IRS. At one time, Frantz found, it had more than fifty suits pending against the IRS and individual IRS employees.

Frantz was also reporting on a second track to find out what had happened in the direct dealings between Scientology and the IRS that led to the sudden reversal of IRS policy in 1993. He found considerable information about this in published statements of Scientology officials, particularly the group's leader, David Miscavige. But he got very little help from the IRS.

According to Miscavige's account in a Scientology publication, he and another church official were walking past IRS headquarters in Washington in October 1991 when they decided to drop in on Fred Goldberg, the IRS commissioner. They told a guard at the door they did not have an appointment but they were certain Goldberg would want to see them. According to Miscavige, the commissioner did indeed meet with them. Soon Goldberg had appointed a special committee of IRS officials to negotiate a final settlement with Scientology.

Miscavige and Scientology also provided some details of the two-year negotiation that ensued, ending with the IRS announcement in October 1993 that it would grant Scientology tax-exempt status. Miscavige announced the final agreement five days before the IRS did in a speech to thousands of Scientologists in Los Angeles. He called it a victory in "the war to end all wars" between Scientology and the IRS. A subsequent article in a Scientology magazine elaborated: "Our attack was impinging on their [the IRS's] resources in a major way and our exposés of their crimes were beginning to have serious political reverberations. It was becoming a costly war of attrition, with no clear-cut winner in sight."

The IRS was less contentious in its dealings with Frantz, but it offered him few facts for his story. Invoking laws and rules requiring it to protect the privacy of taxpayers, the IRS provided no explanation for its policy reversal on Scientology, and no details of its final agreement. Frantz noted that the IRS, in other disputes with religious organizations, including the Reverend Jerry Falwell's *Old Time Gospel Hour,* had required public disclosure of a negotiated settlement of tax disputes. There was no similar requirement for the Church of Scientology.

Using the federal Freedom of Information Act (FOIA), which requires government agencies to make much information about their activities public, Frantz petitioned the IRS for Director Goldberg's office calendar. He got it, but found no reference to the meeting Miscavige had described between himself and Goldberg that led to the final settlement with Scientology. Goldberg, by then a partner in the Washington office of the giant law firm Skadden Arps Slate Meagher & Flom, refused to talk to Frantz.

Frantz did find a lawsuit filed by William Lehrfeld, a Washington tax lawyer, on behalf of a nonprofit group called Tax Analysts that publishes material for tax lawyers and accountants. The suit sought the texts of the IRS's agreements with Scientology and other organizations that had been granted tax-exempt status. The Tax Analysts lawyers were able to take depositions from IRS officials, a helpful source of information for Frantz, as court depositions often are for investigative reporters.

As Frantz neared the end of his reporting, the IRS finally made available two officials for interviews, but Frantz had to accept "ground rules" that prevented him from identifying the officials by name. These "background" conversations helped Frantz confirm that Goldberg had created an unusual special committee—bypassing his agency's tax-exempt-organizations branch—to negotiate with Scientology. A retired IRS official named Paul Streckfus, who had worked in the exempt-organizations division, told Frantz that Goldberg's creation of this committee signaled the IRS's willingness to change its policy toward Scientology.

Ultimately Frantz's meetings with the IRS were more frustrating than illuminating. Frantz recalled the most substantive background meeting he had with an IRS official who was involved in the Scientology negotiations. "He was a nice guy, [but] there were just more questions he couldn't answer than he could answer," Frantz said, "and I left that meeting still convinced that I didn't understand the logic behind the IRS decision."

Frantz decided it was time to talk through the story with an editor. This is another requirement of good investigative reporting that can be satisfied only in news organizations with the staff, time, experience and culture that can support accountability journalism.

"[When] the first images of the picture begin to form, then I'm lucky to have somebody like Dean [Baquet] to sit down with," Frantz said. "By 'somebody like Dean' I mean not only that he's my friend, and therefore I trust him, but because he's somebody who's done this before, he was an investigative reporter. Even the smartest editor I think has difficulty understanding how the investigative process works unless they've done it before. The danger of working [by] yourself on a long, complex project is that you get lost and you miss the forest for the trees."

Baquet usually asked his reporters to begin the writing process by composing a long memo, a narrative describing what the reporting had uncovered. Frantz liked this approach: "It is a very good process, it clarifies the story in my mind as well as providing him with a progress report. It also buys me some more freedom and some more time if I need it."

A narrative memo also fit Frantz's habit of keeping a detailed chronology as he reports a story. This is a tool used by many investigative reporters as a way to see how the bits and pieces fit together.

The biggest question in this case, Baquet said, was "How much [reporting] is enough?" Baquet used a test of his own, developed when he was an investigative reporter, to decide whether a reporter had finished doing the research. "When you start to hear the same stories over and over again, when there are no new incidents of what I would call harassment, when there were no new documents that we were going to get, when Doug felt comfortable and I felt comfortable that we had gone up and down the chain of former Scientology people . . .

"As an investigative reporter," Baquet continued, drawing on his own experience, "you make yourself a list . . . of like twenty things that you've got to do for a story—eight people inside, former Scientologists, defectors, the last four or five IRS commissioners who are now retired, my freedom-of-information requests for these ten documents—once all that stuff is exhausted, which was the case . . . there wasn't anything outstanding, then to me that's nut-cutting time."

The memo Frantz wrote in narrative form was at least 8,000 words long—enough to fill two full pages of the *Times* without any pictures or headlines. Baquet read it. So did Joseph Lelyveld, then executive editor of the *Times,* and Gene Roberts, then the managing editor. Baquet collected their thoughts on the memo and conveyed them, with his own, to Frantz. They talked about how to make the memo into a story, and Frantz began to write it into his computer.

"I do what I always do. I sit down and I write it all. I have to write the lead first"—a reference to the first paragraph of the story, which can occupy a reporter's mind for a long time. Frantz thought he had "the lead from heaven" in the anecdote of Miscavige, the leader of Scientology, telling thousands of cheering Scientologists that "the war is over" with the IRS. "Then," said Frantz, "you go back and review how they won the war."

Frantz's story began:

> On October 8, 1993, 10,000 cheering Scientologists thronged the Los Angeles Sports Arena to celebrate the most important milestone in the church's recent history: victory in its all-out war against the Internal Revenue Service.
>
> For twenty-five years, IRS agents had branded Scientology a commercial enterprise and refused to give it the tax exemption granted to churches. The refusals had been upheld in every court. But that night the crowd learned of an astonishing turnaround. The IRS had granted tax exemptions to every Scientology entity in the United States.
>
> "The war is over," David Miscavige, the church's leader, declared to tumultuous applause.

Frantz then told us how he wrote the story, describing a classic investigative reporter's view of his work. "Before I showed it to anybody else, I would go back through and take an adjective out of every paragraph. Then I'd go back through again and take another adjective out of every paragraph, until I get out most of the adjectives, because I don't like them. Sometimes my stories may read a little flat, but I'd rather be flat than not, I guess, in these stories."

Good investigative reporters often pride themselves on finding the cleanest possible language to tell their stories—no flourishes, just the story, clean and crisp, with the facts speaking for themselves, and without hint of opinion or argument.

"Then," said Frantz, "the last thing that I'd do is make a printout and sit down and check the facts of every single paragraph against the documents and the interview notes that I had and the notes that I'd taken, because I don't want to have to turn a story in to my editor and have him say, 'Boy, this is great stuff, where'd you get this paragraph?' and have to say to him, 'Oh, shit, I got that wrong, it wasn't quite like that.' Because that sets up doubt in the editor's mind, and you don't want the editor to doubt your story, and I don't want to get something that's not exactly right in any form going to anybody outside of myself. And invariably . . . on a story that long . . . you're going to have some nuances that are wrong, and maybe some quote that's wrong. . . ."

"And then I would probably turn it in to Dean. And later in the process, after we figured out which quotes were going to go in, I would call back almost everybody, or everybody who's quoted, and run the quotes past them, to make sure that they're accurate. That doesn't mean I'm going to change every quote, because if somebody says, Well, I didn't mean to say that, or That's not really what I said, or I couldn't have said that, I'll go back to my notes and see, and we may have an argument."

Baquet read Frantz's draft story carefully, inserting questions into the text, suggesting language changes and looking for ways to shorten it. After that, the story got more polishing from other editors and careful scrutiny from the *Times*'s top editors, and from the paper's lawyers. Frantz was impressed and delighted by the attention that Lelyveld paid to his story. He said Lelyveld had good suggestions for strengthening it and insisted the story contain two references, one near the beginning and one near the end, to the fact that granting the tax exemption overturned twenty-five years of precedent for the IRS. Frantz said he complained that this was repetitive, "and Joe said—I'll never forget—he said, 'Repetition for the sake of emphasis is acceptable.' Because really, that was an important element of the story, no doubt about it."

And it was a reminder that Frantz, despite months of hard work, had failed to find out why Goldberg decided to reverse that twenty-five-year IRS position on Scientology, or what the terms of the final agreement were. So Frantz's story, published on March 9, 1997, beginning on the *Times*'s front page and continuing on two inside pages, gave readers a detailed narrative from which they could draw their own conclusions.

After a summary of his principal findings, Frantz quoted Goldberg's predecessor as director of Internal Revenue, Lawrence B. Gibbs, who called the IRS reversal on Scientology "a very surprising decision. When you have as much litigation over as much time, with the general uniformity of results that the Service had with Scientology, it is surprising to have the ultimate decision be favorable [to Scientology]. It was even more surprising that the Service made the decision without full disclosure, in light of the prior background." Obviously, this is an unusual way for a former government official to talk about a decision made by his successor.

Nine months after the *Times* published Frantz's story, more details of the agreement between the IRS and Scientology did appear—in the *Wall Street Journal*. The *Journal* posted the text of the seventy-six-page agreement on its Internet site. Frantz said he also obtained a copy from his own sources, after its disclosure by the *Journal*, and wrote another story about the agreement that appeared in the *Times* on the last day of 1997. Frantz wouldn't say where he got the document or why he thought it finally came out. He speculated that the *Journal* might have gotten it on Capitol Hill, where a congressional committee had recently subpoenaed a great many IRS documents.

The IRS-Scientology agreement required Scientology to pay the agency $12.5 million and make an annual report for the next three years showing that Scientology remained in compliance with the tax laws. The IRS appeared to be concerned that Scientology's revenues go to religious or charitable purposes, not to church officials.

For Scientology $12.5 million was a lot less than the IRS had been claiming it owed in back taxes. Miscavige once said the total could have reached $1 billion. In addition, by granting Scientology tax-exempt status, the U.S. government gave it the legal standing it had been seeking for years—as a church.

In the end the *Times*'s investigative reporting had proved compelling and enlightening, but it had no dramatic impact on Scientology or the IRS. Frantz's largely solo effort was relatively inexpensive for investigative reporting, costing the *Times* less than $150,000 in reporting hours and expenses. Was the Scientology story worth the expense and effort that went into it? Why work so hard on a project that leads to an ambiguous result?

Baquet responded that the story did prove that Scientology "had launched an aggressive campaign against the IRS." And, he said, the IRS secrecy had to be challenged. "I think that when decisions like this get made by a big government agency and they're done in a very secretive fashion, they involve hundreds of millions of dollars, affect lots of people—it affected the IRS bureaucrats who were working on it, it affected the church and its future and its standing around the world. I think when something like that happens and nobody wants to talk about the details, you're almost obligated to try to figure out the details." Because the *Times* pursued this story, Baquet said, "I have a feeling that the next time the IRS does one like this, they're going to be aware of this in the back of their minds, that there might be a big look at it, and they ought not do it in secret."

How does the *Times* pick a target like this for a major investigation? Lelyveld said it isn't as though the *Times* has some kind of "hit list."

"It's typically more a balancing of targets of opportunity," Lelyveld said. "I mean, it wasn't that anybody thought that . . . it was time to do the Scientologists, nobody had done it for a decade or something. It was that here was something that had never been explained and had happened rather suddenly and had never been much remarked upon, and it cost the federal treasury a considerable amount of money. So it was easy to say, Yes, it was big enough and important enough to do it. But you always have to balance it against the stuff you know that's going to need to be done."

Asked if he thought ordinary newspaper readers understood how investigative reporters worked, Frantz said, "I think people don't understand the difficulty in getting information. They really think that the press conferences they see on TV are the way everybody gets every story. But nobody's ever held a press conference for investigative reporters. People really don't know—and there's no reason they should. . . . People don't understand the lengths to which we go to get stories. And I'm not just talking about readers. I think there are editors at this newspaper and other newspapers who don't understand how very hard it is to really get at reporting that answers questions and doesn't just raise questions.

"My definition of an investigative reporter," Frantz continued, "is not somebody who charms sources into leaking. To me an investigative reporter is the person who gets someone to say something that they don't want to say. To get somebody to tell you something that they don't want to tell you . . . takes a lot of spadework, a lot of hard work, and too many people in this business and out of this business don't understand that difference."

Good as Frantz's story was, it had no visible consequences. No congressional committee called hearings to explore what had happened inside the IRS, or why Goldberg made the decision he made. No politician or official suggested the issue of Scientology's tax status be reopened. Journalism can take an issue like this only so far. The *New York Times* had no way to compel Goldberg or the other IRS officials involved in the case to explain why they did what they did.

That does not undermine the value of Frantz's work. The journalist's job is to find out and explain what took place, not to make things happen. It is up to those who hold power to follow up with appropriate action.

## Saving Lives

The *Washington Post*'s investigation of shootings of civilians by Washington police officers was another example of accountability journalism, but it went beyond the usual forms of investigative reporting. The *Post*'s research uncovered a situation unknown even to the commanders of the Metropolitan Police Department. The newspaper's articles described a horrifying reality that would never have been understood without the *Post*'s investigation. Once that reality was obvious, the police department itself moved quickly to rectify it.

The *Post* project involved three reporters, three researchers, two graphic artists and three editors. The basic enterprise was similar to Frantz's: find facts not previously known; use those facts to pry more information out of people involved in the events being investigated, including people who had no desire to reveal that information; bring a huge body of facts and anecdotes under literary control to produce readable articles. The final product, a series of stories covering seventeen newspaper pages over five days in late 1998, could have filled a small book.

The story began with a powerful new reporting tool—the computer—which has opened new vistas for investigative reporting. Many newspapers have hired or developed computer specialists to exploit the fact that much information, especially information collected by governments, is now available on computer tapes or the Internet, and can be analyzed by computer to reveal significant patterns.

The *Post* hired one such specialist, Jo Craven, on a temporary contract in late 1997. Craven had worked at the University of Missouri's journalism school, training students in the techniques of computer-assisted reporting. She told *Post* editors that she had a hunch the FBI was collecting information on "justifiable homicides" by police officers. She came to this conclusion after examining the annual crime statistics the FBI put out on computer tape. Using database technology to look at the figures in different ways, Craven thought she had discovered that the FBI had a category—number 81—for justifiable homicides by police officers, but no statistics from this category were included in the numbers the bureau released to the public.

Craven began to pursue her hunch with the FBI, which was not eager to provide the data she wanted. It took several months of negotiations and the filing of several formal requests under the federal Freedom of Information Act to produce computer tapes that included those category 81s. They were worth waiting for.

Craven's first analysis showed that the Washington police "had the highest rate of justifiable homicides per capita of any [big-city] police department in the country" between 1991 and 1995—three times the rate of Los Angeles, four times that of New York City. She provided these numbers in an initial memorandum proposing that the *Post* pursue this story. The editors then in charge of the *Post*'s twenty-year-old investigative reporting team, Rick Atkinson and Marilyn Thompson, were impressed by her first memo and decided to assign their new star reporter, Jeff Leen, to work with Craven.

Leen, then forty-one, had come to the *Post* two months earlier from the *Miami Herald,* where he had been an investigative reporter for ten years, often writing about the drug culture centered in Miami. He had discovered the existence of the Medellín and Cali drug cartels in Colombia and exposed how drug dealers laundered their ill-gotten millions into legitimate-looking capital. He was a Pulitzer Prize winner, and had become an expert in many aspects of law enforcement.

Leen was stunned by Craven's memo; the number of fatal shootings by police in Washington suggested a very serious problem on the force. "The first thing I did was to read the *Post* clips on police shooting incidents religiously, from 1986 to the present," Leen recalled. The clips—which included accounts of specific shootings and earlier *Post* investigations of the poor screening and training of Washington police officers, particularly those brought onto the force in 1989 and 1990—convinced Leen that an investigative reporting project was warranted.

He was especially struck by the story of Sutoria Moore, an unarmed teenager shot to death in a car in 1994 by a police detective. Then he saw stories on two other fatal shootings by police of people in cars. "I recalled what I had heard from Miami cops: they raised their eyebrows at the mention of an officer who shot at a car to defend himself," Leen recounted. "They told me that shooting at cars could always be justified by claiming the car had 'attacked' the officer. It was, they told me, a variation on the throw-down gun, the infamous practice of officers carrying extra weapons in order to throw them down next to a suspect to justify any shooting."

The best reporters have memories like Leen's. The reporting for one story informs them for the next. Over a long career they accumulate both wisdom and instincts that prove invaluable at moments like that one.

Leen, an intense journalist with a soft-spoken but determined manner, described another crucial episode in his first two weeks on the story in a memo he wrote after the articles were published:

> I called up the lawyers who had sued police over the Roosevelt Askew shooting [the victim was Sutoria Moore]. They were brusque and non-responsive when I called. The case was pending, they were busy and they didn't want to talk to me. I called back several times, trying each of the two lawyers, and finally the younger one in the firm gave me what I needed . . . the name of the expert they turned to when they needed to know about police procedures. I called him. For a week he didn't call me back. Finally the expert called and I convinced him to meet with me for lunch. [This was Bob Klotz, a former deputy chief of the D.C. police department.]
>
> In my first conversation he said several things that were crucial to the project. First he said that he felt the subject was important and should be written about. He said he felt there was a problem with police shootings in the District [of Columbia]. If he had said there wasn't, I'm not sure what I would have done at that point.
>
> He also told me that police officers were more apt to shoot because over the years the cases had gone from officers shooting when they saw a weapon in the suspect's hand to officers shooting at shiny objects to officers shooting at furtive movements. He also said he felt training and the introduction of the Glock hand-

gun [a high-powered, hair-triggered weapon adopted by the Washington police in 1988] played into the pattern. Then he talked about car shootings. He said he noticed a problem and pattern there, too.

Finally, he talked off-the-record about the police shooting cases he had testified on in the District. Several of them were very bad shootings, he told me. After that conversation, for me, the outlines of the project clicked into place: an overall pattern of a high number of shootings, sub-patterns of car shootings, questionable shootings, poor training and Glock accidents.

A well-informed source with a coherent overview of your story is a reporter's dream. Former deputy chief Klotz, part of whose livelihood came from appearances as a paid witness in cases involving his old department, gave Leen expert confirmation of the pattern Leen thought he had seen.

Leen used an FOIA request to obtain a list of cases from the city's legal office in which the government was defending police officers in citizens' lawsuits involving a shooting. To his amazement, this list, which covered a five-year period, had thirty-one entries. Craven, who began pulling the courthouse files on those thirty-one cases, found that several involved policemen shooting at moving cars. Leen began calling lawyers involved in the thirty-one lawsuits. Many would not return his call. One who did, however, gave Leen and Craven "the crown jewels"—a police department document listing every occasion when a police officer had shot his or her gun between 1994 and 1997—a total of 464 shooting incidents involving 576 police officers who fired 2,271 bullets.

Then, in one of the court files for a police shooting case, Leen and Craven found another unexpected document, "a computer printout of the lawsuits in excessive-force cases over a four-year period. It was just sitting in a court file," Leen said. "The attorney [in the case] . . . didn't even know about it, and we were never able to figure out why it was filed there." There were more than 600 lawsuits on the printout. The city had already settled nearly half of them. Another gold mine of information found by chance, but only because the reporters were so thorough.

Atkinson and Thompson began to hold weekly meetings with the reporters and researchers, making suggestions for future reporting. At Leen's urging, first one and then two additional reporters were added to the team. The first was David Jackson, another newcomer to the *Post*, whom Atkinson had hired from the *Chicago Tribune*, a slight, wisecracking forty-year-old who was what journalists call a gifted street reporter, able to chat up just about anyone. The second was Sari Horwitz, then forty-one, a *Post* reporter since 1984, who had covered the police department from 1986 to 1991. Although many of her best sources had retired from the department, Horwitz, with her earnest charm, still had good connections and a reputation among cops as a reporter who understood them.

By summer the scope of the project had become daunting. The team had a web of promising leads not only on incidents of shootings by the police but also on scores of cases in which citizens had accused police of using excessive force—brutality. Data from the FBI and other sources, fed into computers and analyzed comparatively, proved informative yet inadequate. It had too many holes that needed to be filled to present a complete, accurate picture. "The problem with the computer was you couldn't trust it for anything but a lead," Leen said later. "It gave you the surface, but no depth."

Leen filed an FOIA request with the city's legal authorities for a list of all lawsuits charging excessive use of force by police officers that the city had settled out of court. Using this list, five reporters and researchers camped out in the civil division of Washington's Superior Court to sift through case "jackets" that held the records of those civil suits. They found every case on the list from the FOIA request and filled out a form, devised by *Post* researcher Margot Williams, for collecting information from each one. Later, she used these forms to enter the details of each case into the computer.

Finding and reading these cases "went on for days," Horwitz recalled. "It was important because it gave me a real feel for what was out there. Some frivolous suits from prisoners and the like, lots of petty incidents escalating into arrests . . . and classic 'contempt of cop' scenarios." She was referring to the reporting team's discovery that violent cops sometimes lashed out against civilians for no better reason than the citizen's failure to show them the respect they thought was their due.

Ultimately the reporting team created its own databases of police shooting and brutality cases, using the information acquired from the FBI and the city. Because one goal was to compare the Washington police with the forces in other cities, they decided to talk directly to other departments about their numbers, "a task requiring infinite persistence and patience," in Atkinson's words. Figures provided by government agencies could never be accepted without further checking. In nearly every case, the team's own reporting changed or added to the official statistics.

Once Craven and her colleague Ira Chinoy, then the *Post*'s director of computer-assisted reporting, had the raw material they thought they needed, they spent hundreds of hours putting the statistics in order and then analyzing them.

The reporters and editors realized they could be vulnerable to accusations that they did not appreciate the conditions under which Washington's police had to work. The city had become one of America's most violent in the mid-1980s, when crack cocaine first appeared on Washington's streets. Nine policemen had been killed in the line of duty between 1993 and 1998. So the reporters rode in squad cars with Washington police officers, often on the overnight shift. They even went to the police shooting range to test-fire the standard-issue Glock pistol.

Horwitz had the assignment of finding a policeman who had been involved in a shooting who would share with *Post* readers the experience of firing his police revolver. Three times she asked for an interview with officer Keith DeVille, who had killed a man who had killed his partner in a shoot-out; three times department officials said he wasn't interested. Finally, Horwitz got to DeVille directly and explained what the paper was trying to do. He agreed to talk. His moving account gave the final articles a valuable police viewpoint.

Each aspect of the story had to be reported with care. "There was a lot of refinement of everything," Leen recalled, describing "a very slow process of circling the subject." He himself constructed, by hand, the final list of shootings by police, drawing on all the data the team had assembled by reporting and computer analysis. In the end, Leen concluded there had been forty-two fatal shootings of citizens over four years, though the police department's own database recorded only twenty-eight. Leen established that seven cases never got into the police database, and seven more, which were mislabeled, did not show up as fatal shootings.

By examining the criminal records of those involved in these incidents and interviewing police officers and lawyers, the team established that in nine of those forty-two cases, an unarmed person had been shot dead by police gunfire. Lawyers representing citizens suing the city as a result of some of these incidents proved to be particularly useful sources. They extracted hard facts from the police department during pretrial discovery proceedings, when a plaintiff's lawyer can subpoena official data under court order.

The statistics proved conclusively that Washington's police force was dangerously trigger-happy. But the impact of the *Post*'s articles came less from these disturbing numbers than from old-fashioned reporting and interviews. The voices of shooting victims and their relatives, eyewitnesses, police officers who shot or saw their colleagues shoot, and lawyers and prosecutors brought the story to life, making its themes palpable and real. So did vivid graphics, which depicted several shooting incidents so clearly that a reader could imagine the entire scene.

Atkinson kept driving the project with weekly meetings. His colleagues referred to him as their commanding officer or field marshal, in part because of his brisk and efficient military bearing. His father was a career Army officer, and Atkinson had written a best-selling book on the West Point Class of 1966. A key meeting in August, where a final outline of the project was mapped out, required four hours.

Atkinson was proud of the ingenuity of his reporters, and boasted about them in a memorandum written after the project was published:

> For example, when Sari [Horwitz] tried to find former Chief Larry Soulsby, who had disappeared after resigning from the department [under a cloud] in November, 1997, she and [researcher] Margot [Williams] learned through an online public records databank that his ex-wife lived in Spotsylvania County, Va. Suspecting that Soulsby had gone back to her and knowing his passion for golf, Sari drove to a nearby public course and chatted up a few duffers who confirmed that the former chief was a regular. She then waited for him outside the ex-wife's house—wary neighbors, spotting Sari's D.C. tags, called the state police—until Soulsby eventually drove up. The chief agreed to talk for the first time since leaving office, confirming for us that police shootings were "not a hot topic among police officers during his tenure."

That interview confirmed the reporters' suspicion that one reason the shootings had become so common was that senior officers had ignored them.

By late August the team had mapped out a plan for a series of articles, which Atkinson sent to his bosses—Downie, the executive editor, and Steve Coll, who had succeeded Kaiser as the *Post*'s managing editor two months earlier. Ultimately the project was organized around five days of stories. The writing tasks were divided up among the reporters, who began to work on drafts.

The process of turning research into newspaper stories is the chemistry of journalism. As in chemistry, there are formulas that journalists can follow to create a story. The classic formula is a story in the "pyramid" style, beginning with a first paragraph (the "lead") that tells the reader the five w's: who, what, when, where, why. The idea of the pyramid is to put the most important facts as near to the beginning of the story as possible, so that hurried readers can stop anywhere after the first paragraph and still carry away important information from the story. In chemistry the scientist sticks with the formulas or gets into trouble. In journalism we consider the old formulas a starting point for thinking about the material in any specific case. The most striking works of journalism often depart, in some creative and readable way, from traditional patterns.

Jeff Leen drafted the first part of the series on police shootings. It was his job to summarize what the team had learned and to lay it out as clearly and enticingly as possible. If the first story failed to interest a lot of readers, the *Post* would be squandering a huge amount of newsprint and ink over five days.

The hardest paragraph to write, Leen said later, was the second one in the first-day story. "It came very close to being an editorial judgment," something appropriate for the editorial page, not the front page, Leen said. But in the end, he and his editors felt they could make a strong summary statement of their findings that was totally supported by facts and required no leap of faith. "We had marshaled so much evidence, it freed us to write a very strong day one," Leen said.

That story, spread across the top of page one on November 15, 1998, began:

> The District of Columbia's Metropolitan Police Department shot and killed more people per resident in the 1990s than any other large American city police force.
>
> Many shootings by Washington police officers were acts of courage and even heroism. But internal police files and court records reveal a pattern of reckless and indiscriminate gunplay by officers sent into the streets with inadequate training and little oversight, an eight-month Washington *Post* investigation has found.
>
> Washington's officers fire their weapons at more than double the rate of police in New York, Los Angeles, Chicago or Miami. Deaths and injuries in D.C. police shooting cases have resulted in nearly $8 million in court settlements and judgments against the District in the last six months alone.
>
> "We shoot too often, and we shoot too much when we do

shoot," said Executive Assistant Chief of Police Terrance W. Gainer, who became the department's second in command in May. . . .

That was the essence of the investigation. The five days of stories spelled out what had happened in numerous specific episodes. They recounted the experiences of both police officers and citizens they had shot. They explained shortcomings in police training for handling difficult situations and for the use of their guns. The stories demonstrated that the police department did not properly investigate shootings by police officers. They showed how the Glock pistol, recently purchased by Washington police to respond to the heavy weaponry drug gangs had brought to the city's streets, had aggravated the problem with its light trigger.

The impact of this investigative reporting was immediate and substantial. When confronted with its findings, Washington police chief Charles H. Ramsey, recently hired from Chicago to try to rescue Washington's troubled police department, and his top deputy, Gainer, immediately promised improvement. Neither man had understood the full scope of the problem of shootings by police until the *Post* laid it before them. They seized on the series of articles and its impact in the city as an opportunity for promoting reform.

Gainer, a former deputy director of the Illinois State Police, wrote Sari Horwitz an e-mail message on the second day of the articles' publication: "Your series has been outstanding. The articles have been balanced, well researched and useful. . . . Continue to hold us accountable, we will do better for our officers, and, as a direct result, for the people we serve. . . . I have never seen such in-depth, honest reporting. . . ."

Police officials quickly instituted extensive new training for the entire 3,500-officer force, and new procedures for investigating shootings by police. Every officer was required to spend more time at the shooting range to master the Glock pistol. All were taught a "continuum of force" to encourage the use of actions short of firing their guns to subdue unruly suspects.

In 1998 Washington police shot thirty-two citizens, twelve fatally. In 1999, with new training and procedures in effect, there were eleven shootings, four of them fatal. In 2000, after most officers had been retrained, just one citizen was killed by a policeman. The city had deployed a twelve-officer team to respond to the scene of every police shooting incident and conduct a full investigation. Ramsey said the *Post*'s series deserved the credit for pushing the department to change its ways.

. . .

Projects like this one and Frantz's on Scientology are rarer than they should be. Yet when a news organization can do this kind of work, it makes a powerful impression. The best accountability reporting reverberates through the culture, reminding malefactors everywhere that they may get caught and exposed. This is what freedom of the press should inspire.

It is no coincidence that these two projects were conducted by two of the country's best newspapers. With few exceptions—*Frontline* on PBS television is perhaps the most prominent, the best work on CBS's *60 Minutes* is another—television doesn't do this kind of work. Some television journalists (usually off-camera producers, not the "talent" that appears on the air) do investigative reporting, but usually on a much more modest scale. The most intensive investigative journalism is generally produced by the most ambitious, best-staffed and best-edited news organizations. Those belong to newspapers.

## When the Watchdog Fails to Bark

Another way to illustrate journalism that makes a difference is to examine a case in which one newspaper, the *Washington Post*, failed to make a difference. Our failure had significant and enduring importance for the country. We might never have learned about the failure but for a plane crash on Sunday, October 5, 1986.

That day Sandinista soldiers in Nicaragua shot down a C-123 cargo plane carrying four men, three of them Americans. Only one of the four survived the plane's crash landing, a soldier of fortune named Eugene Hasenfus. Soon after his capture by the Sandinista government, Hasenfus appeared at a press conference and said he thought he was working for the CIA. He named two people who ran his operation whom he thought were CIA agents. Hasenfus, it turned out, was a tiny cog in a large wheel—an interlocking combination of secret adventures that came to be known as the Iran-Contra affair, arguably the most egregious abuse of U.S. government power since Watergate. But that wasn't known at the time.

The *Post*, like every other news organization, did not know that Hasenfus was working for a clandestine operation to resupply the Contra rebels fighting Nicaragua's Sandinista government—an operation secretly organized by Lieutenant Colonel Oliver North, then a member of President Ronald Reagan's National Security Council staff, and retired Air Force Major General Richard Secord. No reporter knew that North had raised money to buy arms for the Contras by selling American missiles to Iran. Nor did any journalist know that another purpose of providing missiles to Iran was to ransom American hostages held in Beirut.

The *Post* did know about Colonel North, a Marine officer assigned to the National Security Council. Joanne Omang, then a State Department reporter who specialized in Latin American affairs, had discovered North's close personal relations with the Contras and their supporters in the summer of 1985. Like many conservatives in Washington, including President Reagan, North believed it was imperative that the Contras, whom Reagan called "freedom fighters," overthrow the left-wing Sandinista government, which had been supported by Fidel Castro's Cuba. But the Democratic Congress disagreed—disagreed so strongly that it had passed the "Boland Amendment" banning clandestine U.S. assistance to the Contras.

Before Omang wrote about North, the *New York Times* published a story on August 8, 1985, reporting that an unnamed military officer assigned to the National Security Council had been instrumental in helping the Contras after the Boland Amendment was passed, quoting government officials as saying this was entirely legal. The *Post* published a version of the same story, written by Omang, the next day. Neither story named North, because the White House, at North's request, had asked the *Times* and the *Post* not to identify him, saying North feared for his own and his family's safety.

Downie, then the *Post*'s managing editor, agreed to withhold North's name, but with great reluctance. North was an influential, if then little-known, government official performing important acts in the name of the American government. Hiding his name seemed odd, and wrong. Downie urged Omang to write a full story based on everything the *Post* had learned about North. Then he asked the White House and North himself to explain why the *Post* should not use North's name. Neither provided specific information supporting the melodramatic North's contention that he and his family were in danger. So Omang's long story naming North and describing some of his secretive efforts to help the Contras was published on the *Post*'s front page on Sunday, August 11, 1985.

But Omang had learned only a fraction of the story. She didn't know the full extent to which North and Secord were orchestrating the acquisition and delivery of arms and supplies for the Contras, and no one at the

*Post* knew anything about the arms-for-hostages dealings with Iran. Both these activities continued secretly for more than a year after Omang's article appeared.

When Hasenfus's plane crashed fourteen months later, the Reagan administration denied that it had any connection to the mission of the C-123. Officials said it was being flown by a private organization helping the Contras. Bob Woodward, who was investigating covert foreign adventures of the Reagan administration at that time, recalled how Downie reacted: "Len got into one of his hyperactive states, declaring that the Hasenfus incident was a vital clue and opportunity. Much was being hidden, and here was a way to find it out. He hovered around the national desk, declaring his interest in the story, trying to enlist editors and reporters who would mirror his enthusiasm and go to work. It seemed to be one of the moments when he couldn't or didn't get the train rolling fast enough."

Kaiser, then the assistant managing editor for national news, enlisted half a dozen reporters to chase the story. One went to Miami, home base for the C-123 that had gone down. Others were in Managua, the capital of Nicaragua, where Hasenfus was paraded before reporters four days after he was shot down, and in San Salvador, capital of El Salvador, the location of the American base from which the C-123 had taken off. Facts began to emerge, but agonizingly slowly. Hasenfus revealed that one of the people he worked for was "Max Gomez," who we learned was really Felix Rodriguez, a veteran of the Bay of Pigs invasion of Cuba in 1961 who had worked for the CIA and was close to the staff of the vice president, George Bush. We learned that Rodriguez had met with Bush three times. From our correspondent Ed Cody in San Salvador, we learned that the American ambassador there had eaten lunch with Rodriguez and met with him on several occasions. We established that the airplane was owned and flown by people with CIA connections.

Confronted with embarrassing events beyond its control, the Reagan administration chose to dissemble. Six days after the C-123 went down, Elliott Abrams, the assistant secretary of state for Latin America, was asked in a television interview for "categorical assurance that Hasenfus was not under the control, the guidance, the direction, or what have you, of anybody connected with the American government."

"Absolutely," Abrams replied. "That would be illegal. We are barred from doing that, and we are not doing it." Abrams was referring to the Boland Amendment.

To our frustration and what must have been the relieved amusement of administration officials, their stonewalling was successful. For weeks after the Hasenfus plane went down, the biggest secrets remained secret. North, William J. Casey, the director of Central Intelligence, Admiral John Poindexter, the president's national security adviser, and the other participants in the tangled conspiracy knew what was at risk: the full story of the clandestine, probably illegal effort to supply the Contras; the Reagan administration's simultaneous secret sales of advanced American weapons to Iran for cash and the release of American hostages held in Beirut by terrorists allied with Iran; and, most explosively, the secret diversion by North of profits from the arms sales to Iran to buy weapons and supplies for the Contras in Nicaragua.

Unbeknownst to us, a day after the C-123 went down in Nicaragua, North and others were in Frankfurt, Germany, continuing their secret dealings with their Iranian interlocutors. By the end of October, another shipment of American missiles was delivered to Iran. On November 2, David P. Jacobsen, director of the American University Hospital in Beirut, who had been held hostage for a year and a half, was freed.

But in faction-ridden Iran, opponents of the secret relationship with the United States looked for a way to subvert it. They planted a story that appeared in a Beirut magazine on November 3, revealing the first few details of the secret U.S.-Iran dealings. Still in the dark, we didn't grasp the import of this story, and put our first account of it on an inside page of the *Post*. But quickly thereafter we realized, and reported, the enormity of what had happened. Contradicting all U.S. policies and Reagan's own promise never to negotiate with terrorists, his administration had been secretly selling arms to the Ayatollah Ruhollah Khomeini to win release of American hostages in Beirut.

Reagan's first attempts to deal with the revelations became the worst moments of his presidency. In a speech to the nation and a November 19 news conference, he evaded most questions. Finally, at a second news conference on November 25, after Reagan turned the proceedings over to Edwin Meese III, his attorney general, Meese revealed that money from the secret Iranian arms sales had been diverted to the Contras. He announced the resignations of North and Poindexter.

What a story! Defiance of Congress, trading missiles with the enemy, ransoming hostages, senior officials' heads rolling—an amazing sequence of events. Yet the *Post* and the rest of the American news media had missed nearly all of it. We didn't get one of the biggest stories of the Reagan years until it was handed to us on a platter.

How this happened is instructive. The first reason, obviously, is that we weren't good enough. But we weren't completely helpless, or hopeless. Omang knew North was trying to help the Contras, and so did our readers after we published her story. But encouraged by administration fabrications, we missed more than we knew. Even more tantalizing, in retrospect, was the experience of the *Post*'s senior diplomatic correspondent at the time, Don Oberdorfer. He had gotten a tip earlier in 1986 that something secret and interesting, possibly involving arms, might be going on with Iran. He paid calls on senior officials to ask about this. He met with four members of the National Security Council staff, without knowing that one of the four, Howard Teicher, had been on one of the secret missions to Teheran. Was something up with Iran? Oberdorfer asked them. Nothing at all, Teicher and his colleagues assured him. It's harder to find things out when the officials who know about them choose to lie. These Reagan administration officials had no compunction about lying—directly, bluntly and repeatedly.

The second reason we missed this story is more fundamental. Journalism is an active pursuit, with a deadline every day. Reporters and editors are usually running from one assignment to the next. The stories that are relatively easy to report usually fill the time available. In the modern era, the institutions that journalists cover most intently have learned to feed reporters a steady diet of news, or what passes for news, just to keep them busy. It is difficult to break out of the day-to-day routines of journalism, avoid the ordinary distractions and dig for hidden news. The instinct to do this doesn't come naturally to most reporters.

The fact is that reporters and news organizations, even the best ones, miss a lot of stories, more than we can know. Not knowing what stories you've missed is one of the great frustrations of journalism. The *Post* missed many of the events that subsequently became known as Watergate when they were occurring—everything that happened before the Watergate burglars got caught in June 1972, including many of the dirty tricks that ultimately helped do in Nixon. The discovery of the burglary at the Watergate was, like the crash of that C-123 in Nicaragua, an accident that opened the door to fantastic revelations. How often do those accidents fail to occur? A free press may be an important watchdog, even a bulwark of democracy, but it is very far from infallible.

If the *Post* or any other news organization had disclosed the Reagan administration's very first clandestine dealings with Iran, that surely would have derailed the entire secret enterprise. The country and the Reagan administration would have been spared a political crisis and a mammoth embarrassment. But this didn't happen. The whole truth of the

Iran-Contra affair never did come out. To this day Reagan's personal role remains a mystery. Did all this occur in his administration without his full knowledge and approval? Was he really as obtuse as he claimed when he denied swapping weapons for hostages? And George Bush, then Reagan's vice president, disappeared from the tale, leaving barely a trace. Yet we had many indications that he too was involved. Casey, who was caught up in these shenanigans, had a stroke and died before he could be questioned. The Reagan team, which had mastered the art of deception, ultimately got out of town with many of its secrets intact.

## Was This Love Affair a Story?

Over the last thirty years the country's best news organizations began to pursue a new kind of accountability reporting. Journalists began to examine the personal histories of candidates for president, looking for clues that might bear on what kind of presidents they could turn out to be. One stimulus to this kind of reporting was a 1972 book by Professor James David Barber of Duke University, *The Presidential Character: Predicting Performance in the White House,* which urged journalists and academics to do more to explore the personalities of presidential candidates before they got elected. The *Washington Post,* the *New York Times,* the *Los Angeles Times* and other ambitious news organizations have steadily increased their efforts to introduce presidential candidates to their readers every four years. Not so long ago the *Post* considered one full-page profile of each candidate adequate; in 2000 the paper printed book-length series of articles about the lives and careers of George W. Bush and Al Gore.

In August 1996 the *Post* published a story about the first marriage of the Republican presidential candidate, Senator Bob Dole. In 1948 Dole had married Phyllis Holden, a physical therapist he met in an Army medical center. Dole was struggling to recover from his World War II wounds, which left him with a permanent disability that made it impossible for him to write. Holden had helped Dole get back on his feet, got him through college and law school by writing notes and exams for him and raised their daughter, Robin. Then in 1971, to her amazement, he announced he wanted a divorce. This was quickly arranged and sped through the courts of Kansas by friends of Dole who were lawyers and judges in his home state.

Some Dole supporters angrily criticized the *Post* story as irrelevant ancient history about a marriage that had broken up a quarter century earlier. But the paper's editors thought voters deserved to know a great deal about the character of those who would be president. The way Dole handled this divorce—without prior discussion with his wife, relying on his pals in Kansas to make it happen, leaving both his wife and his daughter in the dark—was revealing.

Angry Dole supporters weren't the only readers who called the *Post*. Kevin Merida, author of the original article, heard from several readers who told him he had missed part of the story: Before asking his wife for a divorce, Dole had had an affair with a Washington woman that lasted for several years.

Deciding what to do next renewed a discussion in the newsroom that had been going on for years. In 1988 every news organization had confronted the Gary Hart scandal, set off by a *Miami Herald* story. Hart had defied reporters to catch him in an extramarital affair, and the *Herald* successfully took up the challenge, catching Hart with Donna Rice. In 1992 the *Post* had to deal with Gennifer Flowers's very public accusations against Bill Clinton. We had come to realize that stories about candidates' sex lives, once unthinkable, were now unexceptional. American society was changing; the line between public and private had certainly moved. Had the *Post* helped to move it? Or was the paper reflecting a change in public mores? That was hard to answer then, and is now.

There did seem to be a growing sense in the country that when a man offered himself as a candidate for an office of unparalleled personal power, the voters ought to know a lot about him. Downie, already editor of the *Post*, had commented publicly in 1995 that "for presidential candidates . . . the American people should know everything" about a man's private life. In a 1996 television interview, Dole seemed to agree: "Once you take that step and say 'I'm running for president,' you're fair game." Including marital infidelity? Dole was asked. "Oh, sure."

Downie's first decision was to ask reporters to find out if the information provided by Merida's callers was accurate. The lady in question agreed, reluctantly at first, to say on the record, in interviews with Bob Woodward and Charles Babcock of the *Post*, that she and Dole had been lovers. When she first met Dole she was thirty-five, working at a local university. He was a forty-four-year-old congressman. She had personal datebooks that recorded her meetings with Dole, and reporters found some of her friends and neighbors at the time who remembered Dole coming to visit her.

Questioned about all this by the *Post*, Dole refused to comment. Officials of his campaign came to the *Post* to argue, off the record, that such an affair should not be considered news because it happened so long ago, was not part of a pattern of behavior by Dole and had nothing to do with his public life.

Republicans had portrayed Dole as an honorable alternative to a dishonorable incumbent president, Bill Clinton. On the campaign trail in the days after he learned that the *Post* knew this story, Dole seemed to be struggling with how far to push the idea that he was the morally superior candidate.

In late September and early October of 1996 Woodward and Babcock drafted several versions of a possible story. They described an affair that was conducted mostly in 1968 at the woman's apartment. She and Dole had a few more meetings during the next two years. After only telephone contacts in 1971 and 1972, the woman ended the relationship when she realized that Dole's divorce would not bring them together. Three years later, Dole married Elizabeth Hanford, who became an important political figure herself.

Confronting the decision of what to do with this story, the two of us realized that our initial, reflexive reactions differed. As Downie soon acknowledged, he realized he didn't really believe that readers should be told "everything" about a presidential candidate's private life. He thought the revelation of a love affair from a quarter century earlier had to be justified by its relevance to the candidate's suitability for the presidency or his past conduct in public office. In this case, he didn't see that relevance.

Kaiser initially was struck by the Dole campaign's effort to cast the senator as a more "moral" alternative to Clinton. "In politics," Dole said in his acceptance speech at the Republican National Convention, "one must never compromise in regard to God, and family, and honor, and duty, and country." In his case, he said, those things were "not compromised and never abandoned, never abandoned." The managing editor thought the new information about Dole's past undermined this aspect of his current campaign, and thus deserved to be aired.

Downie brought a number of other editors and reporters into the discussion, in hopes that an aggressive debate would illuminate the way to the best decision. The discussion in meetings and memos, which went on for several weeks as reporting and writing of the story continued, was serious and lively.

Woodward wrote a 2,500-word memo urging publication, noting that "the *Post* has taken an aggressive position on Clinton and his sex life." He acknowledged that Dole's old affair was a different kind of story, since stories about Clinton's dalliances often involved his official role as governor of Arkansas and bore directly on his political career. But Woodward said that a politician's sexual behavior was an important character trait and he feared the *Post* could be accused of "a double standard." He noted Dole's attempts during the campaign to cast himself as morally superior, and quoted Dole's television interview inviting scrutiny of his private life.

"Withholding the story breaks the contract with the reader," Woodward wrote. "The expectation is that we give the fullest, fairest version of events and people. The presumption is in favor of publication of the truth. Not everyone has to agree on relevance. . . . Any decision not to publish a story we know is true and many believe potentially relevant is rooted in a subjectivity that goes beyond an editor's normal role."

Karen DeYoung, then the assistant managing editor responsible for national news, including campaign coverage, also wrote a detailed memo. She argued for publication, based on Dole's campaign theme that he was the better, more moral man for the presidency. She cited a Dole campaign ad from early October that quoted a voter as saying of the senator, "He's lived the values I want my children to have." She quoted Dole himself: "My word is good. His [Clinton's] is not."

"Publishing this story is not a departure from our past practice as a newspaper; not publishing it is a departure," DeYoung wrote. "The *Post* tradition [is] fully and carefully reporting all pertinent aspects of a presidential candidate's life."

Marilyn Thompson, an editor who supervised investigative reporting, took a purist position: "Our job is to find things out and then publish them," she said. "Why should this be any different?"

Another senior editor, Mary Hadar, said it would be "arrogant" for us to withhold this information from our readers. We should publish the story and let them decide whether it was relevant to Dole's candidacy.

Although most of the senior editors besides Downie favored publication, another important colleague, David Broder, the dean of America's political reporters, adamantly opposed printing the Dole story. Arguments advanced by his colleagues who favored publication were "strong, and in some ways compelling," Broder wrote in his own memo on October 11. "But I still remain unpersuaded.

"Essentially, what is being proposed," Broder wrote, "is that three weeks before election day the *Post* should run a story about an affair a candidate for president once had—an affair that began twenty-eight years ago . . .

and ended a year or two later. . . . I know of no instance in which we have reached back almost three decades and made a news story of a consensual, extramarital affair involving someone in public life."

As to the argument that publication would reveal hypocrisy in Dole's campaign, Broder demurred. He thought Dole had actually steered away from the "character issue" most of the time. The campaign "has been less personal than most of us expected, given the scandals in Clinton's public and private life."

Much of the discussion had been about how to present the information in a story. The pending drafts when Broder wrote his memo began with references to Dole's campaign statements about his and Clinton's character, and referred to the love affair only farther down in the story. In effect the story of the affair was used to undermine the campaign claims that Dole was the more moral candidate.

Broder thought this approach read "less like a news story than like a rationale or defense of the *Post*'s decision" to publish the "nugget of news" it had learned—that Dole had long ago had an affair. If the decision was to publish, he urged, then write the story directly, without beating around the bush.

On October 14 the managing editor, Kaiser, sent a memo to the executive editor, Downie, arguing that deciding to withhold the story threatened to distort the presidential campaign. Dole had known for days that the *Post* had a story, and Woodward's reporting indicated that Dole's advisers were certain the paper would publish it. It was clear that Dole was dancing around the "character issue." Kaiser thought it was obvious that Dole was "paralyzed with anxiety" about the story.

"We have put ourselves in a weird box," he wrote. By reporting out the story of Dole's affair and confronting his campaign with it, the *Post* had altered the course of the campaign. But the readers knew nothing about what their newspaper knew; the *Post* was hiding it from them. "Usually we don't have to think about the consequences of just doing the reporting," he wrote, alluding to Downie's favored strategy of always finding out whatever could be learned about a delicate story before deciding whether or not to print it. "But the jam we're in here is a consequence of simply doing the reporting."

Kaiser also warned that the story of the *Post*'s handling of this matter would come out sooner or later. Too many people in the *Post* newsroom, in the Dole campaign and in the circle around the woman who had been Dole's lover knew what had happened to expect them to keep the secret.

Kaiser worried that it would look as though the *Post* were trying to affect the course of the campaign by holding back the story.

But Downie believed that such decisions should not be based on the anticipated impact of publishing or not publishing, unless a human life or national security was clearly at risk. He had little confidence that we could predict the political impact of any decision we made, and he felt strongly that to make a decision based on an assumption about its impact risked using the newspaper to achieve a desired outcome. He still saw no clear relevance in this old love affair to Dole's qualifications or campaign for president.

The *Post*'s publisher, Donald Graham, also thought the story should not be published, and he told Downie so. Under a "no surprises rule" first established by Ben Bradlee and Katharine Graham when they were editor and publisher, Downie always gave Don Graham advance notice about consideration or publication of a story that could cause controversy or risk for the newspaper. Graham sometimes gave Downie his thoughts, whether or not they were solicited, but he always left the final decision about publication to his editor. Downie had published a number of stories that Graham told him he might not have published if the decision had been his.

In the end, Downie concluded that it was a very close call, but he decided not to publish the story.

A week later, Kaiser's prediction about the sanctity of the secret came true. The weekly supermarket tabloid *National Enquirer* published a strikingly accurate version of the story based on its own interviews with the Washington woman and some of her friends. That story was picked up by the *New York Daily News,* and Dole was questioned about it at a press conference on October 25. Dole responded by testily telling his questioner, "You're worse than they are," a reference to the *National Enquirer.*

Confronted by this public exchange in a campaign press conference, Downie decided it should be mentioned in the next day's campaign story in the *Post,* with an explanation that the *Post* had previously confirmed Dole's 1968 extramarital affair but had initially chosen not to publish the story. The story quoted Downie as saying, "I decided that the information we had about this personal relationship twenty-eight years ago was not relevant to Robert J. Dole's current candidacy for president and did not meet our standards for the publication of information about the private lives of public officials."

Not for the first time, the *Post* had been unable to impose its standards on the other news media. The paper's initial decision not to publish had been undermined by the *National Enquirer.* Nevertheless Downie felt he had upheld the newspaper's standards. He had drawn a line for the *Post.* But after the story appeared in the *Daily News* and Dole was publicly confronted with it, Downie felt the *Post*'s readers were entitled to know what had happened, and what the newspaper knew and had done about it. The whole matter was handled inside a routine news story; no headline referred to it.

Kaiser's anxieties about what might happen when this story became public knowledge proved unwarranted. When the *Daily News* published the story, it quickly died, and had no discernible impact on the last week of the presidential campaign. Many major news organizations ignored it. Perhaps this was because by then Dole was far behind in the polls and looked like a certain loser anyway. This was Kaiser's interpretation. Downie thought the reaction showed that other editors, and American voters, too, did not find Dole's old love affair relevant to the presidential election. Soon after the election, *Newsweek* disclosed the essence of this story, but no one accused the *Post* of trying to influence the election by deciding not to publish the original story.

Journalism can make a palpable difference in the community, sometimes in the entire country or even the world. The best such journalism is often produced by reporters and editors who have the luxury of pursuing topics they think are important without having to worry excessively about how much it may cost to report a story, or whom the story may offend. Those journalists work for news organizations that still have a mission of public service, which has long been the role of America's best newspapers. But that mission, and the future of journalism that really makes a difference, is in peril.

# Chapter Four

# NEWSPAPERS: WHERE THE NEWS (MOSTLY) COMES FROM

S eptember 11, 2001, a day of terror and dread, was, for most Americans, a day of television. We gathered in front of the ubiquitous box, staring at images of horror that were repeated again and again. Nearly every American must have seen those television pictures that day.

But September 12 belonged to newspapers, and reminded us why, even now, decades into the electronic era, newspapers remain so important. On the twelfth, all across America, people who don't usually read the paper bought a copy and devoured it. The *Washington Post* sold a million copies, more than 150,000 papers above its normal press run, and would have sold more if they had been printed. The *Minneapolis Star Tribune* sold an extra 175,000 copies, 50 percent more than usual. John Carroll, editor of the *Los Angeles Times,* said his paper "could have sold just about as many papers as we were capable of printing." It did sell 227,000 more than its normal Wednesday circulation of just over 1 million.

Those papers were filled with information that had not been mentioned on television, or had been touched on only briefly. Much of that was context: the history of terrorism against American targets; the known facts about Osama bin Laden's terrorist network; the history of the World Trade Center and its design. But already on that first day the better newspapers had also discovered new facts: the first information about intelligence linking bin Laden to the terrorists; details about who was on the four crashed planes; the first account of what happened on American Airlines Flight 77, the plane whose passengers forced it to crash near Shanksville, Pennsylvania, before it could hit a target in Washington.

In the days that followed, the leading papers gave their readers the first information on the identities of the hijackers, their movements and preparations prior to September 11, the financial networks that supported them, the diplomatic maneuvering to organize a global coalition to respond and then the attacks against Afghanistan. The *Post* and the *New York Times* discovered and reported details of covert American operations against bin Laden that began in 1998; the *Post* reported on an offer from Sudan in 1996 to turn bin Laden over to the United States or Saudi Arabia, an offer both countries had declined.

Television news organizations did some original reporting of this kind, but never with the depth or context of the best newspaper stories. As is typical, when newspapers published scoops based on their original reporting, the television networks picked them up, repeating their main points on the air. Television gave Americans immediate access to the news, but the journalism that provided the information essential to understanding what had happened was done primarily by newspaper stories. This was a textbook example of how the modern news media work.

We live in the television age, surrounded by other, old and new forms of electronic journalism, but newspapers still do most of the original reporting. In America's towns and cities, the local newspaper sets the news agenda. A few major newspapers do the same for the national news media. Of all the participants in the news business, none is remotely as committed to covering news as the country's daily papers.

This isn't obvious to many Americans. Most people now say they get their news from television, not newspapers, and many Americans misunderstand the vast differences between the way television and newspapers report the news. In fact, the world of news without newspapers would be something like a sleek convertible without an engine. Television news depends on newspapers, as its practitioners freely attest. Radio news is often lifted right out of the newspapers. Government officials and politicians understand the primacy of newspapers and regularly go to newspaper reporters first with important or complicated information. The news organizations maintained by newspapers are what make America's free press meaningful.

Dan Rather of CBS made this point in August 2001 when he was reporting on the speech President Bush had just made announcing his decision to permit limited use of embryonic stem cells for medical research. "It's the kind of subject that, frankly, radio and television have difficulty with," Rather told his viewers, "because it requires such depth into the complexities of it. So we can, with, I think, impunity, recommend that, if you're really interested in this, you'll want to read, in detail, one of the better newspapers tomorrow."

The uniqueness of newspapers begins with the resources they devote to news, and the way they deploy those resources. Television stations and networks employ reporters, as newspapers do, but that similarity can be misleading. Newspaper reporters outnumber television reporters, often by big multiples. The Raleigh–Durham–Chapel Hill "triangle" in central North Carolina provides a typical example. The most-watched television news there is broadcast by WRAL-TV in Raleigh. The station has a reporting staff of sixteen; fewer than a dozen are in the field on an average working day. The *Raleigh News & Observer* has 101 reporters on its staff, nearly all of them working locally. The gap is similar in every significant media market in the country; nowhere are the electronic reporters even close in number to the newspaper reporters. The same situation prevails in Washington. In 2001 CBS and NBC each had about a dozen correspondents based in Washington (augmented by off-the-air reporters called producers); the *Los Angeles Times* had thirty-five Washington reporters; the *New York Times* forty-two.

A serious newspaper sees its mission as more than just covering public events: it wants to uncover hidden information. Newspapers assign their reporters to cover "beats"—institutions like local governments and schools, or subjects like crime, health, the professional football team in town and so on. The best newspaper reporters cultivate sources on their beat, read documents related to it, follow events and personalities over extended periods of time, accumulate expertise in their subject and try to wheedle information out of their sources. Of course the search for information below the surface of events is pursued with varying degrees of determination, skill and success at different papers. Bad newspapers do it poorly. But most newspapers share the same sense of mission.

Most electronic journalists have a different mission. The networks and local television stations have a few beat reporters, but most of their correspondents are generalists who report on events—things that *happen,* primarily things that can be photographed while happening. A network evening news program typically includes five or six short news stories and several more headlines; a local station's half-hour news program at 11 p.m., devoted largely to weather and sports, also reports just a handful of stories. Even a lousy newspaper will have dozens of stories every day; a good one will have scores. The *New York Times* and the *Washington Post* each contain roughly 100,000 words a day—about as many as this book. A typical NBC Nightly News broadcast contains 3,600 words.

The difference in quantity of news is matched by differences in the depth and quality of reporting. You can make this comparison any day of the year in your own hometown. Watch the 6 or 11 p.m. news for its account of a big local story, making note of the points it covers. Then read the account of the same story in the morning paper. Except in the case of lurid crimes or accidents that local television likes to milk dry, you'll almost invariably learn more from the newspaper story than from the television version.

Here's another experiment you can try: Read through the morning paper to familiarize yourself with the stories it contains, then turn on a local morning television or radio news program. You will see how many of the items on radio or television were lifted right out of the paper. In big cities the Associated Press employs someone to boil down the best stories in the newspapers for the AP wire, which most radio and TV stations use as a primary source of news.

We were reminded of the way newspapers usually lead the news pack in August 1999, just as we were beginning work on this book. On August 19 the *New York Times* carried a front-page story that began: "Billions of dollars have been channeled through the Bank of New York in the last year in what is believed to be a major money-laundering operation by Russian organized crime. . . ." The detailed report introduced a colorful cast of characters, including two Bank of New York employees recently suspended from their jobs and an alleged Russian mobster named Semyon Mogilevich. Both the characters and the story line were intriguing, new and unexpected—the essence of a good story.

Competitive journalists jumped on the story. That evening, ABC and CBS television and National Public Radio broadcast reports on the investigation. In their editions of August 20, newspapers all over the world reported on a money-laundering investigation involving the Bank of New York and mysterious Russians. The *Times* had set the hounds running. According to the Lexis-Nexis electronic library of the contents of major American news outlets, they carried 754 stories on the Bank of New York investigation during the next thirty days. During a slow August, this became big news. In Washington, Republicans discovered a political issue—the Clinton administration had been soft on Russian organized crime and the Russian mob's money laundering, some said. Echoes of the *Times* story were seen in the newspapers and heard on the airwaves for months afterward.

Television and newspapers both perform vital public services, but they aren't the same services. Television brings great events to the public, allows us all to participate vicariously in the making of history, allows us to "meet" and evaluate the government officials, celebrities, sports heroes and such who dominate the public life of the country at any given time. Newspapers, at least the better ones, are much more ambitious. Their public service is to bring a rich, detailed account of yesterday in the world to their readers every day, an account that enables citizens to remain in touch with numerous aspects of contemporary life in their community, country and world. A good paper explains big events and puts them in context. Beyond that, a newspaper keeps watch on the powerful people in its immediate neighborhood, checking constantly for competence, honesty, candor and all the other qualities that citizens hope for in the people who run the institutions they depend on. Communities with good newspapers are actually better places to live because the paper performs these functions.

Despite their uniqueness and continued importance, newspapers no longer have the status in society they enjoyed before television became so popular and so influential. There are many fewer daily metropolitan newspapers than there were when we first came into the business, partly because of television's popularity. Those that remain sell fewer copies.

And newspapers have changed, in some respects profoundly. When we started out together at the *Washington Post* in 1964, the *Post* and most other papers had much less space for news than they do today, and their definitions of news were much narrower. Typical coverage was stenographic: just the facts, often just the superficial facts, presented in inverted pyramid style, the most important facts first. The design of the paper was haphazard and confusing. Women were expected to read a thin section of the *Post* called For and About Women. The sports section, aimed unabashedly at men, was much fatter. White men in suits made most of the news in those days. Governments, official agencies and politicians got most of the ink.

In the mid-sixties traditional newspaper journalism began to change. The most exciting experiments were conducted at the old *New York Herald Tribune,* which was struggling to make a commercially viable place for itself against the dominant *New York Times.* This effort failed, but not before the *Trib*'s writers and editors lived up to the paper's advertising slogan of that era: "Who Says a Good Newspaper Has to Be Dull?" They began to write adventurous stories and display them dramatically in the paper, breaking out of the shackles of traditional Joe Friday journalism.

In 1968 Ben Bradlee and his colleagues, influenced in part by the *Herald Tribune,* invented the *Washington Post*'s Style section, a kind of daily magazine containing long feature stories and profiles, gossip, arts news and criticism, television coverage and more. This started a revolution in feature sections in America; soon every paper had something similar.

Now big papers have multiple feature sections devoted to subjects such as food, home decorating, automobiles, real estate, entertainment, health, science and technology. Like a supermarket or department store, a big metropolitan daily now wants to offer something to virtually every possible reader. Tom Brokaw of NBC noted the importance of this transformation of the daily paper: "I think you would feel naked in the marketplace in Washington if you were only to produce the front section of your paper without Sports, Style" and the other feature sections. He was right about that.

A second enormous change in newspapers is their ownership. In the 1960s most American newspapers were still privately owned by local proprietors in the towns where they were published. The paper, its publisher and its editor were usually pillars of the community. This wasn't always good for the journalism. Many owners worried more about their friends at the country club—the other pillars of the community—than about service to readers, and many such owners stifled aggressive coverage of local institutions. The best proprietors rose above parochial interests and encouraged tough-minded, independent reporting in their papers. Both good papers and bad ones had deep roots in their hometowns.

No longer. Today chains own 80 percent of America's newspapers. As noted already, most of the corporations that own newspapers are focused on profits, not journalism. Editors who once spent their days working with reporters and editors on stories now spend more of their time in meetings with the paper's business-side executives, plotting marketing strategies or cost-cutting campaigns. Chain editors now routinely have two titles: editor *and* vice president of a big corporation. Many editors of big papers are millionaires whose compensation is directly dependent on their papers' profitability.

When profits get squeezed, these editors are expected to help their corporate owners revive them, no matter what caused the squeeze. So in late 2000 and 2001, newspapers across America, confronted by rising newsprint prices and an unexpected, sudden downturn in advertising revenue, looked for ways to cut costs. During the last two decades a familiar process has emerged: a downturn in the economy alarms the managers of publicly owned newspaper companies, who instruct their editors to use less newsprint and spend less on salaries to preserve profit margins. Even without a downturn, many corporate owners have put enormous pressure on their editors to get more profit out of their newspapers, which are traditionally among the most profitable businesses in America. Cutting newsprint and personnel means reducing the amount of news published, and the number of journalists covering the news. There is no obvious way to simultaneously shrink a newspaper and make it better. On the contrary, the predictable consequence of such cost cutting is a diminished paper, less interesting and less important to its readers and its community. In the last twenty years or so, many newspapers have declined in quality and shrunk in size, while only a small number have improved. Economic pressures have undermined traditional journalistic standards and values.

Newspapers are vitally important institutions in American life, but most Americans don't seem to know very much about how a daily newspaper is created. Partly this is because of newspapers' notorious and unfortunate reluctance to report about themselves. But even for those of us intimately involved in their creation, the daily newspaper is a wonder, sometimes a mystery—"the morning miracle," Ben Bradlee called it, "because it's a miracle that it comes out every morning."

A good example of the miracle is the *Raleigh News & Observer*. This is an ambitious and aggressive newspaper, one that has actually been getting better in recent years. Though modest in size, it is a complex human organism, like every good paper. Each day's edition has a familiar sameness, but that predictability disguises the elaborate, sometimes tumultuous process that produced it.

Raleigh, center of a metropolitan area of about 1 million people, is the capital of North Carolina and the largest part of the "Research Triangle"—Raleigh; Durham, the home of Duke University; and Chapel Hill, where the University of North Carolina is located. Over the last thirty years the area has boomed, becoming an important center for medical research, biotechnology and other high-tech enterprises. The *News & Observer* is recognized as the leading journalistic institution in the community. There's also a mediocre morning paper in Durham, and three television stations.

The *News & Observer*'s modern history began in 1894, when an ambitious thirty-two-year-old named Josephus Daniels bought the paper for $10,000. It was selling 1,800 copies a day. Daniels built the paper up as he made a career for himself in Democratic politics, serving as secretary of the Navy under President Woodrow Wilson, and as the American ambassador to Mexico from 1933 to 1944 under Franklin D. Roosevelt. Daniels was a Democrat of almost religious intensity and a fervent segregationist. His paper became the principal political organ in the state. Daniels passed the paper on to his heirs, who prospered and ushered the *News &*

*Observer* into the modern era. In 1995 they sold it to the McClatchy newspaper chain, based in Sacramento, California. His heirs cashed in Josephus Daniels's $10,000 investment for $373 million.

McClatchy is also a family company, still controlled by the descendants
of James McClatchy, an Irishman who made his way to California during
the gold rush, failed to find gold but prospered as a newspaperman.
In 2000 the McClatchy company owned eleven daily newspapers, from
Alaska to South Carolina, including the chain's flagship, the *Sacramento
Bee,* and the *Minneapolis Star Tribune.*

McClatchy's acquisition of the *News & Observer* came as "a complete
shock" to its staff, which at first feared the consequences of absentee ownership by a chain, according to Melanie Sill, the paper's managing editor.
The sale followed several years of expansion and modernization under
Frank Daniels III, the last member of the Daniels family to run the paper.

The new owners left all the senior executives in place and encouraged
the newsroom to grow and improve. "We're a better paper than we were
five years ago," said Anders Gyllenhaal, its editor, five years after the sale to
McClatchy. "The newsroom budget has expanded repeatedly," he said; in
2000 it was $15 million. His reporters also express satisfaction with the
new owners. "We have more resources," said Pat Stith, a legendary investigative reporter who has worked for the paper since 1971. "I want a chance
to do my best work, and they give it to me here."

The *News & Observer* is the sixty-seventh largest newspaper in
America, measured by its circulation—about 165,000 copies daily, and
210,000 on Sunday. But it prints a lot of news: on average, about 73,000
words a day and 115,000 on Sunday. The paper devotes significant space to
national and foreign news—ten to twenty columns of type, or 8,000 to
18,000 words, each day, about 11,200 on an average weekday. Many bigger
papers devote far less. The national and foreign news comes mostly from
the Associated Press wire and from the many supplemental news services
the *News & Observer* buys, including the *New York Times* and *Los Angeles
Times–Washington Post* services, which distribute the stories from those
three papers every night to client newspapers all over the world. The
*News & Observer* has its own Washington correspondent, who concen-
trates on the North Carolinians, mostly members of Congress, in the
nation's capital.

The *News & Observer* takes on big subjects with gusto. The biggest of
these in recent years was the North Carolina hog industry, a substantial
part of the state economy. The paper spent months investigating the
state's thousands of industrial-style hog farms and published an alarming

series of articles on the effect of millions of tons of hog waste on the environment, particularly the water supply. These 1995 articles created a new issue in state politics and led to many changes in state government policies. Five years later hog waste was still a subject of hot debate in North Carolina. The articles infuriated the hog industry, which suddenly faced a public clamor for stricter controls and accountability. The *News & Observer* won a Pulitzer Prize gold medal for public service for these pieces.

Another example of the paper's ambitions was a 1999 series of articles by Tim Simmons, an education writer, on a crisis in North Carolina's public schools. This is how the first article began:

> More than four of every 10 students can't do the math expected of them. About half don't read at grade level. One out of two leaves high school without a diploma.
>
> If this were the record of a single school district, its classrooms would be considered academically bankrupt. But it's not the record of a district. It is the record of an entire state. It is a measure of North Carolina's efforts to educate the 400,000 black children in its public schools.

Simmons demonstrated that black children were more likely to be punished than whites, more likely to be put into special education classes and less likely to be placed in advanced classrooms. He also showed that black students did worse than white children regardless of their economic or social class: "Race, not poverty, drives a wedge between the test scores of black and white children." And he showed how teachers and principals often had lower expectations for black children, which became self-fulfilling prophecies.

This was excellent journalism. Simmons bluntly confronted a sensitive subject and compiled powerful evidence to support his findings. He repeatedly quoted black educators and experts who shared his conclusions, a device that helped him avoid some of the pitfalls that confront any American journalist writing about race. Anyone who read Simmons's series would understand both that there was a real crisis and that the state's educators and experts had found no effective way to confront it.

The hog stories and Simmons's series are what newspaper people call projects—large investments of time and energy to pursue a subject in depth. Many American newspapers do no projects, or weak ones, but a surprising number do undertake ambitious project reporting. Even the best papers don't do them every week or even every month. But a good paper like the *News & Observer* defines itself—for its staff and for its readers—by doing stories like these. Publishing such stories sends obvious messages: We are a serious news organization. We care about our community and want it to be better. We take risks to write about difficult subjects. We believe in public service.

A conversation with Melanie Sill provides some clues as to where the paper's spirit comes from. Sill, born in 1959, grew up in Hawaii and came to North Carolina to study journalism at the University of North Carolina. She began her career at the *News & Observer* as a feature writer, then found she loved editing. Her reporters describe her as a stickler for thorough reporting and an enthusiast for storytelling.

"If I hadn't been a journalist, I think I would have been a teacher," she said in an interview. "I think there's a certain amount of the civic do-gooder in me." She's enormously proud of her paper's place in the Raleigh community. "There are some much bigger papers that don't have the relationship or the impact in the community that the *N & O* does. I love the fact that my neighbors talk to me about what's in the paper, and what they care about."

A good paper that does ambitious projects must also perform well on more routine stories, and especially on daily coverage of its own world. This means keeping a close eye on local institutions, sociological trends, sports teams, local businesses and more. Good reporters doing that work will routinely challenge both conventional wisdom and those in authority. In the summer of 2000, for example, the *News & Observer* reported that the chief of the North Carolina State University campus police force had used $2.2 million in "unspent salary and benefit money" accrued because of vacancies on his force to buy fancy computers, flat-screen television sets and a $24,600 pickup truck for the chief's personal use, and to renovate the chief's office (for $17,500). Six days after the story appeared, the chief was fired and his boss in the university administration was "reassigned."

"The fundamental point is to tell people what's going on here," said Sill. The newspaper "should be the thing that doesn't go away, and provides some continuity between what was before and what's coming next. . . . Once people know something's happening, they have the option to get involved in it, or weigh in, have their voice heard. But so many times they don't know what's happening until after it's all done."

The *News & Observer* newsroom is staffed by 260 "full-time equivalents," an accounting term now ubiquitous in the newspaper business that describes how many full-time employees would be needed to fill all the positions on the newspaper. (Most papers use part-timers in some roles, like copy editing.) The paper's 100 reporters are assigned to its various newsroom departments: metropolitan news (about 60), sports (12), features (12), business (10). The *N & O* has 16 photographers, 6 graphic artists and a professional research staff of 8 people.

As at any good paper, these staffs work independently under their own teams of editors, who assign reporters to stories and edit their copy after the stories are written. Although newspaper stories usually appear under the bylines of individual reporters, their creation is a team effort. Editors often participate with reporters in deciding just what to write about, how to construct a story and how much to write. Editors also collaborate with the photo and art departments on illustrations and graphics for the stories they are handling, and with the paper's Web site on breaking news stories. All these people work for salaries comparable to those of employees of the local public schools: reporters were paid $30,000 to nearly $60,000 a year in 2000. Sill thinks the paper should pay the reporters and editors who work under her more than it does. But their willingness to work for relatively modest wages is not evidence of their meekness. On the contrary, the news business attracts ornery, independent, ego-driven individuals who, though they come in many shapes and flavors, often share a crusading sensibility.

Twice a day the paper's editors gather around a conference table in a windowless conference room on the second floor of the old *News & Observer* building on South McDowell Street in downtown Raleigh. The morning meeting begins with a review of that day's paper—what turned out well, what did not. The editors then begin discussion of the next day's edition. At 4:30 they'll meet again to hear about the top stories of the day. At about 6:15, in a smaller meeting held in a small office just off the newsroom floor, they'll choose the stories for the front page and discuss how to handle other items in the news. Between that final meeting and the time the press starts at 11:40 p.m. for the first edition, the real miracle occurs: all the stories are written and edited, and the copy editors clean them up, write headlines for them and prepare them, electronically, for another group of editors on the paper's design desk, who organize and design the paper page by page. Feature sections are designed and assembled by their own staffs, and are usually printed several hours before the main news sections.

The number of human interactions represented by one day's paper is huge, incalculable. A good big newspaper is the product of hundreds of people who know their jobs and do them independently, but almost always in consultation with others—first with the sources of news, then with colleagues in the newsroom. Journalists have to trust one another, and their own judgment. It simply isn't possible for the editors in charge to read everything that will be in the next day's paper; if they tried to, there would be time for little else. Nor, obviously, is there time for the editors to hear about, read or consider the nearly endless stream of material that the newspaper has no room to publish. Both the weeding-out process and choosing the stories that will appear are the shared responsibilities of employees up and down the organization, often acting autonomously. Making choices is a permanent part of nearly everyone's job. The autonomy and sense of responsibility of individual journalists is the key to the morning miracle. Because each knows what to do and does it, the paper appears every morning.

Obviously, the organization necessary to produce a newspaper like the *News & Observer* is fraught with opportunities to make mistakes. What if the reporter covering the governor fails to check in with a key assistant who was ready to tell her about a big story? Or what if the reporter gets that tip, but her editor doesn't recognize its significance, and tells her to save it for another day? What if the wire editor reading the material received from all the news services knows nothing about Japanese politics, so doesn't realize that today's development in Tokyo has enormous implications? What if the top editors are so preoccupied with a big investigative project they're about to publish that they fail to pay attention to something really important happening, unexpectedly, this afternoon? The act of producing a daily newspaper all but invites the participants to make mistakes, and mistakes are common. But it's also amazing that there aren't more mistakes every day. How well would General Motors do if it had to design, engineer and produce a new model car every day of the year?

In our experience, newspaper people are more conscious of the risks inherent in their enterprise than readers might realize. In the newsroom of a good newspaper bright people worry intently with one another over how to handle the news, what leads to chase, how to write and present complex stories.

The way a good newspaper actually gets produced is important evidence in the old argument about the desirability, or even the plausibility, of "objective" journalism. In fact, no human enterprise based on choices and decisions about what is important, what is entertaining, what is wheat and what is chaff can ever be literally objective. Objective means real and tangible, not related to one person's thoughts or beliefs. But a newspaper is the product of thousands of subjective decisions: we will send a reporter out on this story, but not on that one; the reporter will talk to this source, but not that one; the reporter will ask these questions, but not those; we will put these six stories on the front page because they are the most important, or the most fun to read, or the most likely to please readers, and the others will run inside the paper, or not at all. "Objective" journalism is an unrealistic goal; "fair" is more plausible. Fairness is a subjective standard, but it seems easier to explain and to satisfy by answering basic questions: Are all sides represented? Would the advocates or disputants recognize the paper's version of their arguments? Has the paper explained the context?

The *News & Observer* stands out from most American newspapers because of its ambition and its execution. It's easy to put out a daily newspaper that rarely or never does good, original reporting. Editors can fill a weak paper with routine news stories gathered credulously from official sources, feature stories about local people that are little more than personality sketches, coverage of local institutions that flatters rather than explains them, enthusiastic sports coverage that merely cheers for the local teams and stories from the Associated Press or other syndicates that feed the same material into every American newsroom. Weak papers rarely illuminate their community, or open their readers' eyes. They don't provide the stories that give readers the most satisfaction, the journalism nicely described by Paul Tash, editor of the *St. Petersburg Times,* as "stories . . . that make me feel smarter—'Now I get it!' "

A good paper has a culture of excellence. The people who work for it know the difference between thorough, resourceful, tough-minded journalism and pap. A weak paper doesn't challenge itself or its readers. Often a weak paper survives on the strength of its basic service features: the TV and movie listings, the weather and stock tables, the lists of local citizens who have died or made the honor roll or won the swim meet.

Raleigh, its region and the state of North Carolina are all better communities because the *News & Observer* is their newspaper. The paper challenges resident officials to confront serious issues. It brings an honest description of local realities to its readers. It creates a sense of shared experience that strengthens the connections among individuals and institutions in its area. Not incidentally, it enables readers to know what's happening that could affect their lives.

. . .

Broadly speaking, three factors distinguish newspapers from one another: ambitions, resources and values. Ownership is probably the greatest influence on all three.

The owners most likely to encourage their editors' ambitions, give them adequate resources and support aggressive, intelligent journalism are companies controlled by a single family. The modern history of American newspapers makes this conclusion inescapable. Not all family companies are alike, and not all are so beneficent. Some are now publicly traded companies that are still dominated by members of the original owners' families. The McClatchy Company sells common stock, but holders of those shares have no voting rights; a special voting stock is controlled entirely by McClatchy family members. Like the *Raleigh News & Observer,* the McClatchy papers are encouraged to grow and improve, though they are also held to quite strict accounting targets by corporate headquarters. The Newhouse newspapers—including the *Newark Star-Ledger,* the *New Orleans Times-Picayune,* the *Cleveland Plain Dealer* and the *Portland Oregonian*—are entirely owned by the Newhouse family. Of the big chains, Newhouse is the most relaxed about business practices. The company doesn't even give its editors budgets to meet, and encourages them to develop and improve their papers year after year. This doesn't guarantee good papers (none of the Newhouse papers is yet outstanding), but it certainly improves the prospects. And all the major Newhouse papers are improving. The *St. Petersburg Times* is owned by a nonprofit media institute created by its late owner, Nelson Poynter, and controlled by the publisher of the newspaper. Poynter instructed that the paper forever be run for the public's benefit, an arrangement that has allowed the *Times* to become the best newspaper in Florida. The country's leading daily papers, the *New York Times* and the *Washington Post,* are still controlled by Sulzbergers and Grahams respectively, who, like the McClatchys, have issued stock to the public but retain full control of the voting shares that can elect the board of directors.

Family ownership by itself guarantees nothing. The *San Francisco Chronicle* was a family-owned missed opportunity for generations, relying on columnists and local color in place of original, aggressive reporting and meaningful revelation about San Francisco, California and the world. The extended family that owned the *Chronicle* finally succumbed to internecine wrangling and sold the paper, in 2000, to the Hearst Corporation.

Family owners *can* make a positive difference if they use the power of ownership to protect their newspaper from the rawest demands of the marketplace. In practice, that means family companies can resist the pressures most corporate managers now feel to maximize earnings in every quarter of every year and report constantly improving results to stockholders. Instead, they can manage their papers with longer-term objectives in mind.

This is exactly what happened at the *New York Times* in the late 1980s and early 1990s, years when the *Times* was in grave short-term difficulty on its bottom line. According to Arthur O. Sulzberger Jr., the publisher of the *Times* and the fifth member of the Sulzberger family to run the newspaper, in 1987, at a moment of great prosperity for the paper, the *Times*'s board of directors approved an ambitious ten-year plan for future growth. The plan envisioned heavy investments in new printing plants in New York; expansion of the national edition, including remote printing in Boston and Washington; introduction of color in the Sunday newspaper and in all daily sections; creation of new sections for the paper; and expansion of some existing sections. All together, investments in the ten-year plan would total $1 billion, a big number in the newspaper industry.

Three years after the plan was approved by the board, a recession hit nearly all big American papers, and hit the *Times* and others in the Northeast particularly hard. By the beginning of the nineties, *Times* profits had largely disappeared. Sulzberger provided the numbers: In its best year ever, 1987, the newspaper's "earnings before interest and taxes" were $208 million. By 1992 that number had fallen 88 percent, to $25 million. Advertising linage fell by more than a third from 1987 to 1993, costing the newspaper $300 million a year in revenue. This was a body blow, and resulted in a decision to cut hundreds of blue-collar jobs from the nonjournalistic departments of the *Times*. For the first time in memory, the *Times* cut its newsroom budget in 1991, by $300,000. "We were in free fall" in the early nineties, Sulzberger said, "but we stuck with the ten-year plan." Profits or no, the *Times* kept spending millions to improve itself. By the mid-nineties the paper was again highly profitable, and the *Times* adopted another ambitious ten-year plan. In 2001, declining fortunes again prompted the *Times* to trim its workforce and reduce the space for news in some of its feature sections. In an interview in mid-2001, Sulzberger said that declining advertising revenue would compel the *Times* to modify its latest ten-year plan to reduce its costs, but "we still have the same goals" for improving the newspaper.

Unfortunately for America's newspapers, Sulzberger's attitude is atypical. Most of the managers who run newspapers for corporate owners— which means the managers of most American newspapers—are now trapped in a pattern of expectations and reflex reactions that undermines good journalism and threatens the future of many papers. The pattern is simple: In good times, earn and brag about big profits, pretending they will be permanent. When, inevitably, the good times end, make a public spectacle of cutting costs by shrinking your newspapers' staffs and space for news, hoping that Wall Street will reward your discipline by keeping the price of your stock up.

The newspaper business has repeated this pattern twice in modern times. The earnings potential of America's big newspaper companies was first demonstrated dramatically in the boom of the late 1980s, when profits and the selling prices of newspaper properties both soared. But after a sharp turndown in the early 1990s, corporate owners abruptly ordered their newspapers to cut costs to preserve profit margins. The Knight Ridder chain imposed harsh economies on its papers, shrinking the space available for news to reduce consumption of newsprint, freezing hiring and encouraging early retirements. Gannett insisted that its daily papers preserve high profit margins, which inevitably meant reducing news coverage. Even the best papers, including the *New York Times* and the *Washington Post,* cut space for news and held down personnel costs during the early-nineties recession.

Then good times returned with a vengeance. The nineties eventually proved even more profitable than the eighties. Some of the papers that had made significant cuts early in the decade expanded somewhat, though most, including the Knight Ridder and Gannett papers, never restored all the cuts they had made.

Beginning late in 2000, advertisers suddenly began to shy away from spending money. All the news media felt this unexpected decline, newspapers dramatically so. The advertising revenue of big newspapers commonly fell 10 percent, sometimes more, in 2001. Papers remained highly profitable—on average, they are more than twice as profitable as the average big American corporation—but unexpected reductions in profits alarmed corporate managers. Just as they had ten years earlier, the chains ordered more cutbacks. Knight Ridder ordered all its papers to reduce staff by 10 percent. This time the cuts would be permanent—no new staff would be added even when good times returned, the company promised investors.

The chains' dominance in the industry means that most communities' newspapers are now managed by people who put a higher priority on profits than on journalistic impact. Corporate owners take as much of the paper's revenues as its executives think they can while preserving enough quality to enable the paper to maintain a meaningful connection with its readers. That requires reporters to cover local news, a few columnists to give the paper a local personality, a good weather map, sports and comics—enough substance in the paper to bring back readers and advertisers day after day. In bad times, chain owners convince themselves that less news—less space, fewer journalists, less money spent on reporting—is still enough. By instinct, no editor is likely to agree, but instinct can be modified. If the editor's personal compensation is closely tied to the paper's overall profitability, he or she can develop a new appreciation for meeting the corporation's financial goals. And editors of chain papers rarely have the autonomy to resist pressures from corporate headquarters. Like it or not, editors generally make the cuts demanded of them.

At better newspapers the editor was traditionally a revered personage who enjoyed considerable status within the organization, and considerable freedom of action. Both are quickly lost when corporate managers begin to harass the editor to save money. When Gene Roberts was hired as editor of the *Philadelphia Inquirer* in 1972, the Knight newspaper chain that owned the paper dealt with Roberts as the senior executive of the paper, and deferred to him on most subjects. As the years passed, the parent corporation changed (it merged with Ridder newspapers, becoming Knight Ridder), and so did the pressures on Roberts. The *Inquirer*'s fate illustrates the fragility of a fine news organization.

The Knight Company had become a public corporation three years before it recruited Roberts, but the Knight family still controlled it. The Knights believed in high-quality journalism, and they gave Roberts both the freedom and the resources to build a great paper. A charismatic figure beloved by his troops, Roberts assembled a talented staff, emphasizing youth and adventurous journalism. The paper grew, and grew better, through the seventies, then buried its principal competitor, the afternoon *Philadelphia Bulletin*, in 1981. With vast new revenues coming in, Roberts was able to expand, opening national and foreign bureaus while aggressively pursuing suburban readers. "We were in our ascendancy," recalled Don Kimelman, who, in the mid-eighties, was the *Inquirer*'s first Moscow correspondent. In the newspaper business the *Inquirer* was hot—a great place to work, full of spirit and famous for winning Pulitzer Prizes, seventeen of them in Roberts's eighteen years. The *Inquirer*'s circulation grew nearly 20 percent in the Roberts era.

Roberts recalled a powerful symbol of how the company changed after it became Knight Ridder and began pressing its papers to earn more profits: the computer used by Anthony Ridder, then head of the newspaper division of Knight Ridder (and now chief executive officer of the entire company), that made Roberts's life miserable in 1989. Ridder's computer "was faster than the computers in Philadelphia," Roberts recalled, and it allowed him to send "rockets" to the editor on Friday afternoons "asking why we were going to be below budget for advertising that week, or why the circulation department was 2.7 over budget on FTEs [full-time equivalents] for the week." Ridder would demand explanations. "This really started turning editors into accountants," Roberts said. (Asked about this story, Ridder said, "I don't remember ever calling Roberts and having that kind of conversation.")

And then the glory days ended. Economic conditions deteriorated in the late 1980s, just as corporate pressure to control costs and raise revenues grew. After nearly twenty years as editor, "Gene got tired," Kimelman recalled. Once he had won all the battles with corporate headquarters, but by the late eighties he was starting to lose some of them. And each time he still managed to win, "it made my life much more difficult," Roberts said. Facing demands for higher profits and stricter controls on expenses, "in the final analysis I couldn't succeed." In 1990 Roberts abandoned his legendary career as editor of the *Inquirer* and quit.

Roberts's successor was Maxwell King, who had years of experience in the paper's newsroom and had run the circulation department for three years before becoming editor. King had three marching orders from Knight Ridder when he took over: (1) Make the *Inquirer* "more responsive to the local market," King recounted. (2) "The newsroom had to be tighter or more efficient in terms of managing its budget," and the paper had to make a bigger profit. (3) "They wanted the paper to remain an example of excellent journalism." Yes, King acknowledged, these were mixed signals. He tried his best to "keep it [the paper] true to the Gene Roberts values of what makes a newspaper great," which meant specifically to continue emphasizing "enterprise reporting"—original, often investigative stories that opened readers' eyes to things they didn't know. But King understood that the fat years were over; he wouldn't be able to make the paper better, but hoped to prevent it from getting worse. "My objective was to keep the bar from being lowered."

The nineties were a painful decade for the *Inquirer*. It shifted a large number of reporters to cover stories in the suburbs, chasing *Inquirer* readers who were moving farther and farther out of town. Knight Ridder froze all hiring for several years and allowed no growth of staff while pressing for the increased suburban coverage. What had once been a happy, adventurous newsroom lost its sense of mission. Space for news was reduced.

Ashley Halsey, then the national editor, recalled when the "minimum" news hole in the main news section was suddenly cut by a quarter in the early 1990s. A $300 million investment in a new printing plant turned out badly when the new presses didn't work as promised; initially, readers got papers printed early in the evening, before the results of nighttime sporting events could be reported. Demoralized, many of the paper's most talented editors and reporters gave up on the *Inquirer* and moved on. The *New York Times,* the *Washington Post* and other news organizations now benefit from the skills that dozens of journalists developed in Philadelphia.

When Roberts retired, the *Inquirer's* circulation was 520,000 daily, 978,000 Sunday; eleven years later it was 365,000 daily and 732,000 Sunday. The *Inquirer's* profit margins rose from a recession-depressed level of 4 percent in 1990 to just under 20 percent in 2000 in a booming economy. But this wasn't good enough for Knight Ridder, which ordered the *Inquirer* to cut costs still further in late 2000. Using financial inducements, the paper persuaded thirty-two journalists to quit.

But the *Inquirer's* revenues continued to fall in 2001. Robert Rosenthal, who had succeeded King as the *Inquirer's* editor at the beginning of 1998, found himself under intense pressure to cut even deeper. At the end of 2000 he told us he could preserve the quality of the *Inquirer,* but soon afterward he wasn't so sure. By November 2001 he had reduced the newsroom staff by about one hundred people, or 15 percent. He had killed three Sunday feature sections and merged the TV guide into the Sunday magazine. But management wanted more. Rosenthal told us that "too many" of the cuts "were too short-sighted." Ultimately, he said, "my loyalty to the staff . . . may have led me to move more slowly" than his bosses wanted. In November 2001, Rosenthal was fired.

The *Inquirer* is "not a hot paper anymore," in the words of Halsey, the former national editor who is now at the *Washington Post.* In the decade after Roberts retired, the *Inquirer* won just one Pulitzer Prize. The Pulitzers aren't a measure of a newspaper's overall quality, but they do say something about its aspirations. Halsey has a simple explanation for the *Inquirer's* decline: The paper gave its readers less to read than it once did. "If you give people less of anything, they're going to want it less."

But no simple explanation can do justice to the whole story. Although the *Inquirer* under Roberts was certainly a hot paper, it was never a great paper. It had flashes of sheer genius, and produced many elaborate investigative projects, but its daily coverage of Philadelphia, the country and the world was erratic and incomplete. The paper's position in its market was never dominant; when its circulation was highest, the *Inquirer* reached only about a quarter of the households in greater Philadelphia. The flight of middle-class Philadelphians to distant suburbs, many with their own newspapers, undermined the *Inquirer*. And despite all that's happened, the *Inquirer* has remained one of the best newspapers in the country. Several of its investigative projects in the nineties and in 2000 were distinguished by any standard.

But by 2001 the *Inquirer* did give its readers less—less news, less excitement. Its aspirations had shrunk, its resources were fewer, and its focus was more on the bottom line. Already demoralized by events of the 1990s, the paper's staff absorbed new blows in 2001 under orders from Knight Ridder to again reduce staff, space for news and costs. The profit margin had climbed to 19 percent by 2000, but when advertising turned down late that year, corporate headquarters demanded action to preserve profitability. The *Inquirer* once again offered buyouts to encourage departures; this time, the managing editor of the paper, Butch Ward, took up the offer. So did two star reporters, David Zucchino and Gilbert Gaul, who left for the *Los Angeles Times* and the *Washington Post* respectively. Losses like those knock the wind out of a good newspaper, simultaneously depriving the paper of great talent and discouraging those left behind. Knight Ridder's relentless pursuit of short-term profitability has profoundly changed the *Inquirer*.

Ask Anthony Ridder, Knight Ridder's CEO since 1995 (and its president for six years before that), about the *Inquirer*, and he cites statistics showing that the paper's staff and news hole were about the same in 2000 as in 1986. "I have to say I have a very thin skin when I read all this stuff about how we have done all this cutting and slashing and burning and the numbers just simply don't bear that out," he said. But the staff has been shifted to the suburbs, leaving it thinner everywhere else; the space for hard news from the national and foreign desks has been cut, and the news hole has been redistributed to print new and enlarged feature sections. The *Inquirer* budget has been squeezed for years, and the paper has often been subject to hiring freezes and buyouts. Ridder did not acknowledge to us that morale at his biggest paper had fallen, but a conversation with any member of the staff would confirm how dramatically it had.

Maxwell King expressed sympathy for Ridder: "I think Tony Ridder . . . is primarily responding to market pressures, in the way the CEO of a publicly traded corporation has to respond." Critics of the decline of Knight Ridder newspapers—many of whom blame Tony Ridder personally—are missing "the larger forces that are moving our profession," King went on.

"And it's much more instructive to examine those larger forces than it is to demonize Tony Ridder."

The most powerful of those larger forces were, as King indicated, the demands of stockholders and boards of directors for higher and higher earnings. No force is stronger in modern American capitalism than the imperative to enhance "shareholder value." The big corporations that own news outlets are not immune to these pressures even if news is considered a public service. The prevailing ethos was stated succinctly in 1998 by analyst Lauren Rich Fine of Merrill Lynch in a research report that encouraged investors to buy Knight Ridder stock in part because its papers were moving away from a preoccupation with serious journalism: "KRI's historic culture has been one of producing Pulitzer Prizes instead of profits, and while we think that culture is hard to change, it does seem to be happening."

"There's no doubt that there is pressure" to maintain profits, Ridder told us. "They will say, you know, you operate at a 20 percent [profit] margin, and Gannett and the Tribune Company operate at a 30 percent margin, and why is it that you are at 20 and they are at 30?"

To whom was Ridder referring?

" 'They' would be the institutional investors, the analysts."

Jack Fuller, who covered the Vietnam War in the late 1960s as a journalist for the military newspaper *Stars & Stripes,* helped explain the new realities that Ridder described. After a successful career as a reporter and as editor of the *Chicago Tribune* with a second career as a novelist on the side, Fuller went into management. He served as publisher of the paper, then as head of the Tribune Company's newspaper group, which has been extremely successful financially. When we talked in the summer of 2000, the *Chicago Tribune*'s profit margin was something more than 25 percent—that is, net profit was more than a fourth of the paper's total revenues from advertising and circulation. Most American corporations would be thrilled with a 10 percent profit margin, but most newspaper proprietors consider a 15 to 20 percent profit from their monopoly businesses a minimal sign of good health. The Tribune Company reported a profit margin of 29 percent for all its businesses in 1999.

We told Fuller about an earlier conversation with Howard Tyner, Fuller's successor as editor of the *Tribune.* (Later in 2000 Tyner was named senior vice president of the Tribune Company, and gave up the editorship.) Tyner had talked bluntly about the difference between the

*Chicago Tribune* and the *Washington Post.* "We're leaner than anybody else," Tyner said, referring to his news staff of just under 700, compared with the *Post*'s nearly 900. "There's always a price for being lean. . . . We don't have the depth that [the *Post*'s editors] have . . . the layers of really fine people. . . . On my staff I don't. I have top people who are terrific, and here and there I have deputies who are good. But it thins out real fast. And you can see that in the paper. We make more mistakes than we did before. . . . [The *Tribune*] would be edited . . . much better if we had more people there. And you know, it's a box I can't get out of."

In the summer of 2000 we read Tyner's words to Fuller and asked whether, at a time when the Tribune Company was reporting fabulous profits, it might be opportune to let the *Tribune* hire some more people, to give its editing staff more quality and more depth.

"Now would be an odd time to do it," Fuller replied, explaining that the previous year's profits weren't the relevant factor. What mattered was the Tribune Company's recent acquisition, for $8 billion, of the Times Mirror Company, owner of the *Los Angeles Times* and other papers. "We've just made an acquisition that focuses the attention of the investing world skeptically on our ability to perform financially," Fuller said.

Then he provided a lesson in the modern newspaper business. By buying Times Mirror, the Tribune Company created certain expectations for the benefits of the purchase, Fuller said, "but if we fail to deliver on those expectations, the consequences would be a fairly significant drop in the stock price, which would put enormous pressure on everyone." The result for Tyner and all other Tribune Company managers, he said, would be "to crunch"—to cut back—not to invest more.

So "I'd be very reluctant" to help the *Tribune* strengthen its editing staff by spending more money to hire more editors, Fuller said. Yes, the *Tribune* was doing very well. "It's thriving, and if you want to make more investments [to improve the paper], it has to thrive a little more to stay producing roughly the same kinds of earnings that we produce now, which is what the expectation is."

It is possible to make new investments to improve the product, he added, but only "if you can demonstrate that by doing so, earnings in outyears will be enhanced." But how could Tyner demonstrate that better editing of his paper, more depth and more "really fine people" on the staff would directly increase the *Tribune*'s profits? Quality isn't so tangible, so measurable—in itself, or in its impact.

So the *Tribune,* which does brilliant work sporadically and remains one of the country's better newspapers, probably won't be getting many new

resources anytime soon. That means it is unlikely to become more important to the people of greater Chicago, or more compelling to people who
might become regular readers. Its circulation, which drifted downward
from 793,000 daily in 1978 to about 612,000 in 2001, could continue on
that path.

Papers like the *Inquirer* and the *Tribune,* good papers that could quite
easily be better, are not the worst feature of the American newspaper business. Much more serious are the weaknesses of the small and medium-
sized dailies on which most of the country's communities depend for
news—more than 1,000 of them. Most are mediocre, many are much
worse than that.

For years an exception was a medium-sized paper on the New Jersey
shore, the *Asbury Park Press.* It was owned by a family trust and an individual, both of them enthusiasts for aggressive local reporting. We were
introduced to the *Press's* investigative work in 1998 when a project called
House of Cards was nominated for the Gerald Loeb award, a prize given
annually by the University of Southern California for distinguished business journalism. (Kaiser was a Loeb award judge.) The *Press's* prize entry
was impressive. Several of the paper's reporters, using computerized databases and resourceful reporting, had exposed an elaborate scheme by
which the owners of run-down houses in the worst neighborhoods of
Asbury Park and other New Jersey towns were inflating their value artifi-
cially, then getting mortgages on the basis of the inflated value. These stories ultimately won a Loeb award, and several other national prizes.

But even before the last of those articles had run in the paper, the *Press*
printed a bigger story about itself. A front-page story in August 1997
announced the sale of the paper to the Gannett Company, the country's
largest newspaper chain. Fear of the impact of estate taxes and uncertainty about who might succeed the joint publishers persuaded the two
families involved that selling made the most sense. Many other newspaper
families have made similar decisions. Being sold to Gannett is not an
unusual fate; the chain has absorbed scores of newspapers, and in 2001
owned ninety-nine of them. Most are relatively small; the *Press,* with a circulation of about 160,000 daily, became Gannett's sixth-largest paper.

The *Press* enjoyed an unusual status among papers sold to Gannett,
because John J. Curley, Gannett's president at the time of the sale, had
worked as a reporter there early in his newspaper career. Curley was an
old friend of Donald Lass, one of the co-owners of the paper who made

the decision to sell. Lass and his partner, Jules Plangere Jr., noted Curley's connection to the paper in a memo to their staff, adding: "The leadership of Gannett thinks very highly of our operation." Curley himself appeared at a staff meeting on the day the sale was announced, wearing an *Asbury Park Press* golf shirt, according to Arlene Schneider, then the paper's weekend editor. "There was a sense the *Press* was going to be treated differently and maybe much better than other Gannett papers," Schneider recalled. The sale to Gannett "was actually advertised as a good thing for us."

Gannett named Robert T. Collins, publisher of its paper in Cherry Hill, New Jersey, as the new publisher in Asbury Park. Collins introduced himself to the *Press* staff with a tough speech. He promised to "take this newspaper to its next level," according to notes made that day by Rick Linsk, then a *Press* reporter. "There will be change," Collins continued. "You can be part of the process, or you can fight it—the choice is yours. Your names will come to my attention."

Collins made known his view that the *Press*'s newsroom staff was too big. He called in the pagers and cell phones that the previous management had issued to the staff. A memo was circulated announcing restrictions on the use of Federal Express by the staff.

Collins instructed reporters and editors to embrace Gannett policies by writing shorter stories and putting greater emphasis on local news. Three months after Gannett assumed ownership, the executive editor of the paper, W. Raymond Ollwerther, explained to readers in a signed column that the *Press* was changing in accordance with readers' preferences for "coverage of the events, the people, the issues that have a direct impact on the lives of the people of Monmouth and Ocean counties," the paper's home territory. "Quite simply, under our new ownership we are focusing a greater proportion of our resources on that coverage, and giving it more prominence in the newspaper day by day."

The paper launched a promotion offering a free computer each month to a reader whose name would be drawn from a hat. To qualify, readers had to cut off the banner at the top of page one, put their name and address on it and send it in. Collins himself chose the monthly winners. This was followed by the "Asbury Park Auto Sweepstakes," a similar promotion offering the winner cash toward the purchase of a new car. Collins picked the winner of this giveaway, too. A news story about the first winner described his visit to Freehold Toyota, a *Press* advertiser, and showed a picture of the Toyota minivan he was considering on the Freehold lot. A story in the paper quoted Collins as promising more contests in the future: "The objective is to connect with customers, both our readers and advertisers, to show them the value of the newspaper."

The *Press* launched a new feature, a special insert called "Day in the Life," prepared by teams of reporters, photographers and editors who spent "a full day" in one community served by the paper and wrote about what they found. The feature is relentlessly upbeat. "Keyport . . . is a cozy, waterfront town with sidewalks, shops galore, fire companies, an American Legion and rows and rows of houses. Kids grow up with their grandparents and then watch their grandchildren do the same," wrote Gary Schoening, managing editor of the Sunday *Press,* introducing the "Day in the Life" section on that Jersey coast town. This Keyport, Schoening wrote, was discovered by a *Press* team consisting of "17 reporters, 9 photographers and 5 editors."

The Keyport section consisted of brief stories of about 350 words each on local merchants (praised by name), local institutions and local characters. Judging by these stories, Keyport has no social, economic, racial, environmental or other problems. In the words of staff writer Sheri Tabachnik, who used them to end her story about the local high school, "Go Keyport!"

Another story in the package described the hectic scene at a Keyport auto dealer as cars were made ready for delivery to their new owners: " 'You have to make sure it is right,' says James R. Martin, general sales manager for Straub Motors Buick-GMC-Pontiac on Route 35. 'You can't afford to make mistakes.' " Straub Motors is a *Press* advertiser.

*Press* reporters have been told there will be no bad news in the "Day in the Life" stories, no aggressive reporting or attempts to expose problems or wrongdoing. Even under those constraints it might be possible to do revelatory journalism. If, for example, the population of Keyport really is unusually stable, with more families staying there over many generations than in most American communities, that could be the subject of a good piece of sociological reporting. But the *Press* didn't even provide factual evidence of such stability, let alone explore what might be the reasons for it.

Another change in the paper was announced to readers in a column by Lawrence Benjamin, an editorial writer. Under the headline "Making an Obituary Celebrate a Life," Benjamin explained a new approach to obituaries, which he attributed to readers' desires that the *Press* "publish more information about the [dead] person." Henceforth, the *Press* would like to print many more details about the life of the deceased, including "community organizations, any level of education, a full employment record

and military service. The list of survivors can include the names, not just
the number, of grandchildren. . . . We also invite the names of friends
treated as if they were members of the family." Benjamin suggested that
obituaries could be personalized with details like "He was a lifelong Yan-
kee fan who caught every game on radio or television," or, "His grandchildren were the light of his life."

Benjamin announced one other change, a revision in the *Press*'s policy
of providing news obituaries about local residents at no cost (as many
papers do). Henceforth "the *Press* will provide a set number of lines free of
charge," but "there will be a charge for additional lines." By late 2000, the
policy had changed again: the charge was $45 for the first twenty-five
lines, and $4.50 for each additional one. At about five words a line, a
400-word obituary (just under four times the length of this paragraph)
would cost $292. At the *Press,* obituaries, important news stories for the
paper's readers, had been converted into a revenue source.

As the new regime took hold, interest in investigative reporting waned.
Terri Sommers, a thirteen-year veteran of the *Press* who worked on the
prizewinning House of Cards project, said the new management was less
interested in pursuing those stories (which led to the indictments of five
individuals around the state). "It wasn't a priority like it had been before."

As the weeks became months, the new Gannett paper in Asbury Park
began to lose members of its staff. About 60 of the newsroom's 240 journalists left the *Press*. They were not replaced, which was how Collins
reduced the "head count" in the newsroom.

Jody Calendar, who had been the key editor on the House of Cards
project, left the *Press* for the *Bergen (New Jersey) Record,* where she
became managing editor. "I'm very worried about American journalism,"
she said, discussing the fate of the *Press*. "As we lose the independents
[locally owned newspapers], I wonder who's going to watch the government. If we're not watching the government and the community, then I
don't know who the hell is going to do it."

Donald Lass, one of the co-owners who sold to Gannett, acknowledged
two years later that things hadn't turned out as he had hoped. "It's really
hard to look at the *Press* today and [at] what happened in the initial two
years after we sold. . . . I don't see the enterprise [reporting] that should
result from those synergies. [After buying the *Press,* Gannett owned a
cluster of six New Jersey dailies.] I don't see the high-impact local coverage that should result. . . . They do not cover local news the way we did.
They just don't do it."

Rick Linsk, a former *Press* investigative reporter now at the *St. Paul*

*Pioneer Press,* was more philosophical: "It's the system. It's Wall Street. If they're going to tell him [Collins, the new Gannett publisher] to make 25 or 30 percent [profit margins] or else go to Poughkeepsie, what's he going to do?"

We tried to talk to Collins about the changes he made in the *Press,* asking him to respond to his critics. We called three times, and sent him a fax outlining some of their criticisms. He never called back. We also wrote to John Curley, the Gannett executive who started his career on the *Press,* asking to talk to him. He never replied.

Collins's biggest efforts since taking over the *Press* have been in marketing the paper. It has run scores of contests, giving away more than $100,000 a year in prizes, and even stages a giant yard sale open only to its subscribers. Thanks to intense marketing, circulation has risen about 2 percent between 1997, when Gannett bought the paper, and 2001—but the population of the Asbury Park area grew at least that much.

The journalism now being done at the *Press* is similar to the work of dozens of Gannett papers. The corporation, headquartered in the Virginia suburbs of Washington, gives its editors extensive guidance, rates them on their adherence to the guidance and rewards them accordingly. Gannett considers editors largely interchangeable; they are moved from paper to paper, often after brief tours of duty. Most of Gannett's publishers are moved as well, so they are relative strangers in the communities they serve.

Gannett has made one of its newspapers markedly better: *USA Today,* the national daily launched in 1982, known for years as McPaper, long on color and gimmicks, very short on real reporting and news. In recent years it has gotten much more substantial, notably improving its national, foreign and business coverage. But most papers bought by Gannett follow a path similar to that of the *Asbury Park Press.*

In the 1980s Gannett acquired two of the country's best regional newspapers, the *Louisville Courier-Journal* and the *Des Moines Register and Tribune.* These were bigger papers than most previous Gannett acquisitions, and both had long-standing statewide and national reputations for excellence when Gannett bought them. At both papers Gannett's arrival was greeted initially with some optimism. The sales of the *Courier-Journal* and the *Register* followed anxious periods in their newsrooms and faltering economic performances under troubled family ownerships. Gannett initially left local executives in charge as publishers of the two papers.

In Des Moines, Gannett asked Charles Edwards, a member of the Cowles family that had sold the paper, to stay on as publisher. He hired Geneva Overholser as the paper's editor. Initially she embraced changes the new owner wanted to make, including focusing the paper's coverage primarily on the greater Des Moines area after years as a statewide organ. Eventually Gannett eliminated far-flung circulation of the paper. That circulation had been expensive to maintain, so the new policy made the paper more profitable, but it no longer had the same statewide impact.

Over time Overholser became disillusioned by Gannett's efforts to reduce the paper's scope and ambition. This was "all about institutional limitations . . . that just kind of were programmed to reduce the paper to be a shadow of its former self, and to serve readers less well, despite the emphasis Gannett thinks it's putting on listening to readers," Overholser said in an interview. Many of the paper's best-known senior journalists followed Overholser out the door after she resigned in 1995.

In Louisville Gannett took over from the Bingham family, a dysfunctional collection of Kentucky aristocrats who had run the *Courier-Journal* and the afternoon *Times* for most of the twentieth century, maintaining a liberal, integrationist editorial voice in an often-hostile environment. Family discord prompted the sale to Gannett. The *Courier-Journal* enjoyed a reputation that exaggerated its real quality, but it did have a fierce tradition of courage and service to Kentucky. When Gannett took over in 1986 and left locals largely in charge, optimism on the staff initially blossomed.

But it didn't last. Irene Nolan, who became the managing editor soon after Gannett bought the paper, recalled the change. After a brief honeymoon and a change in the corporate leadership of Gannett, "our problems with corporate started in earnest. . . . They thought we thought we were too good for them, and we were. . . . But we tried not to be too obvious about it, and we did try to work with them. But it became an increasingly stifling atmosphere. Right away the efforts to cut back staff and space were started. . . . Every year at budget time, cut staff and cut space. . . . It became increasingly difficult as the screws kept tightening and tightening and tightening, and the space cuts became more and more of a problem." Today's *Courier-Journal* has substantially less space for news than the paper did in the mid-1980s, and fewer reporters too.

As Nolan's remarks indicate, there was a cultural gulf between Gannett corporate headquarters and the proud, independent *Courier-Journal*. This came to a head in 1991, when Gannett launched a program called News 2000, intended to "make dramatic, lasting improvements in our newspapers" by "catapulting [them] into the twenty-first century," in the words of John Curley, Gannett's chief executive officer. The goal, said the authors of News 2000, was to break the habit of running newspapers according to the instincts and interests of their editors, and "allowing the newspaper to be driven by the community and by customers: readers."

"It is time to insist. We absolutely must have more readers," Curley said, introducing the program. Gannett would continue to respect "local autonomy," but "local autonomy can no longer be used as a shield or an excuse to prevent action."

Nolan thought News 2000 was "the basement"—not a plan to improve her paper but a menu for homogenized "reader-friendly" pap that she found deplorable. But she, like every Gannett editor, had to conform, first by preparing a News 2000 plan for the *Courier-Journal* to show how the paper would identify its readers' and community's interests, then how it would satisfy them.

The last straw for Nolan was the evaluation of the *Courier-Journal*'s plan by the former editor of the small Gannett paper in Rockford, Illinois, Mark Silverman, who was transferred to headquarters outside Washington to oversee News 2000. Silverman criticized the *Courier-Journal* for emphasizing "hard-news subjects" and suggested the paper consider "more how-to stories, stories that show how a person or a group of people accomplished something, question-and-answer columns, 'ask the experts' call-in hot lines, and even first-person stories by readers." This was a good summary of the prevailing ethos at Gannett, which pushed its papers to be more alike, more "reader-friendly," but also, inevitably, less aggressive, less revealing about their communities. As Silverman's critique suggested, Gannett headquarters' goal may have been to quote more "local" voices and speak more directly to local concerns, but it did not include deep reporting on complex local subjects, arguably the most useful and rewarding form of local news. This sort of journalism is rarely found in Gannett newspapers.

Silverman's eight-page, single-spaced memo outraged Nolan and her colleagues. "We were all kind of speechless" that this small-town editor would tell the *Courier-Journal* how to change. But Gannett continued to meddle, giving the *Courier-Journal* unsatisfactory rankings on its News 2000 efforts in biannual evaluations, conducted by editors from other papers. Nolan called this "a destructive and diabolical plot" to impose the views of second-rate outsiders on a fine paper that was admired in its community.

So Nolan quit. So did lots of other *Courier-Journal* staff members.

The paper didn't fall as far as the *Asbury Park Press;* it's one of the best Gannett papers. But many old-timers said it had clearly declined. Many in Louisville thought the paper hit bottom in the mid-nineties, when Gannett sent the same Mark Silverman to be its editor. In 1997 he moved on to Gannett's *Detroit News,* and several loyal *Courier-Journal* readers told us their paper had improved.

The *Courier-Journal* and the *Des Moines Register* are symbols of how the American newspaper business has changed. When they were in the hands of the Bingham and Cowles families, respectively, they weren't very successful businesses, though both were influential voices in their states. Some years the profit margins at both papers were in the single digits; the *Courier-Journal* actually operated in the red in some years, according to George Gill, a senior executive under the Binghams and Gannett. Both papers lagged behind industry leaders in modernizing their printing presses and other equipment; both lacked a clear plan for survival in difficult economic circumstances.

Gannett focused both papers on their hometowns, limited their journalistic ambitions, sharply increased advertising rates, invested many millions in new printing facilities for both papers and turned them into highly profitable properties. Circulation fell, very slightly at the *Courier-Journal,* by 30 percent at the *Register,* in part deliberately, to restrict the paper to greater Des Moines. Similar circulation results at other Gannett papers indicate that News 2000 failed in its primary goal of winning new readers. During the year it was named for, Gannett dropped the News 2000 program. By 2000 the *Courier-Journal* and *Register* both had profit margins above 25 percent, an economic stratosphere never visited by their previous owners. They weren't better papers, but under Gannett they were better businesses.

Editors for the profit-driven big chains feel the strongest economic pressures, but they are hardly alone. We interviewed nearly two dozen past or present editors of newspapers and found them all highly sensitized to bottom-line issues. The lucky ones can be conscious of business pressures without being constantly frustrated by them, thanks to proprietors who support newsrooms and don't constantly try to squeeze them. But most owners see newsrooms as money-eating cost items, so most editors feel defensive, and more than a few think they are under siege. It is now broadly accepted in the newspaper business that editors just aren't what they used to be.

John Carroll, now the editor of the *Los Angeles Times,* said, "You can really boil down the important things that an editor does to two things, people and stories"—hiring and developing a good staff, and working on stories to make them better. "And I'm here to tell you, in corporate journalism it's damn hard to find time to do those two things, because there are incessant demands on editors to be businessmen, to be community glad-handers, to be hand-holders at corporate [headquarters], and if you let the forces take their course with you, you won't be an editor and you won't be interviewing people and you won't be doing stories."

Geneva Overholser, the former *Des Moines Register* editor, concluded after studying the status of editors for the *American Journalism Review* that ownership by public corporations has fundamentally and permanently transformed the role of editor. In a survey of seventy-seven editors for Overholser's article, half of them said they spent a third or more of their time on "matters other than news"—marketing, administration and other corporate duties.

Perhaps the most important change for editors is their incorporation into the business side of their newspapers. Today's editors are expected to do things that old-fashioned editors wouldn't have dreamed of, like sitting on their paper's marketing committee. In the jargon of the times, there is also an "upside" to this arrangement: many editors are now remunerated like business executives.

"At this convention, if you gave me a roster [of attending editors], I could probably come up with thirty-five to fifty millionaires, and I mean real substantial millionaires who are worth a hell of a lot of money," Tim McGuire, editor of the *Minneapolis Star Tribune,* told us during the 2000 convention of the American Society of Newspaper Editors (ASNE). McGuire was talking about editors who got stock, stock options and big bonuses from their corporate employers. Some of them struck it really rich when their papers were sold to bigger corporations. McGuire is one of them—McClatchy acquired the *Star Tribune* in 1998. "Without question," McGuire said, "it has made ... top editors heavy businesspeople. ... Those stock options were designed to give editors more of a total stake in the business, and they succeeded. And is it good for the journalism? I still think it is. But that would certainly be ... an interesting debate for somebody to conduct."

There is some question as to whether the millionaire, corporatized editor will think first of service to readers, or be able to identify with ordinary readers himself. Moreover, though there are well-compensated editors whose values have not changed because of their stock options, there has to be a corrosive effect on editors who are judged, formally and annually, on their performance as businessmen. This is now typical in the big media companies that use MBO (management by objective) techniques to goad, grade and reward editors on their contributions to their paper's profitability. Overholser published her own MBO from Gannett in her last year as editor in Des Moines, which gives a flavor of the relationship between corporate managers and editors. Under "People," she was instructed: "Conduct twenty-four brown-bag lunches on various news and issues topics. At least four should be aimed at looking at the future; two should be on legal issues; at least six should bring diverse constituencies from the community into the newsroom." Ideas like these were suggestions first made by Overholser herself; others came straight from her bosses. For example, under "Profits," her MBO said, "Help the company make budget by staying within extremely tight expense budgets, conserving newsprint and participating in intracompany efforts to become more efficient. Stay within budgeted amounts for payroll (eliminating two positions and saving $100,000)." The size of Overholser's bonus depended, in part, on how well she executed these instructions.

The aggressive management techniques of corporate newspaper owners rarely relate to improving journalism. A classic example was the 1995 decision by Mark H. Willes, just weeks after he took over the Times Mirror Company and the *Los Angeles Times,* to abandon the New York City edition of *Newsday,* the Long Island daily paper that Times Mirror owned. *New York Newsday* had struggled for ten years and was finally on the verge of breaking even (after an investment of more than $100 million to establish the paper in the city). *New York Newsday* had a talented staff, and was regularly beating its competitors in New York—the *Times,* the *Daily News* and the *Post*—on significant stories. But to Willes, *New York Newsday* was just a drag on profits. *Newsday* executives dreamed of a bright future, even imagining a time when their paper might be the last surviving competitor of the *Times* on its home turf. Hundreds of thousands of New Yorkers had come to enjoy a lively paper that focused its attention on their city and was clearly superior to the *Post* and *Daily News,* neither of which is economically healthy. But Willes refused to wait for *New York Newsday* to prosper. He killed it.

Everyone who worked for *Newsday* understood the message. Few of the best writers on the New York edition stayed with the Long Island home paper; the best found new jobs elsewhere. Five years later, Anthony Marro, *Newsday*'s editor since 1987, was still angry over Willes's sudden decision to fold the New York paper. "I thought that was a terrible mistake," Marro said.

According to Paul Tash, the editor of the *St. Petersburg Times*, his paper could never have become one of the two biggest dailies in Florida (it is neck and neck with Knight Ridder's *Miami Herald*) if it had been run according to the business requirements of modern newspaper chains. But it had the freedom to invest profits back into the paper, thanks to the terms of the trust set up by the paper's last private owner, Nelson Poynter. Tash called it "remarkable" that "this once-little newspaper based in a sleepy fishing village on the west coast of Florida" became such a big paper in the state, which it did by expanding its home base into four nearby counties over the last twenty years. "All those moves of expansion would have been impossible under the current climate of public ownership, because they would have diminished [profit] margins in the short term. And yet, over the long term, it has been . . . an enormously successful business strategy."

In the 1990s the newspaper industry fell into a siege mentality. Early signs of defensiveness were evident in the eighties, the decade when newspapers all over America copied the color and graphics of *USA Today*, but rarely if ever gained new readers. A more powerful paranoia was born in the recession of 1990–91 and aggravated by a sharp increase in the price of newsprint as the recession ended. Total newspaper circulation declined, gently but steadily, and for some papers precipitously. Newspaper publishers began to pay serious attention to statistics that showed a steady erosion of newspaper readership in American society, especially among young people. Editors were shaken by public opinion polls that showed a sharp decline in the credibility of the news media, including newspapers. Then the World Wide Web on the Internet materialized out of the ether, portending, many in the industry initially decided, gloom and perhaps doom. The doom would follow if online competitors to newspapers managed to steal away classified advertising, the source of 20 to 40 percent of all newspaper revenues.

There is no disputing the fact that newspapers are no longer the ubiquitous, pervasive news and advertising medium they once were. In 1964, 81 percent of American adults were regular newspaper readers; by 2000 that number was 55 percent. Young people were the least likely to read a paper. Conceivably, newspaper readers would steadily die out.

The siege mentality produced numerous attempts to revive news-papers' fortunes. They came in two broad categories. The first, driven by bottom-line considerations, actually had an impact. Corporate owners cut costs and improved efficiency to make papers more profitable imme-diately and, they hoped, to improve their chances of holding on for the longer term. The result was sharply increased profits by the mid-nineties. But more fundamental efforts to attract a larger readership and make papers more popular in their communities were not notably successful. The fact that cutting costs—reducing staffs and the size of the news hole—can actually make a newspaper *less* appealing and important to readers seems not to have occurred to many corporate managers.

In the crisis atmosphere, industry organizations, especially the Ameri-can Society of Newspaper Editors and the Newspaper Association of America, a publishers' group, discussed, studied and proposed changes that might reverse the negative trends for newspapers. New fashions pro-liferated in the industry. One of the most striking of these was the stam-pede toward "market research." For years Procter & Gamble, Gillette and their cousins had used polls, focus groups and the like to consult pub-lic opinion, test products and explore what consumers might want to buy. Newspapers had also conducted some market research, most of it designed to impress advertisers with how much attention readers pay to their newspaper. But now an increasing number of newspapers were using market research to change the paper to attract more readers. Gan-nett was a pioneer with these techniques, which were used to shape the original version of *USA Today*.

Market research has provoked sweeping changes in American news-papers, animated endless debates among practicing journalists and sown deep confusion in the industry. Many of the suggestions market research-ers made for "improving" papers to win new readers failed, when imple-mented, to sell more copies. For example, researchers reported that nonreaders or occasional readers would like the paper to have shorter sto-ries, and fewer stories that jump from one page to another. They wanted more local news, less foreign and national news, the research concluded. Gannett and many other newspaper companies reacted by setting arbi-trary limits for the length of stories, and rules that limit the number of jumps. They have radically reduced the space devoted to national and for-eign news, putting more emphasis on stories about the local community. The effects of these changes are obvious on the pages of the newspapers but negligible in the marketplace. No newspaper has soared in popularity as a result of such changes. Nearly all Gannett papers have followed the general industry pattern of stagnating circulation. All the chain's bigger papers have lost readers. The one exception is *USA Today,* a national paper with no local news at all, and with stories that have gotten longer and denser in recent years.

There appears to be a powerful lesson in the experience of papers that have tried to tailor themselves to suit the desires—as described in market research—of irregular readers, or nonreaders whom they hope to attract. People who don't read newspapers, or read them only occasionally, are probably disinclined to change their habits, but also disinclined to admit as much to a researcher who is asking them questions about what would make them read the paper. Yet when newspapers respond to marketers who suggest simplifying the news, shortening stories, printing more how-to stories and spending less effort on hard news, they can easily alienate their most loyal customers: regular readers. Gene Roberts saw this problem coming years ago. He warned in 1993: "When we started cutting back on substance, we put serious, devoted readers at risk by becoming less essential to them. And this was . . . a very bad trade-off. . . . We are imperiling newspapers in the name of saving them."

Another response to the siege mentality has been to hire business consultants. In recent years all sorts of self-styled experts have paraded through American newsrooms advising managements how to reorganize their staffs, change their cultures, do more with less. A particularly horrific example took place at the *Winston-Salem (North Carolina) Journal* in 1995. The paper, owned by Media General of Richmond, Virginia, hired DeWolff, Boberg & Associates, a consulting firm with no newspaper expertise, to help it become more efficient, and more profitable. After interviewing journalists and asking them to keep precise diaries on how they spent their time over three weeks, DeWolff, Boberg produced a "grid" describing how much time various journalistic endeavors should take. "An A-1 [front-page] story should be six inches or less. A reporter should use a press release and/or one or two 'cooperative sources.' He or she should take 0.9 hours to do each story and should be able to produce 40 of these in a week." The grid survived three months before, mercifully, editors of the *Journal* threw it away, recognizing that creative work like journalism cannot be governed by such arbitrary formulas. By the time DeWolff, Boberg was done, the paper's total workforce of 600 had shrunk by 20 percent.

Consultants have been involved in another response to the siege mentality, the reorganization of newsrooms around teams of editors and reporters covering the same subject. This began at the *Orange County*

*Register* in Southern California and spread across the country. In traditional newsrooms editors and reporters are organized by geography—the city desk, the state desk—and subject, like sports, business and features. The *Register* instead reorganized reporters and editors in teams devoted to topics like entertainment, "making money," "social trends" and "government, health, environment, transportation." Other papers that experimented with reorganization tried to abolish or limit hierarchy, so, for example, the *Minneapolis Star Tribune* for a time had a management group but no managing editor. When asked why they were changing their newsrooms in these ways, editors and publishers gave a range of answers: To get "ideas to bubble up from the front lines," "to get off the assembly-line way of putting out a newspaper," to reach endangered readers, to create a team-based newsroom "that produced a vital, interesting, useful newspaper that said 'me' to readers." Measured by their impact on circulation, reorganizations of newsrooms have been no more successful than shorter stories and fewer stories that jump from one page to another. Many of the early experimenters eventually returned to more conventional newsroom structures.

Another idea for addressing the ills of newspapers that caught on in the 1990s was civic or public journalism. This came in many flavors, all related to the idea that newspapers could be positive catalysts for change, not just passive, cynical and critical observers. The diagnosis that led some editors to civic journalism was essentially this: Readers are tired of newspapers that repeatedly tell them what's wrong with their community, the country and the world without ever explaining how problems might be solved. Some saw civic journalism as an antidote to the outdated journalistic tradition that reporters cover institutions—city hall, the police department—instead of the concerns of citizens. Others thought newspapers should actively participate in civic affairs, convening public forums and inviting citizens to meet with journalists and officials to discuss community issues and how to address them.

Most civic journalism blurs a line we'd prefer remain bright and clear: the line that separates journalists, who are constitutionally protected observers of the world around them, from the people they are often observing, those who hold power in the community. Newspapers as deliberate community boosters make us uncomfortable. In fact a good newspaper, without making any special effort, does boost its community enormously, by giving all its residents a rich diet of useful information about what is happening around them. The better its newspaper, and the more the community knows about itself, the more "public knowledge" its citizens can share.

Civic journalism developed into something of a cottage industry. The Pew Charitable Trusts created the Pew Center for Civic Journalism, which provided money to papers and television stations for specific civic journalism projects. Letting an outside funder pay for news coverage seems like a dubious proposition for a supposedly independent news organization, but dozens of them sought this cash. A number of small and mid-sized papers took up the cause of civic journalism. Again, there is no tangible evidence that newspapers that have undertaken civic journalism projects have been rewarded with higher circulation. The underlying trends that held down newspaper circulation in the nineties proved stronger than any of the responses the industry devised to try to counter them.

This does not mean newspapers haven't benefited from the trauma of the last decade. On the contrary, self-examination and debate within the industry have altered the opinions and practices of most of the country's editors, and enlivened many papers, including the best ones. Papers do seem more responsive to readers, more interested in discovering what is on their minds (a form of old-fashioned reporting) and more inclined to experiment with new features and sections to appeal to and inform a broader range of readers, especially women and younger adults. The market researchers taught us that women often read the paper less than men, and liked its traditional news content less, but did appreciate serious news about subjects like health, education and personal finance. Many papers have improved their coverage of those subjects.

As businesses, most American newspapers, whether chain-owned or still independent family enterprises, are much smarter, more efficient and more resourceful than they were a generation ago. And although it remained easy to find pessimists about the future of newspapers, you couldn't base that pessimism on the performance of newspaper companies at the end of the twentieth century. Profits in 1999 and 2000 were at historic levels for many papers, though the economic slowdown that began at the end of 2000 foretold smaller profits in 2001. The newspaper industry's share of all the dollars spent on advertising remained high, about 21.5 percent. Broadcast and cable television combined had 23.3 percent, and magazines 5.3 percent. American newspapers took in a total of $46.3 billion in advertising revenue in 1999.

The news is less good regarding high-quality journalism. The trendy experiments of the nineties produced no dramatically improved paper. There are improving newspapers, such as the *News & Observer,* but not many. And they got better by raising their sights and improving their execution, not with gimmicks. John Carroll of the *Los Angeles Times* observed, "I've always regarded all of these things like civic journalism and so on as a dodge to avoid facing up to the fact that putting out a good paper is *hard* and requires a lot of work and vision, and not many people know how to do that."

Carroll is right. It is much easier to hire a consultant than to motivate a newsroom to do great work. It's easier to reorganize than to actually produce revelatory stories that open readers' eyes to situations they hadn't previously understood, or that make them laugh, or cry. Like all creative professions, newspaper journalism attracts people of varied talents. The best reporters, writers and editors are wonderful—and rare.

The proprietors who experimented with the journalistic fashions of the nineties usually avoided one obvious avenue to improvement: spending more money on covering the news. Like Jack Fuller at the Tribune Company, many newspaper executives whose companies were raking in cash at the end of the last decade remained disinclined to spend much more of it to improve their papers. Too many papers in the nineties followed the *Philadelphia Inquirer* model, squeezing staff and space for news instead of increasing them. At the big companies, there is no sign of interest in expanding news staffs or the size of newspapers, or pursuing more ambitious journalism. "Realistically," Tony Ridder of Knight Ridder told us even before the late-2000 downturn, "I don't see the number of people we have in our newsrooms changing much." Then, in 2001, he ordered further reductions in all his papers' news staffs.

Just spending money can't compensate for a paucity of talent or energy, but newspapers do improve when money is spent on them. Merely adding space for more news can make a mediocre paper better by making it more complete. Adding employees allows a paper's ambitions to rise and gives all staff members more time to do their job more carefully. Management that supports its journalists with resources will bring out their very best. Managements that cut and squeeze demoralize their people as they shortchange their readers.

Ironically, publishers and editors across America demonstrated the connection between spending more money and improving a paper's quality in the aftermath of the September 11, 2001, terrorist attacks. Every daily newspaper in America increased the amount of space it devoted to news to cover those attacks. In other words, they used more newsprint to cover a big story. The budgetary impact was mitigated in the first days by the closure of the stock market and suspension of professional sports, allowing papers to save space usually devoted to stock tables and sports results, but still, covering this huge story generally cost newspapers more money. News coverage is costly.

Reading the newspapers published in those dramatic days illuminated the vast differences in quality that now separate America's daily papers. Events of enormous importance cannot convert bad newspapers into good ones, as many of the country's papers demonstrated in the days after September 11. A newsroom with little or no experience handling stories about an important, complicated national and international event can't learn how to do so on the fly, when a catastrophe happens. So citizens trying to understand these events who depended on the *Omaha Herald,* or the *Helena (Montana) Independent Record* or the *Lewiston (Maine) Sun Journal*—to cite just three examples—got very little help from their newspaper. Like many others, those three printed numerous emotional human-interest stories but very little hard reporting about the foreign context or reaction to the events of September 11, Osama bin Laden, the history of Arab terrorism or the investigations into the terrorist acts. In some papers—the *Montgomery (Alabama) Advertiser* was one—the international aspects of the story were given almost no serious coverage at all. Many papers tried relentlessly to "localize" the story, emphasizing hometown connections to the victims in the Pentagon or World Trade Center. Some papers downplayed the news itself, emphasizing instead local reactions to it. The main—and only—news story on the front page of the September 12 *Akron Beacon Journal* began like this:

> As we huddled in shock around our television sets, most of us agreed on what we were watching: our second Pearl Harbor.
>
> September 11, 2001, will surely take its place next to December 7, 1941.
>
> A new century, a new Day of Infamy.
>
> This time, we got the news much faster. . . .

At the opposite extreme, many papers did a magnificent job, and not just the famous national dailies, either. The *Burlington (Vermont) Free Press,* a Gannett property, published a wonderful newspaper on September 12, making extensive and intelligent use of meaty stories from the news services of the *New York Times,* the *Los Angeles Times* and the *Washington Post* in a thirteen-page main section cleared of advertisements. It published poignant local reaction stories in its Metro section. The *Phila-delphia Inquirer* served its readers well, exploiting the sophistication of its best reporters, many of them former foreign correspondents. The *Wall Street Journal* published a series of compelling papers despite the fact that it had lost its headquarters (located across the street from the World Trade Center) and was publishing from makeshift facilities in New Jersey.

When editors are asked what makes a good newspaper, the best ones all have similar answers. None of them mentioned shorter stories or fewer jumps (the continuation of a story on another page). A good newspaper "gives them something that they can't get anywhere else, that's vital," that makes readers think "I've got to have it," said Robert Rivard, the editor of the *San Antonio Express-News,* not long ago an awful newspaper that Rivard is improving substantially.

Rivard's case is interesting. The *Express-News* is owned by the Hearst Corporation, a privately held company "that does not have a distinguished journalistic legacy," as Rivard put it diplomatically. In 1999 Hearst executives in New York read in the *New York Times* that Rivard, a former *Newsweek* correspondent in Latin America who had been their editor in San Antonio for just two years, was the leading candidate to become the new editor of the *Miami Herald.* They found Rivard by telephone at the Dallas–Fort Worth airport, on his way from Miami to San Antonio, where he planned to resign from the *Express-News.* Hearst's senior executives persuaded him to stay in San Antonio by offering to increase his news budget by several million dollars, add space for news and allow him to hire several dozen new reporters over three years.

During 2000 Rivard began raising the salaries of his most important people, and hiring new reporters, "senior reporters, good people who were talented, who were attracted to the whole buzz [about change in San Antonio, which got a lot of attention in the newspaper trade press]." Now, Rivard said, his paper can give its readers "more investigative reporting, more hard-hitting government reporting" and news from "more bureaus in the state [of Texas] that we've opened up." He expressed special pride in a reporter hired from the *Trentonian* in New Jersey to write about demographics in the predominantly Hispanic San Antonio area, explaining the changing population to readers. He has hired Spanish-speaking reporters. He has devoted more space to national and foreign news, and enlarged the daily business section by two pages. "I expanded my [weekly] entertainment tabloid by four to eight pages." He now has space for special projects on issues like light rail transit, which San Antonio voters were to vote on, or the city's new sports arena. In other words, Rivard's idea for how to create a better newspaper is to make it meatier, more interesting, more important to its readers. In the first reports after instituting these changes, circulation of his paper went up slightly.

"Our secret is to tell people things they don't know," said Tim McGuire, editor of the *Minneapolis Star Tribune.* "It's so simple it sounds stupid at first, but when you think about it, it is our fundamental advantage. We've got to tell people stuff they don't know." This means information acquired by creative reporting, conveyed by good writing, digested by smart analysts who know what to make of it. It means high-quality work.

"People demand quality," said Sandra Mims Rowe, editor of the *Oregonian* in Portland, an improving paper, and one of the few in the country whose circulation grew during the nineties. Newspapers, she said, have to be "the high-quality provider" of information. A good paper is "essential to readers in terms of providing news they can't get anywhere else, or providing it at a depth or a detail or with the sophistication they can't get elsewhere. . . . There are lots of different ways to be essential. We do that by being authoritative, which means we actually have to know what the hell we write about."

And not just Portland politics or the Oregon state budget. One of her proudest accomplishments, Rowe said, was a new weekly section called Homes and Gardens. Starting from scratch, it has become one of the paper's most popular features. Portland is "a gardening-crazy place," Rowe said. When the section announced it would give away 100 rosebushes, 15,000 people clipped and sent in the coupon that qualified them for the drawing, an amazing response to such a promotion. Over the first three years of its existence, the section's advertising grew every month, and "has brought over 300 advertisers who had never advertised in the *Oregonian.*" Rowe sees such feature sections as central parts of her newspaper. "I believe this is a section that helps people think the *Oregonian* is a better newspaper than it was," she told us. "It's a very important section, and its [readership is] mostly female."

In a fine paper, the gardening section is as good—as authoritative, as fun, as useful—as the front page, or the sports section, or the business section. Any medium can provide the ball scores; only a good newspaper will give a serious fan the explanatory account of the game that helps him or her understand what happened, the way the players and coaches understood it. The radio will tell you that the president gave a speech today on his new plan for Medicare coverage of prescription drugs, and may provide one sentence describing the plan. The network news might give you ten sentences. But a good newspaper will explain the plan thoroughly, so all Medicare recipients and their children, every pharmacist and every doctor in the community can know just what the president is proposing. The newspaper's role is to be definitive, authoritative about all the subjects it covers. That doesn't mean ponderous; on the contrary, ponderous journalism can rarely reach its readers, and will never touch them. Good journalism has to be intelligent, careful and correct; it has to put events in an accurate context. Newspapers, even the best ones, don't always achieve that standard. But that is the goal they should all be pursuing. That is the way newspapers can preserve their place in a fragmented media world.

Consider the modern supermarket: It has a meat department for meat eaters, but lots of vegetables for vegetarians; it sells frivolities like potato chips, and fundamentals like flour; it even sells garden furniture and *People* magazine. The owner doesn't care if it's the meat or the mayonnaise or the magazines that draw in the customers, just so they come. A good newspaper is like a supermarket. Some readers buy the paper for the local, national or foreign news, some for the sports, some for the comics, some for gossip about celebrities, some even for the advertisements.

But the news is what makes it a *news*paper. In 1998, one of the leading market researchers for the newspaper industry, Christine Urban, emphasized the point in a report to a group of editors: "News coverage needs to be better and more intelligent. *News* is the primary reason people buy the paper."

Using gimmicks to revive the fortunes of newspapers evades the need for better news coverage, but trying gimmicks is so much easier than really improving coverage. Urban, who has surveyed readers for many papers, noted this too, criticizing a feature many small and medium-sized papers have embraced—sections about teenagers written by teenagers. (The *Asbury Park Press* has one.) "On the continuum from easy to hard, the industry stays too much on the easy end. [It] employs concepts like teen magazines borrowed from other newspapers. These don't cost much time and don't upset many apple carts. By definition, they'll have little impact, which fuels the engine that [says] we can't do anything about readership."

It was heartening to discover from other newspaper editors how broadly they shared our sense of what is most important to the success of a newspaper. Sandy Mims Rowe of the *Oregonian* distilled the essence of a successful paper into three adjectives: "authoritative, engaging and essential." The goal, said Gene Roberts, is "to put out a paper that people have to have." Howard Tyner of the *Chicago Tribune* put it this way: "The successful papers are the ones that have quality."

And if newspapers are to retain their place in the news food chain, if they are to continue to be the most important sources of new information, then nothing is more important than their ability to be authoritative. "Authority is going to be our selling point," said Gregory Favre, former senior news executive of the McClatchy chain. "The authority in sports, the authority in news, the authority in criticism and commentary."

This may sound like wishful thinking from old editors resistant to the realities of the modern marketplace, but we don't think so. Roberts points out that the marketplaces in a number of cities made choices over the last twenty years or so between more and less ambitious newspapers. In each of these cities where one of the two newspapers had to fold (or barely survives) after losing a competitive battle, the winner was the superior paper, the one with deeper and more aggressive coverage. Roberts listed the examples: Philadelphia, Boston, Washington, Little Rock (where Gannett bought the stronger paper, then found itself bested by a feistier, meatier competitor) and, especially, Dallas.

The conservative, family-owned *Dallas Morning News* was at risk of losing out to the rival *Times-Herald,* acquired in 1970 by the Times Mirror Company. A new chief executive of the *Morning News,* Robert W. Decherd, hired a new editor, Burl Osborne, an executive of the Associated Press, and began to invest in the paper. Its staff grew in size and quality; "it went from strength to strength," as Roberts put it. The *Morning News* added to its Washington bureau, added foreign correspondents, added reporters around Texas and covered the news aggressively. In 1986 Times Mirror acknowledged defeat and sold the *Times-Herald,* and in 1991 its new owners gave up and closed it. Today's *Morning News* is one of the best, and one of the financially strongest, regional papers in the country.

Is it really plausible that higher quality can mean greater success? John Carroll thinks so. "You could make an argument that taking the highest of the high roads in terms of doing journalism that is of the highest quality and puts public service first—it really does pay in the long run. But nearly everybody [now] depends on [the financial results in] the next quarter, or certainly on the next year. There is no long run. If you or I owned a paper, we would go for the long run, and we'd make a barrelful of money, but it might come in barrelfuls some years, and nothing some years, but over the years it would be great and you'd enlarge the franchise. But only a few people have that luxury now."

One such is the *Washington Post*. We are not the *Post*'s sternest critics—
in fact, we're probably blind to many of its shortcomings—but it certainly
is an example of an ambitious newspaper that has endured some difficult
years and then prospered mightily when times were good. The *Post* is
a consistently successful newspaper business, with profit margins regularly exceeding 15 percent and often going above 20 percent of total revenues, which now exceed $700 million a year. It is read in nearly half the
households of greater Washington every day, and in two-thirds of them
on Sunday—figures not matched by any other big-city daily (though circulation has declined slightly in recent years). According to the *Post*'s market research, a majority of the paper's readers did not graduate from
college. Yet they seem to like a newspaper filled with serious political,
business, economic and foreign news, technology news, sports, feature
stories on the human condition, three pages of daily comics and two or
more feature sections every day of the week.

Creating compelling, authoritative journalism *is* hard work. We are
vividly aware of the daily failures of the *Washington Post* to achieve a uni-
form excellence in its work. As the worlds it covers become more and
more complicated, real expertise and authority become painfully difficult
to achieve. Our biggest challenge is finding the people who will report,
write, photograph, illustrate and edit at a high level of professionalism,
and who will make the effort to master difficult subjects, from computer
science to international economics, from the business of sports to the lan-
guages of China.

One disadvantage facing newspapers is the traditional pay scale for
reporters and editors. In 2001, the best newspaper journalists on the best
big papers earned $100,000 and more, but the much-lower salaries at the
*Raleigh News & Observer* are more typical. And even at $120,000, a senior
reporter is earning less than the salary of a new associate in a major East
Coast law firm. To persuade the very brightest, most resourceful young
people to invest a lifetime in journalism is, in this materialistic age, a challenge in itself.

Tim McGuire, editor of the *Minneapolis Star Tribune,* put the matter
bluntly. "I think people [on newspapers] are building expertise," he said,
"but there's no question that, especially in an area like business or science,
at $65,000 a year [the salary his paper pays senior reporters] you're not
going to get people who can comfortably sit with a CEO and go one-on-

one with him . . . you're not going to have a CEO-caliber thinker. So authoritative coverage, I think, is an issue in our business."

Salaries are far from the only factor limiting authoritative coverage (and some $65,000-a-year journalists are undoubtedly smarter than some CEOs), but reporting and writing with authority is a constant challenge. Consider the example of the *New York Times* story on money laundering through the Bank of New York, cited near the beginning of this chapter. We used that story to illustrate the point that newspapers still provide most of the original, revelatory reporting in the United States. But the same story is also an example of how hard it can be to get complicated stories right.

The *Times* story was revelatory but, as it turned out later, not authoritative. It described "what is believed to be a major money-laundering operation by Russian organized crime," a scheme to use the Bank of New York to turn mobsters' ill-gotten gains into liquid investment capital. In the weeks that followed, official investigators and reporters for other papers filled out a quite different picture. The *Wall Street Journal,* which did the best follow-up reporting, discovered that the real story was "an ingenious scheme to skirt a tangled thicket of tax, customs and other regulations that governed . . . Russia's business with the outside world." Its authors, the *Journal* reported, were "a tight-knit group of ambitious young bankers and traders," not mobsters, and their principal clients were Russian businessmen eager to deceive Russian tax authorities about the extent of their import-export business. These schemers did indeed misuse the Bank of New York, and they did help secretly transfer billions of dollars out of Russia, but clear evidence of a criminal money-laundering operation never materialized. American and Swiss investigators were still trying to find a connection to Russian organized crime in 2001. Two Russian-born employees of the Bank of New York pleaded guilty to various charges, one of them to a charge of money laundering.

As noted, the original *Times* story was echoed by news media all over the country and the world. The more careful, more accurate reporting of the *Journal* made less of a splash. Months later the *Times* did report developments that undermined its original story, including the confession of a Bank of New York executive who organized the scheme, but the paper never explained where that first story's emphasis on gangsters and criminal money laundering had come from. The first *Times* story and the wave of stories it provoked in other media must have left a lot of people with the impression that the Bank of New York was tied up somehow with Russian mobsters. No evidence supporting that idea has ever emerged.

Covering stories like this one is extremely difficult. Reporting on secret criminal investigations often makes reporters dependent on sources who by instinct are tendentious—usually lawyers, prosecutors or defense attorneys, whose culture emphasizes fierce advocacy for their positions and clients, not a judicious search for complex truths. The *Times* got burned earlier covering the crash of TWA Flight 800 by listening too much to the FBI agents investigating the crash, who were convinced terrorists could have caused it, without paying more attention to the experts from the National Transportation Safety Board, who were skeptical from the beginning that any sort of terrorism was involved. Ultimately all the investigators agreed that the crash was caused by a spontaneous explosion in a fuel tank on board. But for weeks *Times* readers got the impression that someone probably planted a bomb on the plane. Later, Stephen Engelberg, a senior *Times* editor, made an elegant confession of the paper's error: "Our coverage, driven by the views of experts and law enforcement personnel, tilted too far toward a theory for which there was little or no evidence."

America needs more outstanding news organizations, more great newspapers. More American communities deserve aggressive, thorough, intelligent coverage and revelatory accountability reporting.

Sadly, the visible trends in the news business are mostly pushing in the opposite direction. The great national papers are thriving; many of the Newhouses' twenty-six newspapers and the McClatchy chain's eleven dailies seem to be improving. But in the newspaper industry more broadly, "the drive for ever-increasing profits is pulling quality down."

Those were the words of Jay T. Harris, publisher of the *San Jose Mercury News,* who caused a sensation in the newspaper business in March 2001 when he resigned in protest against the economic pressures from his paper's parent corporation, Knight Ridder. Harris, a former editor and a popular figure in the newspaper world, accepted an invitation from the American Society of Newspaper Editors to explain his resignation to its annual convention in April 2001. He gave a speech that no editor who heard it will forget.

Harris articulated the crisis of confidence that has afflicted many of America's best journalists. The company he joined in 1985 (as executive editor of the *Philadelphia Daily News*) appealed to him because of its traditional emphasis on its newspapers' obligations to the public, Harris said. "It was the conviction that newspapers are a public trust that brought me to Knight Ridder." But when company executives told him in March that he would have to make painful cuts at the *Mercury News* to try to achieve what he considered an unrealistic target for higher profits, he realized the company had lost its way, Harris said. He had watched for years as profits supplanted public service in Knight Ridder's hierarchy of corporate values: "I had lived as long as I should or could with a slowly widening gap between creed and deed. . . . I had watched a long train of abuses against the traditions and core values of a great profession and a great company. I had witnessed enough."

The last straw, Harris told the editors, was the round of meetings in which Knight Ridder's corporate executives demanded that his paper meet a specific profit margin, an exact percentage figure. (He didn't say what it was; we learned later the target number was in the upper twenties.) In the course of very rough meetings, Harris said, "little or no attention was paid to the consequences of achieving 'the number.' There was virtually no discussion of the damage that would be done to the quality and aspirations of the *Mercury News* as a journalistic endeavor, or to its ability to fulfill its responsibilities to the community." The discussion was utterly focused on the number, "and essentially blind to all else. It was like watching a loved one commit suicide, unintentionally."

Harris said he explained to the Knight Ridder people why painful cuts in the newspaper to adjust to an unexpected loss of advertising revenue made no sense. The cost savings the bean counters wanted could be achieved, he said, but "those savings would be more than offset by a long-term diminution of the vitality and potential profitability of Knight Ridder's Bay Area franchise."

Three months earlier, in December 2000, Tony Ridder, Knight Ridder's chief executive officer, had promised investors that the chain's profit margin, 20.8 percent in 2000, would grow "into the mid-twenties within three years." The unexpected downturn made hash of that forecast (Ridder later revised it), but the company was still trying to preserve every possible percentage point of profitability. That was possible, Harris was saying—he would just have to weaken an extremely successful and profitable newspaper's long-term prospects.

That is what has been happening for many years now to Knight Ridder's papers, to Gannett's and to many others. Anyone who travels around America knows how mediocre most of its daily papers are. Even mediocre papers can make big profits, thanks to their status as print-advertising monopolies. But it seems improbable that mediocre papers that are steadily getting worse will hold on to their readers or their advertisers in an increasingly competitive, multimedia era. As a small number of fine papers prosper, it seems all too possible that most American daily newspapers will sputter downward in the years ahead, steadily relinquishing what should be a powerful position in their communities.

In his speech Jay Harris described his efforts to persuade Knight Ridder's executives to let him keep improving the *Mercury News* instead of undermining it. "Despite my best efforts," he reported, "they could not or would not hear the warning."

Several weeks after he gave his speech, Harris told us he had received an outpouring of calls, letters, e-mail messages and personal congratulations. "It's really been much more than I expected," he said, "and has been surprising both for its size and its passion." Many who contacted him praised Harris for confronting issues so pervasive in the industry "in a national forum, without equivocation." Harris said he agreed with many of his correspondents who expressed hope that his speech could help "enlarge and extend the debate" about the future of newspapers, and "draw in the public."

Meanwhile, Knight Ridder quickly found a replacement for Harris at the *Mercury News,* and the new publisher pursued Knight Ridder's instructions to cut costs. By the end of 2001, the paper's newsroom staff would be 10 percent smaller than it had been at the end of 2000; space devoted to news would also be down 10 percent; the newsroom operating budget (covering items like travel by reporters) would be at least 25 percent smaller than a year previously. The *Mercury News* killed its Sunday magazine and a weekly feature section and shrank its book section to save money.

What Knight Ridder did in San Jose in 2001 is precisely the opposite of what newspaper companies will have to do to preserve their place in a crowded media environment. Newspapers must get better, not worse, to retain the loyalty of readers, and thus the dollars of advertisers. If they fail to get better, newspapers will continue to shrink—in size, in quality, in importance. This would be tragic, because no other news medium can fill the role that good newspapers play in informing the country.

# Chapter Five

# THE NETWORK NEWS

T his is amazing, truly amazing," said Dan Rather, staring at a youthful version of himself reading brief news items into the camera. Rather was sitting in his cozy, windowless office just off the main CBS newsroom on West 57th Street in New York, from which he broadcasts the *CBS Evening News.* The room was dark and comfortably furnished; an aromatic candle burned on a side table. With rapt attention, Rather watched himself delivering the news of March 25, 1981. What amazed him was the number of brief news items— eight in all, each of ten to fifty seconds in length—that he simply read facing the camera, without fancy graphics or any other diversion. This, said Rather, would never happen today.

His surprise had begun with the first items on the old broadcast, an eighty-second report from San Salvador, where the American embassy had been attacked by terrorists, and a four-minute-forty-second story from Washington about a power struggle in the new Reagan administration involving the then secretary of state, Alexander M. Haig. Later a correspondent gave a two-and-a-half-minute report from Poland. "No one among the big three [networks] would run this long at the top [the beginning of the show] with these kinds of stories" now, Rather said. Nor would there be so much foreign news. If he tried to do a similar newscast now, Rather said, CBS executives would tell him, "Dan, you cannot lead with El Salvador and take the broadcast through an inside Washington power struggle and go to a piece about Poland. . . . There was a time when you could do that, 1981 was the time. But if you do it today, you die, and we die."

The three network news shows together still attract a bigger audience each evening than any other regularly scheduled program on television. And when a big story breaks, Americans still turn to Rather, Tom Brokaw on NBC and Peter Jennings on ABC, who have been our national masters of ceremonies since the early eighties. After terrorists flew jetliners into the World Trade Center and the Pentagon, most American adults turned to the three major networks to follow the story. There was no measurement of the daytime television audience on September 11, 2001, but that night, at least 80 million Americans were watching ABC, CBS or NBC throughout prime time (8 to 11 p.m.). Before the terrorist attacks, the three evening news shows were watched by 20 to 25 million people each night.

But their longevity and the size of their collective audience disguises the fact that all three networks, and their nightly newscasts, have survived tumultuous changes during the past two decades. Brokaw, Jennings and Rather actually lost about 40 percent of their audience between 1981 and 2001. This remarkable decline reflects increasing competition for viewers as the television universe was transformed by cable and satellite services, giving Americans scores of alternatives to the three broadcast networks. Viewers were also lost to new lifestyles and changing tastes. Under new economic pressures, the networks themselves have been reconstituted: all three have gone through wrenching ownership changes since 1985; ABC and CBS have had two of them. New owners transformed the status of network news.

To explore the fundamental ways network news has changed, we asked all three anchormen to look at tapes of their broadcasts from the first month that each of them sat in the anchor's chair. Then, in the spring of 2000, we asked them to explain what had happened in the years since.

When the tape of the March 25, 1981, *CBS Evening News* broadcast ended, Rather explained how he had altered his approach to the news. Like the other two anchors, Rather is a senior editor of his broadcast as well as its lead performer. He and his executive producer collaborate in deciding the program's content, subject to guidance from CBS executives.

"I want to go home at night saying, Well, we had in the broadcast at least a mention of those things we consider to be the most important and the most interesting of the day," Rather said. Some days what's most interesting was also most important, so it was easy to decide what the main story was. But "there are other days when the most interesting things are not the most important, or, indeed, one may question whether they are important at all." For example, "We do have more celebrity news in the broadcast than I would like to have."

Rather's preference is for strongly presented stories on serious subjects from overseas and from Washington. In 1981 such stories provided the meat, potatoes and often the gravy for the *CBS Evening News.* The 1981 newscast contained, after commercials, twenty-three minutes, twenty seconds of news; of that, nearly seventeen minutes was devoted to stories from Washington or overseas.

In 1981, Rather said, when confronted with a story like the civil war in El Salvador, "we wanted at least two correspondents assigned there with at least two camera crews and at least two producers. . . . The key point is that nobody said, 'Well it costs too much and we can't afford that.' . . . Those decisions were made on the basis of, Is it important? Is it interesting? . . . That's changed quite a bit."

By 2000 foreign stories rarely got one CBS crew, let alone two. The once-vast network of CBS correspondents and bureaus around the world was a small fraction of that. If Rather tried to cover more foreign news in 2000, he said, his bosses might point out that NBC had the most popular evening news show, and "they do the least" foreign news. And of course, "it's the most expensive; international news costs more than others."

The 1981 broadcast also included a five-and-a-half-minute report on two toxic dumps near Buffalo, New York, the famous one at Love Canal and another nearby. A correspondent introduced a cast of worried local residents, a reassuring executive of the company whose hazardous chemicals went into the dumps, local officials and more. "A piece like this is as close as we could come to a mini-documentary," Rather said as he watched. "Today we rarely do something four and a half minutes—maybe twice a year . . . and there would be a lot of discussion whether we should do it at all."

The new approach emphasized shorter pieces, softer stories, less reporting from Washington and abroad. "I myself remain unconvinced" that viewers actually preferred this diet to harder coverage, Rather said. But he also acknowledged the limits of his ability to win these arguments. When we asked him who at CBS had the ultimate power to make the important decisions, he replied, "They're all on the corporate side."

We watched the 2000 version of Rather's *CBS Evening News* on the night of our interview with him—June 16—to see how it compared with the 1981 broadcast, and how it reflected the new realities he had discussed with us. The 2000 broadcast was faster-paced and shorter. The longest story took up two and a half minutes. The show still filled half an hour, but the time actually devoted to the news had fallen from 23:20 in 1981 to 18:20 in 2000. More than ten minutes was devoted to commercials, and Rather spent eighty seconds on "teases"—brief previews of what was still to come on the program to persuade viewers to stick with CBS through its four commercial breaks, each lasting two minutes or more.

The lead story was hard news: Authorities had found two computer hard drives containing sensitive nuclear secrets that had been "lost" at the Los Alamos National Laboratory in New Mexico. Next came "an exclusive CBS News report" on Osama bin Laden, the Saudi terrorist, from Jim Stewart, CBS's Justice Department correspondent in Washington.

This story demonstrated how television has moved away from classical definitions of news. It conveyed a smidgen of information, and a lot of ominous implication. Stewart began this way: "If you thought Osama bin Laden's terrorist activities were limited to the Middle East, then consider the plight of these twenty-one foreign tourists entering their third month of captivity in the Philippine jungle." He showed a grim snippet of videotape depicting weeping hostages, one of whom says, "We are finished. . . . We—we—we cannot face this anymore."

This reference to the hostages in the Philippines provided a reason to use that bit of gruesome videotape. And it created a bridge to the real subject of the story, anxieties about terrorism at the Olympic Games in Sydney.

Stewart quoted the Philippine defense minister saying there was "a link" between bin Laden and the Philippine hostage taking, evidence supporting the fear that bin Laden allies were operating "in several countries" in Asia. Stewart reported "serious concern within the FBI" about the potential for terrorism in (relatively) nearby Australia during the Olympics. Twelve FBI agents had been sent to Australia, Stewart reported. Then he continued:

"Australian security forces have begun virtually nonstop counter-terrorism exercises, worried that bin Laden, without ever leaving his Afghanistan hideout, has earned the loyalty of terrorist groups throughout the Pacific."

He spoke "behind" videotape that might have come from a Hollywood movie. It showed what were apparently Australian commandos attacking a hotel in helicopters, then seizing control of an airliner with pistols drawn.

An apparent expert, identified only as Peter Chalk of the Rand Corporation, was shown next, saying, "In the Philippines and in Thailand, that [apparently a reference to loyalty to bin Laden] has manifested itself in a wave of outpouring of support for bin Laden. He was lionized amongst militants."

Then Stewart concluded, "Giving him not only the influence, but now also the reach of the world's first truly global terrorist." Various still photos of bin Laden filled the screen as these last words were spoken.

We found much to wonder about in this two-minute-ten-second report, beginning with its opening line. Why would anyone think bin Laden's terrorism was "limited to the Middle East"? Bin Laden became notorious after allegedly organizing attacks on U.S. embassies in Africa, and American authorities suspected him of trying to organize incidents in the United States to welcome the year 2000. His scope of activity was never confined to the Mideast. So where was the news?

Stewart's report contained only one new fact: that the FBI had sent twelve agents to Australia. The idea that bin Laden might target the Olympics was not new, and Australian papers had earlier reported that the government there had asked for FBI assistance. The rest of this report consisted of vivid, ominous video, most of it not fully explained, accompanied by rather dark speculation. Was there really a link between bin Laden and the Philippines hostage incident? That was not made clear. What are "virtually nonstop counterterrorism exercises"? Not clear. Are there in fact "terrorist groups throughout the Pacific" loyal to bin Laden who could threaten the Olympic Games? Not at all clear. What was the viewer meant to take away from this story?

It was followed by a two-minute report on rising gas prices. The other major stories in this broadcast were all features: drought in Minnesota (2:30); the potential benefits to heart-disease patients of folic acid (2:10); a flawed version of the new golden dollar coin that would be worth a lot of money (1:50); and the eighteenth birthday of Britain's Prince William (2:30)—the only story of the broadcast reported from overseas.

Only in one respect did this 2000 newscast resemble its 1981 ancestor: Rather again read a great many brief news items into the camera. There were ten, every one illustrated with some kind of graphic. His goal to at least mention "those things we consider to be the most important and the most interesting of the day" was met, thanks to these ten brief items. The next day's New York Times and Washington Post had only one good story that Rather had missed. Israel that day had completed its withdrawal from south Lebanon after an occupation that had lasted twenty-two years. Rather noted every other major story covered in the next day's papers. Of course he gave just a headline for most of them, a reminder of how sketchy the television news is.

## Tom Brokaw

Tom Brokaw revealed none of Rather's nostalgia when he watched the *NBC Nightly News* broadcast for September 23, 1983. Brokaw has made an easier adjustment to the new forms of network news. He talked less about the old days than Rather and offered a vigorous defense of the new version of his program.

The 1983 NBC broadcast resembled Rather's 1981 *CBS Evening News* in many respects. Brokaw in 1983 also began with a foreign story—from Beirut, where U.S. forces had intervened. A correspondent's report from the scene lasted nearly three minutes. The next story, also nearly three minutes long, described continuing demonstrations in the Philippines against the government of dictator Ferdinand Marcos. There followed two Washington stories, one on calls for the resignation of James Watt, President Reagan's Interior secretary, the other on President Reagan's courtship of Hispanic voters. All together, fourteen minutes and twenty seconds of that broadcast (which devoted twenty-two minutes, ten seconds to news) was spent on stories from Washington or overseas.

The program included three features, stories not pegged to the day's events, with a human-interest angle. One, lasting not quite two minutes, reported on an attempt by employees of a West Virginia steel plant to buy the company before it went out of business. The story was confusing and incomplete, conveying no real sense of the workers' prospects for success. A second feature, two minutes long, was devoted to the "doomsday" jetliner that was supposed to carry the president away from a nuclear attack on the United States. The third, just over two minutes, reported on a reunion of now-elderly men who had worked in the New Deal's Civilian Conservation Corps. It was sentimental and easy to look at and contained no real information.

Brokaw watched all this in a conference room lined with promotional posters for top-rated NBC shows on the third floor of NBC headquarters in Rockefeller Center. The world, American society and television had all changed since then, he said—"both quantitative and qualitative changes." In 1983 the news was dominated "by white middle-aged men" and subjects that interested them. Now his newscast is self-consciously diverse, often aimed at women, "because we know that women still are probably our most loyal viewer base."

In 1983 NBC could rely on the news of the day to fill the show. In 2000 it had to construct a program to appeal to viewers who, the producers assume, may already know the headlines of the day by the time they sit down to watch Brokaw. So NBC produced feature stories that could be broadcast whenever Brokaw and his producers decided such segments would help a particular program. "We know . . . beginning on a Monday about what we're going to have on that week in the back end of the broadcast," Brokaw said. "We try to almost do it thematically.

"Every feature that we do has a purpose, it's not just entertainment or because it's interesting," he said. "The features that we're doing we think have real application." Brokaw was critical of the features in the 1983 show because they were too thin and lacked purpose. The piece from West Virginia "shouldn't have been on. . . . It had no context whatsoever."

Brokaw said some things have not changed. "We'd sure as hell be doing today" a big story equivalent to the Beirut and Manila stories of 1983— "probably do more on them today than they did" then. But the news isn't always that compelling, he said—a subjective judgment, certainly, that easily allowed for the sharp reduction in foreign reports on the *NBC Nightly News.*

But Brokaw's philosophy of foreign news had changed. It wasn't necessary, or desirable, to track each developing story incremental step by incremental step. "What we try to do episodically is a two-and-a-half-minute piece that puts it in some context and wraps it up," he said. Such a report might contain 440 words, the length of a short newspaper story.

"I think our role still is to do as much as possible to give people at the end of the day a snapshot of their world," he added. But more than a snapshot, too—"value added" reporting on subjects of interest to viewers, he said, is now a regular part of the program. "More and more of it is in the medical and scientific field."

"Dan [Rather] is always complaining about the hard-news thing," Brokaw said. "Well, what does that mean? That's become a kind of mantra or a liturgy, if you will. And some hard news—so called—has almost no meaning."

The challenge, Brokaw said, is to seize and hold an audience in this era of multiple channels and remote control devices. "We get one crack, we've got to get them, they've got to stay with us." In a simpler, less-competitive era, the producers of the 1983 show "didn't have to worry about somebody going 'click.' "

To newspaper editors like us, one of the most striking aspects of a television news broadcast is the fact that any single item can turn off a viewer, sending him or her to another channel. Our readers can browse through the newspaper looking for items that catch their eye, skipping those that bore them. But television viewers have no such freedom: They are stuck with the sequence of items the producers decide to provide. They can't skip a story or skim through the program until they find something appealing. So every item on a broadcast carries the weight of the entire program. One false step and you've lost a viewer, or a million of them.

So how does NBC try to grab and hold an audience? We watched the *Nightly News* the evening we had talked to Brokaw, May 18, 2000. The show began in a wall of flame on NBC's futuristic set; the flames were from forest fires in New Mexico. Brokaw stood, full length, beside the crackling, flame-orange and smoke-gray conflagration. "It was a government blunder of colossal proportions," he began. "And the financial and emotional price tag still is being calculated. The wildfires in New Mexico, which are still burning tonight, began as a deliberate policy of the National Park Service. Today the government acknowledged the complete failure of that plan."

A correspondent then recounted the day's news against a backdrop of more footage from the fires, pictures of raging fires and destroyed homes. His report lasted nearly three minutes.

Next came a weather story from the Midwest, which apparently earned its place in the broadcast because NBC had acquired an extraordinary home video of a tornado crossing the Nebraska plain. For more than two minutes viewers saw the giant, spinning funnel of a classic tornado speeding across farm fields, occasionally setting off a lightninglike flash when it tore through electrical wires. The impact of the twister? The correspondent reported, "One house destroyed, major damage to two more. Several farm buildings ruined as well. But miraculously, no one seriously injured."

Great video, but no real news.

Next came two and a half minutes from Washington on maneuvering over legislation on U.S. trade with China, a straightforward account that showed viewers a range of opinions on the issue.

Most evenings the Brokaw broadcast included a segment called "NBC News in Depth." On this broadcast it was devoted to more on the New Mexico fires—specifically the difficulty owners of destroyed homes will face when trying to collect damages from the federal government. A correspondent recounted (with more grim video of fire damage playing on the screen as he spoke) how most victims of a California fire caused by a government mistake nine months before still had not collected a penny, explaining why the red tape makes it take so long. This in-depth report ran two minutes, fifty seconds. A transcript of it contains 501 words.

The longest piece in the broadcast, three and a half minutes, was a feature in an NBC series called "Best Medicine." This one described the Cleveland Clinic, a leading center treating heart disease. The Clinic gave NBC correspondent Robert Bazell and his camera crew access to the operating room while open-heart surgery was under way, which produced marvelous footage. Bazell himself dressed in surgical greens, including a hat and mask, to lend an air of authenticity to his report. The story included a mini-drama of its own as it followed one case in which the patient consulted with the surgeon, then was shown undergoing innovative heart-valve surgery. Finally viewers saw the surgeon telephone the patient's wife to say all had gone well.

There was little real information in this story. Why was the Cleveland Clinic so good? Viewers got this explanation from Toby Cosgrove, a doctor on the clinic staff: "We're building a great team. You know, the same goes on whether you're building the New York Knicks, or the Yankees, or, you know, the Cleveland Indians. You have to have chemistry that works together." Later Bazell (briefly) offered other reasons: All the doctors work for fixed salaries, the clinic gets great experience from the large number of operations it performs, and it emphasizes "research and innovation."

NBC had decided that medical features add to the appeal of its broadcast. Brokaw's *Nightly News* often included two of them. On this occasion, the second was about the fate of chimpanzees used in medical experiments. "They really are our next of kin," began a correspondent. And they can live to age fifty, "at a cost of several hundred thousand dollars apiece." How should we take care of them? The correspondent reported conflicting views on this subject, concluding: "Eventually, Congress will have to resolve" the question.

All together Brokaw covered seven news stories in nineteen minutes of news, mostly with brief headlines. There was one story from Washington (China trade), which lasted two and a half minutes. The only foreign news in the broadcast was a twenty-second "read"—Brokaw announcing Pope John Paul II's eightieth birthday. Five other pieces lasted more than two minutes: three on fires and weather, and the two medical features.

NBC chose not to report these stories that were covered in the next day's *New York Times* and *Washington Post:* The Senate's close vote against a provision that would have forced an early U.S. withdrawal from Kosovo; the decision by the opposition candidate in Peru's presidential election to withdraw from the race because, he said, it was rigged; the U.N. Security

Council's decision to impose an arms embargo against both Ethiopia and Eritrea, and the Ethiopian army's successful offensive in Eritrea that forced hundreds of thousands of Eritreans to flee their homes; the victory of the opposition candidate in the Dominican Republic's presidential election; the World Bank's decision to resume lending to Iran after seven years, over U.S. objections; the final vote by the South Carolina legislature to remove the Confederate flag from atop the state capitol; the announcement by Time Warner and Disney that they had settled an argument that temporarily caused Time Warner cable companies to drop ABC television signals; a new study by psychologists at UCLA, which found that men and women react quite differently to stress; and finally, a new computer virus, akin to but more damaging than the "Love Bug," that had begun circulating on the Internet, infecting many computers.

## Peter Jennings

In his office filled with stacks of books, just off the newsroom of ABC News, Peter Jennings confronted the videotape of his *World News Tonight* newscast of October 6, 1983, as an analytical challenge. Like CBS and NBC newscasts from the early 1980s, this one emphasized foreign news. Its lead story was from Nicaragua, about the crash of a cargo plane carrying arms to the Contra rebels (two years before the Hasenfus plane crashed). That story filled the first two minutes, forty seconds of the broadcast. There followed a one-minute-forty-second report on peace efforts in Central America, then two and a half minutes on controversy surrounding the impolitic James Watt, Reagan's short-lived secretary of the Interior. Next was a one-minute-forty-second report making sport of a House of Representatives debate on a pork-barrel water-projects bill.

All together this broadcast devoted five minutes to news from Washington, and more than eight minutes to news from abroad. The longest foreign story, 3:20, was a report by Barrie Dunsmore, an experienced correspondent (now retired), on the tenth anniversary of the last Arab-Israeli war. Dunsmore reviewed the history of that decade and the prospects for peace in 1983, packing a lot of information into those 200 seconds. The only feature story took up the last minute and forty seconds of the broadcast, a report on a San Diego zookeeper's efforts to save a newborn Emperor penguin.

When the tape was over, Jennings wanted to talk first of all about technology and technique. "Production capabilities in the main have much greater potential, so the technology of production, the graphics . . . the ability to do maps and things . . . has much greater capacity today than it did then," he said.

Redone today, the stories in that 1983 broadcast "would all be more accessible, to use that word of the nineties," Jennings explained. "They wouldn't be as heavily written. We would strive to put more sound in them, we would strive to put more effect in them, because I think increasingly . . . we are mindful of . . . the variety of competitive universes in which we operate. . . . Competition for the viewer's attention has become greater."

What does that mean in practical terms? He said the stories from 1983 "seemed longer than we would give them on the air today." If they were redone now, "I think [the broadcast] would be slightly edgier . . . slightly more staccato. . . . It [the '83 show] seemed to have a kind of potential to let the mind wander . . . which I think we would avoid now."

Under some prodding, Jennings acknowledged that the subjects addressed on his broadcast had changed too. Despite his own interest in such stories, "we do not do a lot of 'process' pieces out of Washington," stories explaining what the government is up to. And "there's a lot of foreign news on that [1983] broadcast that you would not see on a regular basis on an evening newscast today."

How had the presence of ABC News overseas changed since Jennings made his own reputation as a foreign correspondent? "Much slimmer. Much slimmer. If I recall correctly, off the top of my head, we then had correspondents . . . in London, Paris, Rome, Frankfurt, Tel Aviv, Cairo, Moscow, Beijing, Tokyo, Hong Kong, Johannesburg. . . . Today, London [but] no Frankfurt to speak of. No Paris to speak of, no correspondent. No Rome. No Cairo. No Hong Kong. At the moment we have two correspondents who cover Asia for us—two shorter than you could keep running on a full-time basis."

Why the cutback? Jennings blamed money, technology and "national confusion" about the importance of foreign news. And "our own uncertainty [at ABC] about who we are and our commitment in this new marketplace" was also a factor. The network's attitude toward spending money had changed profoundly, Jennings said. "When we send a reporter into the field today it has to be costed out before the reporter travels. . . . In other words, if we want to send a reporter to Libya, our accounting department wants to know in advance how much is it going to cost."

What was the purpose of the evening news broadcast in 2000? "I think our mission . . . is to try to stay with the major national and international stories of the day which are relevant to and/or important to Americans. And on a more provincial basis, we are very conscious . . . [of] trying to put stories on the air which have some resonance in Oregon as well as in Massachusetts."

Definitions of news were changing, Jennings said. "There's much greater demand for personal news . . . about health and personal finance," for example. He said he was trying to emphasize technology news, and he was proud that ABC has a religion correspondent. "We try to do something on business every day." Generally, he said, "we've tried to pick up on what the country's interested in at the moment and tried to accommodate it, if not follow it."

The *ABC World News Tonight* on the night of our conversation with Jennings, April 24, 2000, felt more like a traditional hard-news program than the other two, in part no doubt because of its timing. This was Jennings's first broadcast after the early Saturday morning raid by the Immigration and Naturalization Service to seize Elián González, the young Cuban, from his Miami relatives' home. The first seven minutes of the program was devoted to three items about the raid, all of them informative and aggressively reported. The business story of the day was about Microsoft—its stock fell on Wall Street as its troubles with the government continued. The program included one purely visual feature story: two minutes, forty seconds of beautiful pictures from space taken by the Hubbell space telescope—no factual information, but remarkable photographs.

The longest item on the program, just over four minutes, was also its only foreign story, another ominous report on terrorists affiliated with Osama bin Laden. This was the nightly feature called "A Closer Look," normally the longest segment of the broadcast.

Like the CBS report on the same subject, this one conveyed very little hard information and a lot of generalized anxiety. A correspondent reporting from highly photogenic mountainous regions on the Afghan-Pakistani border told viewers there were "more than a dozen training camps" in the area, "producing a new generation of Muslim fighters: thousands of young men learning to fight the enemies of Islam. Often that means America and its allies." The story included a brief interview with an unnamed "Taliban official" who denied the existence of these camps.

What were these "Muslim fighters" trying to accomplish? The correspondent, standing outside one of the training camps, answered that question this way: "On a wall surrounding the camp we noticed this graffiti: 'Yesterday we broke the Soviets. Tomorrow we break America.' "

A man named Ahmed Rashid, described as the author of a book about the Taliban faction ruling Afghanistan, was quoted confirming the widespread anti-Americanism among the Muslim militants in training. "Even if Americans get bin Laden tomorrow," Rashid said, "there are hundreds of bin Ladens sitting inside Afghanistan." And then the correspondent read his sign-off line: "Hundreds of young men for whom America and its allies are the enemy."

This story had no "peg"—nothing had happened to make it particularly timely. Nor did it have many confirmed facts, or any new facts at all. Its appeal was its locale—remote and exotic to look at—and, evidently, the implicit threat against the United States it described. It was, obviously, a warning of things to come in September 2001.

In all Jennings touched on seven events that had occurred that day. His program included seven distinct segments, plus four "reads." There was 19 minutes for news, 1:10 for teases and 9:50 for commercials.

This wasn't a particularly heavy news day, but ABC did skip a number of stories that could be found in the next day's *Washington Post* and *New York Times:* a Supreme Court argument on whether California could allow voters to participate in primary elections of parties to which they did not belong; the first formal charges in a Los Angeles police corruption scandal brought against three officers; Kenneth Starr's successor, independent counsel Robert Ray, subpoenaing White House e-mail; a pledge by four U.S. foundations of $100 million to support African universities; George W. Bush and Al Gore both campaigning for president; Kofi Annan, secretary-general of the United Nations, criticizing U.S. nuclear weapons policies at a United Nations conference called to review the Non-Proliferation Treaty; the Government Accounting Office release of a report concluding there was no factual support for dramatic accusations of gross misbehavior by IRS agents made at heavily televised congressional hearings two years earlier; Secretary of State Madeleine Albright punishing two officials and changing security procedures after the disappearance from the State Department of a laptop computer containing sensitive intelligence information.


Television now permeates American life so thoroughly that it is easy to forget how recently it changed us all. It wasn't until the sixties that television became Americans' principal source of news. Only in the seventies did color sets outnumber black-and-white. Cable television didn't become commonplace until Reagan was president. By 2000, 281 million Americans owned nearly 250 million television sets, and (according to various surveys and polls) they watched, on average, four to seven hours of television every day.

The impact of television on news would be difficult to exaggerate. Not only did it alter news reporting and the definitions of news, but more profoundly, television transformed Americans' relationship to the news. Before television, great events occurred *remotely*. Interested citizens could read about them in newspapers, or hear about them from friends and neighbors who read the papers. Later everyone could hear "the news" on the radio. But news then was almost invariably something that happened out of sight, which was reconstructed by journalists for a public that could then try to imagine the events described.

As television evolved, that definition became obsolete. Perhaps the moment it expired forever was on November 23, 1963, when millions of Americans mourning the death of John F. Kennedy in front of their television sets watched in amazed horror as a Dallas nightclub owner named Jack Ruby shot and killed Lee Harvey Oswald, the suspected presidential assassin, outside a Dallas police station. Television showed this event, as it occurred, to every citizen who was watching.

Such moments eviscerated the distance between the citizenry and "the news." Soon Americans were watching presidential news conferences, violent confrontations between civil rights demonstrators and southern policemen and, most dramatically, a war in Southeast Asia, all from the intimacy of their own living rooms. Just weeks before Kennedy's assassination, CBS had extended its evening news broadcast to thirty minutes (NBC quickly followed), allowing for fuller reports, made vivid with moving pictures, of the day's events.

This immediate and direct exposure to the dramas that we call news altered America. Suddenly every television-watching American was empowered. Each of us got to "know" the presidents and kings, legislators and corporate executives, celebrities and unlucky citizens whose exploits or disasters constitute so much of the daily diet of news. The tube made them all our intimate acquaintances, regular visitors in our own homes. We became, over time, a nation of armchair experts.

The rise of television was accompanied by the decline of the institutions and individuals that, in a pretelevision age, served as intermediaries between statesmen or big events and the public at large. Politicians and their networks of supporters, sometimes called their organizations, or machines, played this role for much of pretelevision American history. Precinct captains, city councilmen and the like connected voters to higher political powers. So did community leaders, preachers and teachers of many kinds. Many Americans relied on such intermediaries, and gave them special status and respect in return. But when television gave everyone the same exposure to national and international leaders, and provided eyewitness access to all the big events of the day, those intermediaries lost their role, and their status. Your precinct captain (if you still had one) wasn't your connection to the governor or the president; Walter Cronkite was.

For all its powers, though, television never actually claimed the ability to make citizens well informed. On the contrary, the great statesmen of television regularly warned that television alone could not provide a full account of the world's important events. Cronkite, perhaps the most influential personality of the great age of television news during the 1960s and 1970s, described the purpose of his broadcast this way: "We were essentially a headline service attempting to give our audience an overview of the day, leaning . . . on the hope that we would inspire them to consult their newspapers for fuller details." Tom Brokaw has quoted Reuven Frank, the president of NBC News from 1968 to 1973, and again from 1982 to 1984, who described television as a means to "transmit experience"— that is, convey the sense of being present at great events, which is of course different from transmitting a lot of facts.

Television, like radio, is a relatively inefficient conveyor of factual information. The text of Cronkite's evening news, after eliminating the commercials, would fill just over half the front page of a full-sized newspaper. A typical network evening news show now mentions from half a dozen to fifteen or so different subjects, some in just a sentence, whereas a good newspaper has scores of different news items every day. A big story on television might get two minutes, or about 400 words. The *Los Angeles Times* coverage of the same big story could easily total 2,000 words.

A news piece lasting a minute and a half leaves no real room for writing, said Howard Stringer, a former president of CBS News and the CBS broadcast group. "That's the dark secret of news, and it's why great news on television isn't as satisfying as great news in print."

Pictures, of course, convey a different kind of information than words do, and television's pictures can powerfully enrich the news it broadcasts. Watching the Berlin Wall crumble and fall under a battering from young Germans is certainly a more memorable experience than reading a news dispatch on the same subject. The best writers among our newspaper colleagues can bring such moments vividly alive, but there's no disputing the television camera's natural advantages in those situations.

Yet many aspects, including often the most important aspects, of big news stories are not visible, cannot be photographed or recorded by a television camera. Motivation is not photographable, but the motives of actors in big public dramas are usually vitally important. Events easily photographed can also be easily staged, while the important meetings, deals and so on that actually made the news most often occur out of view. So, for example, the public image of a big corporate merger often comes from those staged "photo ops"—Steve Case of AOL, in a suit and tie, embracing Gerald Levin of Time Warner, wearing an open-collar shirt. But the phone calls, meetings and tense negotiations that actually produced that merger occurred in secret over several previous months.

The relevant background to an event, obviously, doesn't emerge from its visual appearance, yet without the background and context, what is visible usually has much less meaning. What, for example, would videotape of the fall of the Berlin Wall do for a viewer who knew none of the history of the Cold War?

Indeed, what is visible can be profoundly misleading. For example, the television audience that watched Lieutenant Colonel Oliver North spin fantasies to the joint congressional committee investigating the Iran-Contra affair could not possibly have grasped what had really gone on in the episodes North purported to describe. Yet North, for all his dissembling, was a compelling witness—a fabulous performer for the television cameras. His testimony altered the course of the Iran-Contra investigation, because members of Congress worried that he had made such a good impression on the public that they didn't want to challenge him aggressively.

The ability to make a good impression on television has become one of the most useful talents for ambitious Americans, particularly in public life. We have had no homely or egregiously inarticulate presidents in the television era, which is surely not a coincidence. The presidents who failed to win re-election during the last thirty years were all less than terrific television performers (Ford, Carter and Bush), also not a coincidence. In presidential politics, a handful of televised events—especially the candidates' acceptance speeches at their party conventions and the debates— now provide the principal occasions for voters to assess the candidates.

So television has become enormously important in our national life, but it has never been a fully effective information medium. Everyone who works in television knows this. Jennings, for example, put it like this: "It's going to be a very unsatisfying experience if you get all your news from television ... because it's just not fulfilling enough, it's not broad enough, it's not deep enough." Yet Jennings, like Cronkite before him and all the other modern network anchormen, have not been able to significantly enrich the diet. In fact, television news has evolved in ways that have actually reduced its effectiveness as a provider of detailed, reliable information about important events. Today's television news could be a lot better than it is.

Brokaw, Jennings and Rather all agreed on that point in our conversations. Rather was bluntest. A generation ago, he recalled, the executives in charge of CBS News hardly noticed ratings or profits. Speaking of Bill Leonard, the president of CBS News in 1981, Rather said, "What he cared about was the integrity of what we were doing covering the news."

By 2000, Rather went on, for Leonard's successors at CBS and the other networks, "the driving force every day" was "delivering the profit." And when integrity is displaced by profit, "it's inevitable that a lot is going to go out of your organization ... and a lot is going to go out of yourself. And that's what has happened to television journalism as a whole, and it's what's happened here [at CBS]. . . . Once we begin to see ourselves as more of a business and less a public service, the decline in quality is accelerated."

The history of American broadcasting, the unphotographable context for the reality Rather described, helps explain what has happened to network news.

The American broadcasting industry grew up in the 1920s and 1930s as the radio became a ubiquitous presence in the country's living rooms. When Congress passed the first laws regulating broadcasting—the Radio Act of 1927 and the Communications Act of 1934—it legally enshrined the idea that holders of broadcast licenses were required to operate in "the public interest, convenience and necessity," in return for their use of the publicly owned airwaves. But the specific content of the public interest commitment was never spelled out in detail. Broadcasters made elaborate promises about how they would serve the public interest when they applied for a license to use the airwaves, but they routinely ignored their promises once the license was granted.

As television spread in the 1950s, the owners of networks and stations were rarely harassed by government authority. The Federal Communications Commission, created by the Communications Act of 1934, did enforce a "fairness doctrine," which allowed persons who felt they were abused on television to demand broadcast time to respond. And the commission upheld a broad equal-time rule that broadcasters understood as a requirement to give roughly equal time to politicians competing for the same office. The Supreme Court upheld the government's right to regulate broadcasters because of their use of the public airwaves.

This was enough to keep the broadcasters on their toes—and jumping on the rare occasions when regulators in Washington actually asked them to adopt a new policy or change an old one. The best example of this followed the quiz show scandals of the late 1950s, when the networks were caught rigging on-air contests that had held the country in thrall. The FCC and members of Congress suggested that the networks should show penance for these sins by re-emphasizing news and public service broadcasting, and they rushed to comply. Probably the best series of prime-time documentaries ever made for television, *CBS Reports*, grew directly out of the quiz show scandal.

But no stricter "public service" requirements were ever formally established. When reformers, including some government officials, periodically suggested that the broadcasters should be required by law or regulation to do more noncommercial, educational or public service broadcasting, the increasingly wealthy broadcast industry had no difficulty beating the reformers off. They would voluntarily respond to some political pressures, but never had to accept legal requirements for more public service. On the contrary, by the first Reagan administration in the 1980s, broadcasters had succeeded in persuading the FCC to drop most of the public service, equal-time and fairness requirements under which radio and television had operated for years.

At the very beginning of the television era, the entrepreneurs who were creating this new medium treated the news with some deference. The owners of the networks saw their news divisions as a way of paying the debt television owed society for the opportunity to profit by using the airwaves. "These networks were licenses to print money, they really were monopolies," as Brokaw put it. "We [the news division] were their conscience money. . . . If they [network executives] got jerked down to Washington for a private session at the White House or called before a hearing, they would say well, [look at] our news division, and they would shovel the money at us." In those days network executives didn't think of news as a profit center, though according to early news executives at CBS, news did make money almost from the beginning.

In the early years the networks' only money worries involved how to count it. Starting in the fifties, television advertising began to demonstrate an unprecedented power to sell consumer goods. CBS, NBC and ABC became giant money machines. They could afford to be generous in funding their coverage of news.

And generous they were, particularly at CBS and NBC. ABC didn't get serious about news until the end of the 1970s, when a driven redhead named Roone Arledge, long the president of ABC Sports, took control of the third network's news division. William Paley, who ran CBS for more than fifty years, from the late 1920s to the 1980s, first used radio news as a way to compete for prestige and audience before and during World War II. Edward R. Murrow, the most distinguished broadcast journalist of the forties and fifties and for years a close friend of Paley's, became the symbol and embodiment of a news tradition that set CBS apart for decades. In his day Murrow was an enormous celebrity, at least as famous as any television news personality since.

Murrow won his fame as a radio broadcaster, particularly for his nightly reports from a besieged London in the first months of World War II. Some radio personalities could never make the transition to television, but Murrow did. Initially he was the central figure in CBS television news. But this did not last. The story of Murrow's personal fate is instructive.

Murrow was rightly famous for his high journalistic standards, but even he could not escape the two great forces—economics and entertainment—that shaped and still dominate the television business. Starting in the early fifties he was compelled to augment the traditional (and often distinguished) journalism he did for CBS with forays into what would prove to be perhaps television's most powerful genre of programming, the promotion and exploitation of celebrity personalities.

Murrow launched a program called *Person to Person* that consisted of a half-hour visit with monuments of the popular culture, such as Marilyn Monroe and Mickey Spillane. The guests were told in advance what they would be asked, so they could prepare their answers. The program converted Murrow, a chain-smoking, romantic war correspondent, into the equivalent of the guests on his show: another celebrity.

In tandem with *Person to Person* Murrow did more traditional journalism in a second weekly half-hour show, *See It Now*. On these broadcasts he burnished his reputation for hard-hitting, original reporting and analysis. But *See It Now* was controversial, especially after a famous program Murrow did in 1954 attacking Senator Joseph McCarthy, the Republican senator from Wisconsin who made himself famous by claiming to find Communists spread throughout the American government.

A year after that broadcast, CBS reduced the presence of *See It Now*, changing it from a weekly half-hour broadcast to an hour-long program appearing eight times each season. A year after that, it was moved to Sunday at 5 p.m. And then, in 1958, it was killed outright. Paley, once proud of his friendship with Murrow, now saw this outspoken celebrity correspondent as a liability to his burgeoning money machine, CBS television.

Totally demoralized, Murrow accepted an invitation in the fall of 1958 to speak to the annual convention of the Radio and Television News Directors Association, the association of broadcast journalists from the country's local television and radio stations. Reading Murrow's text more than forty years later, you can feel the emotion rise from the page.

"I am seized with an abiding fear," he told that audience, "regarding what these two instruments [radio and television] are doing to our society, our culture and our heritage. Our history will be what we make it. And if there are any historians about fifty or a hundred years from now, and there should be preserved the kinescopes [the early equivalent of videotape on which television programs could be recorded] for one week of all three networks, they will there find recorded in black and white, or color, evidence of decadence, escapism and insulation from the realities of the world in which we live." The ruling ethos in network television, he said, was that "we must at all costs shield the sensitive citizens from anything that is unpleasant."

Murrow introduced that speech with two prescient sentences: "This just might do nobody any good. At the end of this discourse, a few people may accuse this reporter of fouling his own comfortable nest." Yes, and they included Murrow's bosses. Paley was livid. His anger played out over another year, but then Murrow was gone from CBS.

Murrow's inelegant exit from television more than four decades ago was perhaps the first dramatic demonstration that in this medium, old-fashioned news values would always be at war with commercialism and entertainment. Murrow put this well in that same speech: "One of the basic troubles with radio and television news is that both instruments have grown up as an incompatible combination of show business, advertising and news. Each of the three is a rather bizarre and demanding profession. And when you get all three under one roof, the dust never settles." The network executives, men "trained in advertising, research, sales or show business" who "make the final and crucial decisions having to do with news and public affairs . . . frequently . . . have neither the time nor the competence to do this."

Yet good television news did not die with Murrow's departure. On the contrary, his leaving was followed by a golden age for news on television, led by CBS and NBC. It wasn't that Murrow was proved wrong, or that the pressures of advertising and entertainment he described suddenly disappeared. But the United States was entering a period of excitement, then turmoil and chaos, that Murrow could not have foreseen in 1958. The sixties and seventies provided one astounding news story after another. They also provided fantastic profits for network television. It was this combination that made possible a golden age of network news.

After the expansion of the evening news from fifteen to thirty minutes in 1963, in the tumultuous sixties and seventies the world seemed to play into television's hands. The big stories were dramatic and splendidly telegenic: the struggle for civil rights in the South, then riots in black neighborhoods of the North; Vietnam and the antiwar movement at home; the assassinations of two Kennedys and Martin Luther King Jr.; the disintegration of a once-staid national culture under the pressure of war, sex, drugs and rock 'n' roll. First Chet Huntley and David Brinkley on NBC, then Cronkite on CBS, served as masters of ceremonies at a banquet of compelling stories.

In those two decades television news settled comfortably into extravagant habits. Salaries were two or three (or more) times higher than those earned by the ink-stained wretches of the newspaper business. (Most early television correspondents were former newspapermen.) Television correspondents flew first class, as did their soundmen, cameramen and producers; the networks maintained huge bureaus around the world, and elaborate facilities for transmitting film and, later, videotape. By the mid-seventies the networks, at considerable expense, could transmit their stories by satellite, allowing them to broadcast pictures of the same day's news events from every corner of the globe.

In those years all three networks regularly produced serious documentaries on important subjects and broadcast them in prime time. They maintained expensive corps of foreign correspondents across the globe. They provided "gavel-to-gavel" coverage of the Democratic and Republican conventions every four years, and turned over prime time to election returns every two years on the first Tuesday in November. The networks devoted hundreds of hours of daytime coverage to Congress's Watergate hearings in 1973 and 1974. The extensive coverage of the Iranian hostage crisis at the end of the seventies led to the creation of ABC's *Nightline,* one of the best news programs on a major network.

As befitted a golden age, large personalities emerged as leaders and symbols of television news. Some became national celebrities, like Cronkite and Eric Sevareid. Others operated off-camera as producers and managers. One of the most important of these was Richard Salant, a lawyer turned news executive, who was the president of CBS News through nearly the entire golden age. A difficult, complicated man, Salant was a stickler for journalistic ethics and standards. He insisted that CBS News be straight, and hard, and without frills. He permitted no music on news shows, no showbiz gimmicks.

One of Salant's monuments is a collection of rules and policies called "CBS News Standards." They commit CBS to the best possible journalistic behavior, and could easily be embraced in any good newsroom. Salant wrote a preface for this rule book that included the hallmarks of his own purist philosophy—no show-business tricks, no pandering to public tastes. "We in broadcast journalism cannot, should not, and will not base our judgments and our news treatment on our guesses (or somebody else's surveys) as to what news the people want to hear or see, and in what form. The judgments must be professional news judgments, nothing more, nothing less."

And then everything changed—not immediately, but over the course of the eighties and early nineties. The economics of television, the technology of television, the very nature of news were all transformed.

An early harbinger of change was the success of *60 Minutes,* CBS's combination of investigative reporting and celebrity interviews built around popular correspondents—initially, Mike Wallace and Harry Reasoner, later Morley Safer and Dan Rather. First launched in 1968, it took years for *60 Minutes* to build an audience and advertiser support, but by 1975 it was a big success. That year CBS added the program to its prime-time schedule on Sunday nights, and soon it was the first news program to regularly finish in the top ten prime-time shows, according to the Nielsen ratings that measured television audiences. "By 1981 *60 Minutes* had become the proverbial cash cow—and a Holstein of a cash cow," Rather recalled. Its success demonstrated to the executives of all three networks that news could make serious money.

At the end of the seventies the networks began competing with one another in a new way. Arledge wanted to convert ABC, the third network, into the best. He began by hiring numerous producers and directors from CBS, key personnel who had helped make CBS the leading news organization in television. Then he tried to persuade Rather to become the anchorman on ABC. CBS responded by promising Rather that he would succeed Cronkite as its anchor, and by offering him more than $2 million a year. Rather decided to stay at CBS.

This was an unprecedented salary. Cronkite's last salary as anchorman was about $950,000 a year. And Rather's new contract was only the beginning. Arledge went after other CBS stars, and got some of them. NBC and CBS started bidding against each other for "on-air talent."

"It was devastating," recalled Ed Fouhy, who was executive vice president of CBS News at the time. "We started losing first-class correspondents and we almost didn't know what had hit us." Fouhy recalled that "we started to exceed [our] budget because . . . we had to pay people a lot of money to keep them." But corporate headquarters didn't increase the budget to cover the higher salaries, Fouhy said, so the money to pay for them came out of the budget for covering news.

A time of troubles had begun for institutions that had been, heretofore, calm oligopolies. The competition among the networks for talent and the spike in salaries was, Fouhy said, a profound change for the old system. "I would put that right up with the advent of cable as being a highly significant factor in changing the face of network television news."

By 1980 cable television companies had wired 20 percent of America's homes. By 1983 the number was 35 percent, and by 1990, 60 percent. Cable finally gave the networks real competition. This was demonstrated by falling ratings for the three network evening news programs, which had peaked in the 1980–81 television season.

Steady erosion of audience was part of a great transformation of the television industry. The money machine no longer worked on automatic pilot. The makers and syndicators of programs, and the owners of local network outlets (which became competitors with the network news as their own news programs began to use national and international stories, often those provided by the network), kept making big money, but network ownership no longer ensured vast wealth. Suddenly, in the mid-eighties all three networks changed hands. NBC and ABC, acquired respectively by the General Electric Company and an upstart media company called Cap Cities, lost their independence, while CBS, taken over by New York investor Laurence Tisch, lost its way.

These new owners were determined to rationalize the expenses of their new possessions, a determination that often led them to the news divisions. Everyone in the news business understood that the networks spent money like drunken sailors. In the golden age, producers and executives said, and believed, and acted on the belief, that money was no object. Gordon Manning, a charming and hard-driving CBS executive, told his people when he was vice president of CBS News in the early 1970s, "Don't ever let me catch you missing a story because you wanted to save money." By 1982 the CBS News budget was $212 million and growing. With ratings declining and new owners eager to maximize earnings, the news divisions in the eighties had a rough confrontation with new realities. First, all the networks endured painful layoffs; the most painful were at CBS, where the news division lost nearly 400 jobs, but all three absorbed substantial reductions of manpower. Partly as a result, the networks began to change the way they deployed reporters.

Traditionally, the three news divisions assigned reporters to beats much the way the best newspapers did. They each had a London correspondent, a Moscow correspondent, a Supreme Court correspondent and so on. Though always encumbered by the paraphernalia of television and the need to get pictures for their stories, these correspondents could operate like traditional newspaper reporters, cultivating sources on their beats, reading up on the subject matter they covered, developing a real expertise over time.

Each network still retains a few such correspondents, most of them in Washington, but the system has changed. The change is most obvious overseas, where the networks have essentially abandoned the old practice of keeping resident correspondents in major capitals. As Rather told us, "the whole concept has changed. . . . These days . . . the correspondents live in a kind of base camp and you fly out from the base camp" to the place where news was happening. A correspondent new to the story and the country usually couldn't file the sort of report a resident expert could produce. "The kind of coverage that was the backbone of our reputation as a world-class international news-gathering organization no longer exists," Rather observed. Nor does that world-class news organization.

"What's changed is, there is a much—and I emphasize the word *much*—higher consideration given to competition," Rather told us. "It is much larger and it is much more ferocious than it was when I came to the broadcast [in 1981]. And I do want to emphasize the word *much*."

"Much" was measured in two currencies: audience ratings and profits. The two were intimately connected, since the networks charged more for advertisements on the highest-rated shows. Rather recalled that when he started as anchor, "we looked at the ratings probably every week, but I'm not even sure every week. We tended to want to see a trend line [over] three or four or five weeks. . . . Now the ratings are looked at overnight, and looked at every day." In fact, Peter Jennings said, they were now measured "minute by minute," so it was possible to see when viewers decided to leave the broadcast to look at something else. And the demographics of the audience could be minutely examined—the networks could trace when young people turned the channel, or women over fifty, Rather said. By 2000, ratings had come to "dominate."

"Another thing that's changed is . . . talk about money," Rather said. Profits might have been mentioned "once a year" when he first became anchor. "Now this is talked about at least every day, and most days more than once." And it affected the broadcast. In the old days "assignments for coverage were made strictly and entirely on the basis of, Do we think this is important enough and/or interesting enough to cover? . . . Nobody said, Well, it costs too much and we can't afford that." In 2000, cost considerations affected decisions about what to cover.

As the three anchors made clear during our conversations, the people responsible for assembling network news programs were designing them to win and hold audience. This was their priority.

"Now it's popular to say in television journalism . . . What we need is a rich mix," Rather said. What is a rich mix? "It's going to be entertainment and news all in a kind of bouillabaisse, and we do a lot of stuff that is pretty far over the line in the direction of entertainment, and we will mix in enough news that we will still call it a newscast. That's my definition of a rich mix."

The network news shows always had to make arbitrary choices about what to put on the air in the limited time available. The traditional approach was to let the day's news shape the broadcast, based on what Richard Salant called "professional news judgment." By 2000, a television news organization might be influenced by the nature of the news, but it imposed its own order. It underplayed stories with bad pictures or "boring" subject matter; it overplayed fires, crashes and tornadoes. It covered fewer news stories and did more features—a rich mix.

Brokaw told us that he was constantly "trying to construct a program that has a kind of beginning, middle and end," a program "that plays to all these . . . constituencies that are out there." Increasingly the networks seem to be using "news"—or information gathered from the real world—to construct entertaining, engaging news shows.

It's no secret that the networks exchanged "infotainment" for harder news in pursuit of ratings and profits. Rather lambasted this phenomenon in 1993, on the thirty-fifth anniversary of Murrow's famous speech to the Radio and Television News Directors Association. Rather was invited to the same convention, where he unveiled a new U.S. Postal Service stamp bearing Murrow's likeness. Rather used the occasion to try to echo Murrow for a new era.

"How goes the battle . . . to make television not just entertaining, but also, at least some of the time, useful for higher, better things?" Rather asked rhetorically. "The answer, we know, is 'not very well.' In too many ways we have allowed this great instrument, this resource, this weapon for good, to be cheapened. About this, the best among us hang their heads in embarrassment, even shame. We all should be ashamed of what we have and have not done, measured against what we could do. . . . Our reputations have been reduced, our credibility cracked, justifiably. This has happened because too often for too long we have answered to the worst, not the best, within ourselves and within our audience. We are less because of this. Our audience is less, and so is our country."

The villain, said Rather, was fear, particularly in the executive suite. "Fear leads them to depend on thoughtless, lifeless numbers to tell them what fear convinces them are facts. 'American audiences won't put up with news from other countries. Americans won't put up with economic news. Americans won't put up with serious, substantive news of any kind.'

"Bull feathers. We've gone on too long believing this nonsense. We've bought the lie that information is bad for news."

Rather's blast didn't cause much of a stir, considering the message and the messenger. It took the *New York Times* two days even to report it. Perhaps by 1993 his message was already old news.

The fact that Rather could make that speech, then return for many more lucrative years as anchor of the *CBS Evening News,* then speak as bluntly as he did in our interview with him reveals a lot about him personally, but even more about television news. It had become a cynical business. Rather's bosses couldn't like his outspoken criticism of what they do, but they tolerated it. At all three networks it was said of the anchormen, "He's the franchise." All were outsized, overpaid celebrities (they each made about $8 million a year) treated with kid gloves in their own domains. None protested that he was overpaid.

Granting each of them the foibles that often accompany fame and fortune, Brokaw, Jennings and Rather are all good guys. They care about news, care about this country and the world. If each of them was emperor of his realm, the network news would be better. Prime-time documentaries would still be broadcast, as they were regularly in the golden years. The networks would still have bureaus and correspondents scouring the country and the world for news.

But in 2000 the anchormen most decidedly were not emperors. They were highly visible hired hands working for mammoth corporations that expected the network news, like all their enterprises, to make lots of money. The corporations, not the anchormen, decided how the news divisions would operate, how much money they would spend gathering news, how much time they would get on the air for broadcasting it. The history of network television news can actually be reduced to a pair of compact sentences: *As audiences declined, network executives decreed that news had to become more profitable. So news divisions sharply reduced their costs, and tried to raise the entertainment value of their broadcasts.*

In important respects this worked. Network news staffs cost less than they used to. The new versions of the network news were more entertaining than the old ones—faster-paced, better pictures, more drama. They were also much shorter (to make room for additional commercials) and much less informative. If you watched every news program on every network week after week, and never read a good newspaper, magazine or book, you'd have a passing acquaintance with the biggest news stories but no real sense at all of the world around you. Television news people know this; the best of them are reading all the time.

The television networks haven't been in the business of making citizens well informed. Their business is assembling big audiences to whom products can be marketed by advertisers. Aggressive coverage of the news was never central to that mission, and in the nineties it became less important than ever before. By 2000 the news was an opportunity, not an obligation—an opportunity to draw more eyeballs to the networks' commercials.

But in one important respect the networks' new approach to news had failed. The audience for their flagship programs, the evening news broadcasts, had withered—in 2000 it was barely 60 percent of what it had been twenty years earlier. Nevertheless, in a fragmented television market, when advertisers were prepared to pay much higher rates to reach a mass audience, the evening news broadcasts were more profitable than they had been twenty years before.

Using elements of the news to pander to the public in hopes of making money was hardly a revolutionary development; the publishers and editors of the notorious "yellow press" were doing this a century ago. Nor was it surprising, considering how much of their audience they had already lost, that the three networks were looking for ways to stem that decline. What was surprising was the loss of confidence this process caused.

Brokaw brought us up short when we asked him to explain the mission of NBC News in 2000. Without missing a beat he answered, "To survive." In fact, in 2000, the only network news division to make big profits was that of NBC—nearly $300 million, thanks to the popularity of the *Today* show on weekday mornings and *Dateline,* its weeknight "magazine" show. But Brokaw remained uncertain about the future. He quoted his boss, Andrew Lack, then the president of NBC News and now president of NBC, as reassuring him that "we're good to go for about ten more years at least."

"There may come a time when CBS News will not do an *Evening News,*" Rather said. "The confidence in our ability to get and maintain an audience large enough for survival, much less to thrive, has gone."

Jennings said he and his colleagues "sit around here now having, I think, no real sense of what it is the audience wants. . . . I don't think we have the vaguest idea on many days who it is we're broadcasting to."

With diminished confidence in their own judgment and abilities, and particularly in their traditional standards for what constitutes news, the networks tried to figure out the appetites of the potential audience and then to satisfy them.

How was confidence lost? Jennings offered one answer that involved the O. J. Simpson trial. At ABC, he said, he and his producers "decided that we would . . . not devote any more time to the O. J. Simpson trial every day than we thought the case on the merits warranted—in contrast to NBC, which created an enormous hole in its broadcast into which it fed simply everything about O.J., and the more theater the better. I don't mean to diminish the impact of theater, because that was an important part of the trial. But when we got toward the end we suddenly realized that NBC's ratings were going up and ours were going down. And it was clear in a changing television audience universe [what] it was costing us to do what we thought was the right thing. Other people would say, Well, you didn't do the right thing, you were just pompous about it, and didn't do enough theater. And who knows who is right? But it did cost us in terms of audience, and we had to chase NBC for a very long time."

Jennings's memory was faulty. ABC's *World News Tonight* was in first place when the trial began, in January 1995, and it was still in first place when the trial ended that October, by a full ratings point. ABC was still ahead by a full point (the equivalent of 959,000 households) in July 1996. NBC, the network some called "All O.J., all the time," did *not* increase its audience during the Simpson trial.

"I'll have to revise my thinking," Jennings said later, when told the actual history. "But when the O. J. Simpson trial was over . . . we were indeed horrified by the big hole in NBC every night [five minutes or more of the *NBC Nightly News* had been regularly devoted to the trial]. . . . [We] thought NBC was doing a more populist broadcast—indeed, there was a movement here to become more populist, à la NBC . . . believing that was the more successful formula."

What did he mean by "populist"?

"It's a little hard to describe in any specific terms, but you know it when you see it," he replied. Populist news includes more stories aimed at specific categories of viewers, more coverage of health, "more stories that focus on 'the comedy and tragedy of life.'"

Rick Kaplan, who was the producer of Jennings's *World News Tonight* through the O.J. trial, left the program soon afterward and later left ABC. He told us he thought ABC made a tragic mistake by trying to mimic NBC at that time, relinquishing the core audience of hard-news consumers. "When does number one copy number two?" Kaplan asked.

Jennings was right about one important point: his broadcast on ABC did lose the lead to Brokaw's on NBC. But this happened nearly a year after the O.J. trial ended, after ABC had changed its newscast to make it more "populist."

Election night in November 2000 brought the networks their worst embarrassment in years. Their interest in politics had declined greatly by then. None of the big three gave extensive coverage to the 2000 conventions, and the standards that had evolved in the 1990s prevailed during the 2000 election cycle—less time for the candidates on the evening news, less attention to the campaign than had been typical in the seventies and eighties. But in 2000, when the election was remarkably tight, all three decided to expand their election-night coverage. What happened that night was grim evidence of how the competitive pressures on the purveyors of television news could lead them to defy good news judgment, and even common sense.

Since 1980 the networks have used computer models, exit-poll surveys of voters as they leave their polling places and early returns to project the winners of presidential elections, state by state. In the fat days when network news divisions spent money freely, each of the big three did its own exit polls and independent analysis. But by the end of the 1980s, when all three had been put repeatedly through the cost-cutting wringer, they decided to collaborate on election-night efforts, to save money. So the networks jointly created the Voter News Service (VNS), an independent organization that would conduct exit polls, create and maintain computer models and decide, for all three, when it was appropriate to call the result in a particular state. All three got the VNS projections at the same instant, so no network could get a competitive advantage with an earlier call. VNS also sold its findings to other news organizations, including newspapers, to further reduce costs for the networks. All together, the savings from this arrangement added up to millions of dollars.

The agreement to share the same projections lasted only until 1994, when ABC decided to create its own decision desk, which used VNS information with other data to make independent ABC projections of election results. On election night in 1994, ABC made several high-profile projections before its competitors. ABC's competitive success drove CBS and NBC to take the same path in 1996. With the networks creating their own panels of experts to judge the information, VNS became principally the data provider.

The networks were not generous with VNS, whose exit polling and collection of early vote totals was considerably less enterprising than the efforts each network made in their glory days. In 2000 VNS was still using old computer technology that was difficult to operate; a new system was being tested, but the money hadn't been forthcoming to fully launch it. Many of its most experienced employees had left VNS. Some voting data on which VNS computers based projections was incomplete or just wrong. For example, VNS assumed that 7.2 percent of the Florida electorate would vote by absentee ballot. In 2000, 12 percent of Florida voters actually did so. The VNS system could not catch irrational errors in vote totals reported by election officials in at least two Florida counties—errors that were eventually corrected but not before the networks had made their humiliating wrong calls.

These facts did not become known until after the debacle of 2000. The best evidence, on which we have relied here, was an after-action report prepared for the networks by Murray Edelman, editorial director of VNS and a veteran of many years in this business. He had worked for CBS before VNS was created. Edelman's analysis of how the networks could have been so wrong in Florida included an admission that the networks' system was incapable of providing a reliable basis for predicting the outcome of a very close race. The imprecisions in the system, what the statisticians call the margins of error, meant that in an election closer than 3 or 4 percentage points, projecting a winner on the basis of exit polls and incomplete returns was a journalistic roll of the dice. Normally, these are the races described as "too close to call."

On election night 2000, however, a combination of structural flaws in the VNS system and human error created the impression that Florida was not that close. At 7:50 p.m. EST, when the first projection was made giving the state to Al Gore, the VNS model projected him 7.3 percentage points ahead of George W. Bush. Two hours later the error had become obvious, and all the networks withdrew their Florida projections.

Amazingly, the humiliation of that reversal had no apparent impact on their appetite for calling the Florida result. Shortly after 2 a.m., first Fox and then the networks made their second and more serious wrong call, giving Florida to George W. Bush. VNS itself joined in the wrong first call just before 8 p.m., but at 2:15 a.m. its experts realized there were too many uncertainties about the vote count to make a projection. This didn't deter the networks, which, using the data VNS provided, all declared Bush the forty-third president of the United States. Their confidence was infectious. A number of newspapers, including the *New York Times,* published editions declaring Bush the winner. Gore called Bush in Texas to concede the election.

But the networks were as wrong the second time as they had been the first. As more returns came in, the difference between Gore and Bush in Florida dwindled to hundreds of votes. At 3:50 a.m., the networks began withdrawing their calls again.

By then, though, the country, or that part of it still awake, had digested the idea that Bush had won. So had Bush and his jubilant inner circle, the more so after Gore's phone call. So when Gore, realizing that Florida was really too close to call, telephoned a second time to withdraw his concession, Bush was furious. It was a tense, unsatisfying phone conversation for both men.

The networks had altered the course of history, setting up first one false expectation, then another, in the process sorely exacerbating relations between the two candidates' camps. The tensions this caused played out for more than a month, as the Gore and Bush campaigns dueled, in court and in the public arena, over who had really won Florida.

Their mistake had devastating consequences for the reputations of the network news divisions. All three rushed to apologize. Brokaw caught the spirit of the moment when he said, on the air, "We don't just have egg on our face, we have an omelet."

Making the call was the networks' last big contribution to the presidential campaign. Their investment in coverage of politics and government had declined substantially, but they still spent millions of dollars to be able to make these projections, which established their importance in the theatrical performance of election night. On that night, they enjoyed a special role that even leading newspapers were willing to acknowledge. The network computers could decide who won the election. Or so everyone thought before November 2000.

The decline of serious, ambitious television news over the last two decades of the twentieth century cannot be called surprising. Ours had become a celebrity-besotted culture, with television the single most powerful promoter and ratifier of celebrityhood. Entertainment, which once occupied an important place on the edge of American life, moved, over the course of the twentieth century, to the center of American life, in no small measure because of the power and reach of television. Television became big business, throwing off billions of dollars.

In the first decades of network television the owners and managers cared about things other than the maximization of profits, and they indulged expensive network news coverage. They needed goodwill, from the public and the government, as they tried to insinuate this new medium into the mainstream of American life. Feeling the gaze of government regulators, they wanted to demonstrate qualities of good citizenship and public service. The three individuals who built the networks—Paley, General David Sarnoff of NBC and Leonard Goldenson of ABC—had pride of ownership and also some self-consciousness about how much money they were making once television took hold. When, during the 1960s and 1970s, the country was gripped by turmoil in the streets and had been riven by war in Vietnam, the news mission had a compelling importance that even cynical network executives had to acknowledge.

But in the eighties and nineties all those considerations fell away. Television thrived; Congress and the FCC, beginning in the early 1980s, effectively ended public service requirements for broadcasters; the original pioneers of network television passed their creations on to a new breed of corporate owners; the news became less compelling and less scary. At the same time, prodded by a wave of mergers and acquisitions, American capitalism was transformed. A new ethos of maximizing stockholder value came to dominate businesses of all kinds, including the television networks. By the beginning of the new century the attitudes and business practices that had built the networks and their news divisions seemed quaint. Now "the driving force every day," in Rather's memorable phrase, "is delivering the profit."

Yet when Brokaw argued that nostalgia for a lost, golden age depended in part on the use of a "rosy rearview mirror," he was right. Even in the best times, network news was uneven and vulnerable to the temptation to put entertainment values ahead of news values.

Even when it was impossible to argue that the networks made the best possible use of the power of television to inform and educate, that power hadn't been lost. Television allowed all of us to participate vicariously in great events all over the world. Television still covers wars and natural disasters with great impact. There are still some serious network reporters, such as Bob Schieffer on Capitol Hill and David Martin at the Pentagon, whose reporting holds powerful people accountable from behind a microphone and camera. And in times of crisis or great excitement, the country still turns to network television to share the experience.

This was dramatically the case on September 11, 2001. Just ten months after the election-night fiasco, all three networks put on what must have been the finest display of television journalism the country had ever seen. Particularly on that first day, confronted by a bewildering series of unimaginable events in multiple locations around the country, the live coverage on all three networks remained calm and careful, as well as vivid and dramatic. It would have been extremely easy to contribute to or even create a sense of national hysteria that day, but the three anchormen remained cool and professional. The producers, directors, technicians and writers working behind them performed admirably.

We talked to each of the anchors several weeks after September 11, and all of them were proud of what their organizations had done to report on what all agreed was the biggest story they had ever covered. Typically, Rather was the most blunt:

"To be utterly frank, I'm not only pleased and inspired by it, I'm also somewhat surprised. I believed, and I know I'm not alone in this belief, that we had moved into an era of softer news. . . . News as we had known it in most of my lifetime was in real and present danger of being completely overwhelmed by entertainment values." But on September 11— "within minutes," as Rather put it—hard news was back in the forefront.

All of them spoke of the role their organizations played in helping the country cope with a national trauma. "We were all reminded in large and small ways how important a national broadcasting service is," Jennings said. All of them praised their corporate bosses for seeing at once that commercials should be taken off the air and all energies devoted to the story. "One of the things that has been put to rest," Rather said, "is 'All those guys think about is money.' In this case they have cared about the country and they have cared about good journalism."

"This has been a reminder of the traditional role of network news," said Andrew Heyward, president of CBS News. A television network is "an institution that can knit the country together in a time of crisis by being not only an honest broker of information, a sifter of rumor from reality, but also a conveyor of shared experience."

The networks stayed on the air with the terrorist story for four days without commercial interruption. This cost them hundreds of millions of dollars, and won them plaudits from many sources. Perhaps more important, it won them viewers, scores of millions of Americans who sat for hours, then days, in front of their televisions. There had never been such an audience for news coverage before. The Nielsen company said its true size could never be fully counted, since so many people watched in their offices, where Nielsen has no meters, and because so many cable channels rebroadcast the signals of the major networks.

Not every American eager to follow the story turned to the three major broadcast networks, of course. Millions tuned in to the cable news networks that provide news all, or most, of the time. The cable news operations are evidence of the transformation of television news in recent years.

For the first four decades of the television era, from 1950 to 1990, news was unabashedly aimed at a mass audience by networks that put primary emphasis on their evening news broadcasts, and also regularly devoted slices of prime time to documentaries and other news programs. Since 1990, news has increasingly become a niche product, one taken most seriously now by the cable news networks, CNN, MSNBC and Fox. This is a huge cultural change. The existence of multiple cable outlets devoted primarily or exclusively to news guarantees that big stories will be instantly addressed on television. Devoted consumers of news know they can find pictures and reportage from a big breaking story on CNN or Fox or MSNBC right now—they don't have to wait for the network news at 6:30 or the local news at 11. The three principal cable providers compete fiercely to be first on the air with live pictures from a significant breaking story. They can give viewers immediate and compelling coverage of those stories.

It may seem to the regular viewers of CNN, for example, that they are watching a network similar to the older, better-known ones, but there is one profound difference: the size of the audience. In the fall of 2001, when more than 20 million people were watching the three networks' evening news programs, CNN, Fox and MSNBC were being watched in about 3.5 million homes, according to Nielsen figures. Nor can cable news compete for audience during a big story. On the night of September 11, 2001, the networks had more than 80 million viewers; the cable news channels had about 14 million. CNN's most-watched program, *The Larry King Show*—a talk show sometimes *about* the news, rarely a program providing news—draws an audience of less than a million viewers during prime time each night. No prime-time show on a broadcast network would survive with an audience that small. Even when two-thirds of American homes subscribe to cable or satellite television, the network audience, for news as well as entertainment, is many times bigger than for cable.

Cable news is best understood by looking closely at the actual content of cable programming. Ted Turner, the sports and television entrepreneur who founded CNN, long held out the promise of a first-class news operation but never achieved it. CNN is notorious for its parsimonious salaries, paying a few stars well but skimping on other personnel, especially off-camera editors and producers, whose skills set the standard for any television news operation. CNN has never developed a culture of authority and excellence in its news coverage.

The network's strength is its commitment to transmit video from important news events as they are occurring, wherever they may be, or, if live pictures are impossible, to provide recorded images as soon as possible. CNN, and now the other cable news outlets as well, have made it possible for everyone to join the audience for big, breaking stories. This is an important element in the voyeuristic culture of our times. It can be fascinating and sometimes highly informative to be able to see big news being made.

But CNN reporters have rarely broken a story or challenged a powerful person or institution with original reporting. CNN's most famous scoop was based not on revelatory reporting, but on technology and resourcefulness—Peter Arnett's reports from Baghdad at the beginning of the Gulf War, when the broadcast networks could not get their correspondents into Iraq. Occasional forays by CNN into investigative journalism have not been fruitful, and have sometimes been embarrassing. The network had to retract one much-publicized investigative report alleging that U.S. forces had used nerve gas in Laos in 1970. CNN fired two producers after that mistake. On September 11, 2001, a CNN producer happened to be in Kabul, Afghanistan. He reported breathlessly on a fire at an ammunition dump on the edge of town apparently caused by an American cruise missile responding to the attacks on the World Trade Center and the Pentagon. But it quickly emerged that the fire was caused by Afghan rebels; no cruise missiles had been fired.

Most CNN correspondents rush from one breaking news story to another and are unable to add much context or expertise to their reports. CNN coverage of big stories is often heavily larded with interviews with newsmakers and the opinions of talking-head observers, leaving the viewer to try to sort out fact from hot air. At its best, CNN coverage is as good as the best on the broadcast networks, but it isn't any better. Typically what CNN and the other cable news networks provide is a headline service, a sort of radio news with pictures, heavily reliant on news agency reporting from the Associated Press and Reuters.

By 2001 CNN, newly merged into the conglomerate formed by America Online's takeover of Time Warner, was in difficulty. MSNBC and, quite dramatically, the Fox News Channel were both gaining viewers at CNN's expense, and a new team of CNN managers decided they had to respond. The nature of their response was revealing. They announced layoffs of about 10 percent of the CNN workforce of 4,300 people. They created a series of new nightly talk shows built around personalities, hosts they hoped would become popular the way Larry King did fifteen years earlier. This meant there would be less reporting of news on CNN, and more talking about the news—already the norm on cable television. Jeff Greenfield, host of one of the new CNN talk shows, described the challenge the network faced: "We need to keep the effort going to find new modes of making news interesting and compelling entertainment." How to make news into entertainment—that was the conundrum, at least until the terrorist attacks on America.

The most profitable information channel on cable television by 2001 was not one of the general news channels, but CNBC, an NBC offshoot specializing in business and financial news. Riding the wave of interest in the stock market that swept the country in the eighties and nineties, CNBC provided a steady diet of stock tips, market reports and experts' commentary that often outdrew CNN and its rivals. CNBC's success seemed to confirm the idea that on cable, at least, news was becoming a niche product for special-interest viewers.

CNBC was also part of a successful restructuring of NBC, which has combined broadcast and cable in a new organization that offers good commercial prospects for the future. For NBC, news is increasingly a cable product. When challenged about their decision to provide only a few hours' coverage of the national political conventions in 2000, executives at NBC replied that their MSNBC channel was providing more coverage than ever, hours of it each day. The ratings for CNN's convention coverage fell by more than a fourth from 1996 to 2000, while MSNBC claimed a burgeoning audience by using its star NBC newsmen, led by Tom Brokaw and Tim Russert. MSNBC, a joint project of NBC and Microsoft, which includes a popular Web site as well as a cable news network, quickly became an integral part of NBC News. Network executives planned to allocate the costs of the entire NBC News operation to the cable operations, which, they said, would be profitable early in the new century. Cable programming can be lucrative because local cable systems must pay a small fee to the provider of the program for every household the system serves.

This economic arrangement will apparently guarantee the survival of cable news networks indefinitely, but it won't help them attract audiences that might rival broadcast television's. Instead they seem to be becoming a kind of utility, similar to all-news radio stations or news sites on the Internet, a place to turn to periodically when you want to monitor the news.

Of course this is the way many Americans use television news of all kinds, which may explain why survey research has begun to show television news losing audience to online news providers. If you want to check out the headlines quickly, reading them online is much more efficient than waiting for a broadcaster to read them to you, and depending on that broadcaster to read the ones you're interested in.

One of the biggest promoters of cable news, ironically, is a network news executive, Andrew Lack of NBC. As president of NBC News from 1993 to 2001, he was instrumental in NBC's expansion into cable through two new networks: CNBC, and MSNBC, a news channel and Internet Web site. In 2001, Lack was promoted, becoming president of the NBC network, responsible for entertainment programming as well as news.

Andy Lack is a man of infectious energy and enthusiasm who talks with his hands as well as his booming voice. He is charming and persuasive, and a great enthusiast for his work and his network. We talked to him at length when he was still president of NBC News. He struck us then as the archetypal network executive. So it was no surprise when the big bosses at the General Electric Company, owners of NBC, put him in charge of the entire network several months later (in May 2001).

Lack wanted to persuade us that the network news of 2000 and early 2001 was terrific—better than any previous version. He was encouraged in his enthusiasm by concrete facts: his NBC News had the top-rated show in the morning *(Today),* the top-rated show in the evening (Brokaw's) and the top-rated prime-time news show at night *(Dateline).* CNBC and MSNBC were both profitable, and MSNBC.com was one of the most popular news sites on the Internet. Lack's news division made hundreds of millions of dollars for NBC—nearly $300 million in profits in 2000 alone. "I am America's news leader," he once told a *New York Times* reporter in a moment of exuberance.

Lack is a creature of the television age, which sets him apart from the three anchors, who all grew up in the age of radio, and are old enough to remember when *The Howdy Doody Show* first came on television. That was in 1949, when Lack was two. His own biography seems apt for a man so wrapped up in modern television.

That biography includes an early drama, the murder of his father, whom Lack described in an interview as a gambler and a rogue, "a charming guy, a Damon Runyon figure." In 1953, when Lack was six, his parents split up, and a year later his father was shot dead in Detroit during a card game that turned ugly. "I remember vividly, at seven years old, the photographers from the *Daily News* climbing up the side of the apartment [house] that we lived in in New York to get a picture of me and my brother and my mother. And we were the front-page news for the *Daily News* on this Memorial Day weekend when my father was killed."

His mother didn't tell her sons much about their father's demise, and Lack developed a powerful curiosity about what had happened. When he was thirteen he talked his way into the *Daily News* library and found the papers from that weekend on microfilm. "I read all the reporting of the murder."

Lack's first idea for what to do in life was the theater, which he studied at Boston University, but that didn't pan out. He did better in advertising, becoming an accomplished maker of soap commercials. "I learned craft there," he recounted. "I did learn that in thirty seconds you can communicate a hell of a lot to people."

But this didn't satisfy either. "I realized very early on that I'd much rather work in nonfiction than fiction. . . . The real stories worth telling in life were the true stories, not the made-up ones. . . . The human condition and what makes us tick, what makes society go round, is the stuff of great theater and the stuff of great nonfiction. The news business is maybe the greatest theater to operate in, because it's really what happened."

So he began knocking on the door of Mike Wallace, star of the new hit storytelling show on CBS, *60 Minutes*. He wrote Wallace letters and called him on the telephone, and finally Wallace agreed to meet him. Eventually he helped get Lack his first break in television, a job on a new CBS show called *Who's Who*.

"It was a personality show," Lack recounted, "based a little bit on the popularity of *People* magazine. . . . And it was considered by the CBS News purists as 'Aw man, they're going to junk this joint up with that personality crap. . . . They've even hired some asshole from advertising to be a producer on it.' " That would be Lack himself, who did get hired as a producer on the show, partly on the strength of his "pitch reel," a roll of film of his work that included "a couple of Liquid Prell commercials."

This was an appropriate beginning to Lack's network television career—working for a controversial new "news" show that was more entertainment than news. Ever since—though he has done a lot of serious television, including prizewinning documentaries on difficult subjects like nuclear weapons—Lack has been associated with programming that stretched the definitions of news, and often ignored traditional news subjects. He got his big break in 1985, when CBS launched his new magazine show aimed at younger viewers, *West 57th*. This too was controversial among CBS News traditionalists, because it used modern camera work, featured informal young correspondents and covered subjects from everyday life that were rarely examined on network television news shows. Though never a hit, it lasted four seasons, and had a big influence on subsequent television magazine shows. After *West 57th*, Lack's star at CBS lost some of its luster. But he went on to produce *Face to Face with Connie Chung* and *Street Stories*, two more shows out of step with the straitlaced conventions of the old CBS News.

Then, in 1993, Lack's fortunes turned. NBC was reeling from a scandal involving *Dateline*, the network's prime-time newsmagazine, which had staged a rigged truck accident it then used in order to accuse General

Motors of producing a defective pickup truck. The previous president of news had resigned. Tom Brokaw had been courting Lack as a possible new producer of the *Nightly News,* but when Bob Wright, the president of NBC Television, met Lack, he immediately had bigger ideas. This was the man to run NBC News, Wright decided. When Lack's appointment was announced in April 1993, his CBS colleagues were amazed.

The O. J. Simpson case arrived in June 1994, in the second year of Lack's tenure at NBC, and the network claimed the story as its own. "The O. J. Simpson trial was a very interesting story, frankly, in my perception of race, and many of my colleagues think that we overplayed it here at NBC," Lack told us. "I wished I could have done more with it. I had O.J., I didn't have my cable channel. I didn't have MSNBC [which was launched in mid-1996]. So I wished I could have been in the court with that case, that was the real first cameras-in-the-courtroom [for a big trial]." Lack wanted even more O.J., more of the time.

When we asked him whether, on his watch, NBC News had become softer, less interested in hard news, less interested in foreign stories or politics, Lack firmly rejected each of these suggestions. He has always respected the highest news values, he said emphatically. "I have always believed we have a public trust to protect."

Under questioning, Lack acknowledged that his personal definitions of news weren't always the traditional ones. He described many reports from Washington and overseas as "process stories." Telling viewers that the secretary of state flew to the Middle East yesterday was a process story, but "that doesn't make it news," Lack said.

Stories from Washington and overseas were just less interesting to Lack than stories about families, health and science. "I just think that the under-covered stories in our newsroom have invariably been stories that affect families, and women in particular, because these newsrooms have been subtly, or not so subtly, ruled by men who aren't really interested in breast cancer until their wife, sadly, or their mother gets it. . . . I point to the areas of health and science because they've always been the unglamorous stocks in the newsroom. But in fact they are the real news in people's lives." The other networks broadcast more foreign news than NBC, but Lack's team broadcast much more about health and science—more "real news." And on Lack's watch, NBC broadcast less of the 2000 national political conventions than ABC or CBS, letting MSNBC carry the political load on cable.

Had entertainment values corrupted the news? Absolutely not, Lack replied. "My job is not to entertain, there's nothing in my mission about entertaining people. Informing is my mission." At the same time, "engaging people" was important:

"Engaging . . . is not about entertainment, it's about helping to inform. It's exciting to me to make the choices about how I'm going to organize this information in a way that makes you feel the importance of it, makes you see the importance of it, makes you understand the importance of it, makes you look at it a little bit differently."

In pursuit of engagement, Lack encouraged creativity in storytelling, new approaches to old situations, reliance on compelling visual images. The "marriage" between words and images was critical: "It's the execution of that marriage that is the challenge every day." But this was not entertainment, he repeated. "I'm not interested in making you laugh or amusing you or making you cry. I'm interested in being true to the information and offering it to you as interestingly as I can. Some people are uncomfortable with that. They think, you know, get out of the way of the information, just tell me: 'Yesterday three people issued a report and this is what the report said.' . . . [If] you want your news that way, go get it that way. There are places . . . that's what you'll get."

Lack made no apology for NBC's decision to eliminate most of its foreign correspondents and bureaus. In the old days, before satellite communication became commonplace, "I couldn't get a picture out of Rome or get to Rome fast enough to get the picture that I wanted, so I needed somebody to be there. In this age you don't need that. But the dirty little secret, even in that age, was that those people were not very productive. . . . I was at the old CBS Paris bureau and the old CBS London bureau and there were an awful lot of guys sitting around and going to Savile Row and buying fancy-looking suits. . . . There was a noblesse oblige in the bureau system that was a waste of money, and bullshit. . . . That level . . . of waste was pulled out of the system," Lack said. He was referring to wave after wave of cutbacks at NBC News during the eighties and early nineties. But NBC News remained "a very aggressive and vigorous news organization that has no trouble covering the world and getting the best stories on the air," Lack said.

"And they don't need a bureau in Rome to do it. I can tell you, in the seven years that I've been here, if I had a bureau in Rome I wouldn't have gone there once [for coverage of a news story]. I can't think of a reason to be there, you know? To cover the Pope? And when the Pope dies, God bless his soul, I'll have those pictures without having to have a Rome reporter. And I'll have plenty of intelligent people to talk about the subject without needing my beat guy in Rome."

When Lack made this comment about a Rome bureau he had been the president of NBC News for just over seven years. In that period, the *Los Angeles Times* (a newspaper that is serious about foreign news) printed more than 320 stories under a Rome dateline. These were the years when the Italian neo-fascists became a force in Italian politics and a nationalistic media magnate became a new political power; Italy was rocked by the prosecution of dozens of senior officials for corruption, an investigation that destroyed its once predominant Christian Democratic Party; the Pope spoke and traveled widely; Italy surprised Europe by qualifying for membership in its new currency, the Euro; and refugees from Kosovo and elsewhere flooded into the country. In other words, by traditional news standards, there were plenty of good stories that a Rome correspondent might have covered, if NBC had been interested in that sort of news. But it wasn't.

The issue was not cost, Lack said. "NBC is spending more money doing more news, producing more news and pursuing journalism with more people . . . than they ever have in the history of this company. Ever." This was surely true, at least until NBC announced layoffs of up to 10 percent of its workforce early in 2001. But the size of NBC News reflected the growth of NBC into a cable and broadcast enterprise offering twenty-four-hour news more than a commitment, for example, to news from overseas, or to the kind of beat reporting that newspapers rely on. As Lack's commentary made clear, his kind of news was visual, dramatic, engaging—in other words, the news you could see every evening on the *Nightly News* in the years Lack ran NBC News and made it the leading network news division.

In early 2001 Lack thought the future was bright—and on cable. He realized in the mid-nineties, he said, that "the future health of NBC News was going to be competing with CNN, not with ABC News or CBS News." NBC would satisfy the public interest, give viewers lots of news, cover government and politics, but these things would be done primarily on cable television. This implied that news would increasingly become a specialized, niche product for a small, specialized audience.

The terrorist attacks on the United States in 2001 reopened all the old questions about the future of news on television. The anchors and presidents of the news divisions knew, in October 2001, that something big had happened, but were far from certain what it might mean for the future.

"I think it's a great moment in American journalism," Rather told us three weeks after the attacks. "Now, whether we can make this moment last, and how long we can make it last, these are the open questions. . . . I'm mildly optimistic, but the italics must be on *mildly*."

Peter Jennings of ABC, also speaking shortly after the attacks, expressed similar uncertainty: "The world has changed, at least for now, in very significant ways, and that's a huge, huge, huge news story, and I hope our employers let us continue to cover it. We have had nothing but support so far." Jennings's boss, David Westin, president of ABC News, echoed his anchorman's caution. Speaking of the intense post-attack coverage, Westin said: "I'm very reluctant to say this is the way it's going to be from now on."

Rather predicted the early return of the network executives "who were saying before this happened, 'You just can't survive, much less thrive, without dumbing it down, sleazing it up, going lighter, going softer.' Those voices are bound to return. Now the question is, How many of us listen to them and what I consider a false gospel, and how many of us try to hold the line, and then among those who try to hold the line, how many will succeed?"

One prominent television executive was openly contrite. Walter Isaacson, a former managing editor of *Time* magazine who had recently become chairman of CNN, had been planning changes to soften CNN's news coverage to try to compete for viewers with the Fox News Channel when the terrorist attacks altered his plans. Television news, he said soon after September 11, had lost its way before the attacks. "I think this has been a wake-up call to the public and to all of us in the news business that there are certain things that matter more than the latest trivial thing that can cause a ratings boost," Isaacson told the *New York Times.* "It's helped all of us regain our focus."

But Paul Friedman, executive vice president of ABC News, was not so sure: "I don't know that the current interest [in international news] will continue much beyond this story, however long it lasts."

Questions about money loomed for all news organizations: covering wars costs big money. Initially the corporate owners of all the major networks behaved impeccably: none questioned the expense of covering the story or tried to hold down costs. But the journalists knew this forbearance would be temporary. "The reality is, there will probably be some tightening up" of the news budget, Brokaw said. "How severe or draconian it will be, I don't know," he added in October 2001.

Jennings, acknowledging previous cutbacks in coverage of foreign news, wondered if these cataclysmic events "mean they will put more money into [ABC News], or continue to make it difficult to cover the world in the manner which we would like. I don't know the answer. It's just simply hard to know whether an event of this magnitude will alter the business structure of the major news organizations."

Lack said, after the attacks, that he thought they would force Americans generally, including television journalists, to re-examine their priorities. "You could watch [television] news over the last six, seven, eight years and say to yourself, Gosh, what's going on in America?" Lack said. The America that viewers had seen on the news—"that face that we all saw in the mirror"—was not an appealing one, Lack thought in October 2001. "The mirror was shattered, arguably, on September 11, and I hope that forces us now to go back and take another look at ourselves, and yeah, rearrange some priorities, and what's important to us."

But terrorist attacks against the United States could not wipe away the history of the previous fifteen years, which had taken a toll on network news. The traditions that prevailed when Brokaw, Jennings and Rather came into the television news business had been displaced, as all three of them acknowledged.

We asked each of them if their successors would have the same standing and influence within their networks that they enjoyed, and still sometimes exploited to preserve traditional news values. No, they all agreed. Rather said he thought it likely that future CBS management would decide it was "better to have somebody who will concentrate on the presentation of the news" in the anchorman's chair—a news reader, not a reporter and editor who is also trying to shape the broadcast, as all three anchors do now. Today's anchors are "brand names," Rather added, so "management has to be careful" not to disagree with them publicly. He's less hopeful about future anchors, and future managements: "I think in the future there's a very strong possibility what you're going to have [in management] is somebody who doesn't give a damn" about news values.

Jennings said the next anchormen won't have had the extensive reporting experience that shaped him, Brokaw and Rather. "Experience equals authority," Jennings said, so future anchors won't embody the same authority.

Brokaw said future anchors and producers would come from a new milieu, where traditional news values were not so important. "Curiously, the people who are coming to us [to work at NBC] are smarter than they've ever been, well educated. . . . They're children of television and they really want to come to work here. And a lot of them, unfortunately, don't give a shit about the news. They want to do magazines or they want to do talk shows."

Speaking in the spring of 2000, Rather went further: "Certainly . . . journalistic business organizations have stopped believing [in public service] to a very large measure. And . . . we stopped believing that the public cares. . . . At one time [we believed] . . . if you don't sort of radiate with a sense that . . . what you're doing . . . has to do with public service . . . you're going to pay a price. Now the fear is that if you *do* that, you will pay a price."

In the autumn of 2001, after the terrorist attacks, Rather was a little more hopeful: "I do think that some news organizations, in the wake of this, will change considerably, substantially," and that those changes would be "lasting." He obviously hoped CBS would be one of them, but wasn't sure.

Rather has long been ready with an idea for a substantial change at CBS. He told us in 2000 he thought the day might come when an aging baby boom generation would want "integrity-based news, and what used to be called 'gatekeeper' news" on television—a broadcast that would sort through "the flood of information coming in" and make sense of it.

He imagined a one-hour broadcast. "My own preference [would be] to have it on at ten o'clock and make it the combination of *The CBS Evening News, 60 Minutes* and *Nightline* at ten o'clock. I think somebody is going to do that. And I think . . . [the] first outfit that does it, I think they're going to do good, and do well. They may not win the time period for ratings, but they will do quite well."

For Rather this would be his long-dreamed-of "newspaper of the air," an attempt to redeem the reputation of CBS News in particular and network television in general. "I think we have diluted and diminished our brand name," Rather said poignantly when we talked with him. "There was a time [when] CBS was the overarching brand name." He'd like to see that again.

Is this a pipe dream? All over Europe big audiences tune in to prime-time newscasts, many of them much more serious and richer in content than any American television news broadcast. But the trend away from serious network news is deeply entrenched now. Rather acknowledged this, too. "You should know," he said, after predicting that a prime-time news program could be successful, "that I am the only person that I know of in this world who believes that."

When we talked to Brokaw shortly after the terrorist attacks in 2001, he also raised the subject of a one-hour broadcast, which NBC had created for him for several days after September 11. "It was so gratifying . . . to have an hour [with no commercials] to deal with these serious issues for an audience that was seriously interested in them," he said. But that was not to last. "For me," Brokaw said, "the saddest thing is that I will probably leave this job and it still will probably be only half an hour for the network evening news."

# Chapter Six

# LOCAL TELEVISION NEWS: LIVE AT 4, 5, 6 AND 11

W e are not finding dead fish."
        Brenda Mallory, producer of the 5 o'clock news-
        cast on WRC-TV, Channel 4, hovered over a speaker-
phone in the station's noisy newsroom listening to the disembodied voice
of reporter Mary Alice Salinas, speaking from a satellite truck somewhere
in scenic Rock Creek Park, which slices through the middle of Washington, D.C.

"Any other locations where we might find dead fish?" asked Frank
Caskin, executive producer of all four of WRC's evening newscasts, at 4, 5,
6 and 11 p.m.

"Did she have a location to look for dead fish?" Mallory asked in
return.

"She's been to a number of locations," Caskin said with resignation. It
was already 3 o'clock, the minutes ticking away to airtime.

The news was slow that Friday in the spring of 2000, so Channel 4's
evening news producers were counting on the contamination of Rock
Creek by a mysterious toxic substance. It had all the elements that a producer looks for in a good local television news story: a hint of danger (the
National Park Service had warned local residents to stay away from the
popular creek during the forthcoming weekend), environmental damage
(tens of thousands of fish had died along eleven miles of the creek), the
mystery of the nature and source of the poisonous substance (authorities
were checking a number of businesses near Rock Creek Park), potentially
vivid video (competing Channel 5 had already aired footage of dead fish
on its noon news) and an opportunity for a reporter to appear "live" at the
scene of the story on the evening news (Salinas and her camera crew had
been hurrying from place to place along the creek for several hours in
search of dead fish).

But WRC, an "owned-and-operated" affiliate of the NBC network, one of the most-watched, most-profitable and best-staffed local television news operations in the country, had been fumbling the story all day. Beginning at the first morning news meeting at 9 o'clock, the producers had difficulty finding a reporter to send out on the story. WRC had a relatively large news staff of 120 people, but only 30 of them were news, sports and weather anchors and reporters. The others—camera operators, videotape editors, technicians, producers, directors and managers— were needed to get the news on the air. So, like most television stations, Channel 4 had fewer than 10 reporters available to cover the entire city and fill three and a half hours of evening newscasts each day.

At the 9 o'clock meeting, held on leather sofas in the comfortable office of the station's news director, Bob Long, some of those reporters joined assignment editors and producers for the four evening newscasts to discuss a list of potential stories. It was near the end of May, a ratings "sweeps" month, one of several periods each year when audience ratings are used to set advertising rates. "I'd like to give us a little goose at the end," said Long. He prided himself on the high ratings of WRC's newscasts, which accounted for 60 percent of the station's market-leading advertising revenue and profits.

A warm morning sun was bouncing off the leafy trees that filled the view outside the office's big picture windows, but assignment editor Bill Starks said that severe thunderstorms were forecast for that afternoon— another potentially good television story. His list of possible stories included a new computer virus being reported by the wire services and the scheduled media preview day for the annual military air show at nearby Andrews Air Force Base, which would attract hundreds of thousands of Washingtonians over the weekend. The Rock Creek contamination warning was on the list because someone whose dog got sick after drinking water in the creek had called the station. Also on the list was the collapse of a recreational pier that killed several people in Philadelphia; the NBC station there had informed WRC and other NBC-owned stations in their daily conference call that its coverage from the scene would be available to them.

Story possibilities gleaned from the morning newspaper and press releases received by the station were also mentioned. And a reporter whose responsibilities included covering the city government said he was checking on the vacancies for school superintendent and fire chief. Unlike newspapers, where much of the news is discovered by beat reporters, who then tell their editors about it, in television newsrooms the editors decide where to send the reporters. This makes it less likely that a local television newscast will contain original journalism about a subject not being covered elsewhere.

This is one of the many ways that local television news is severely limited in what it can tell viewers each day about their community and the world around them. Others include the relatively small size and modest ambitions of each station's news operation, its dependence on complicated and expensive technology, its hunger for audience-grabbing visual and emotional impact and its preoccupation with high audience ratings and profit margins. Survey after survey has confirmed that although their audience is shrinking, local television newscasts remain the primary source of news for most Americans. Yet those newscasts don't cover many stories and don't cover them in much depth.

"Who wants to step forward?" Starks asked reporters in the room. "I want somebody at the [Andrews] air base. I want somebody at Rock Creek."

Several of the day's stories had been assigned to the handful of available reporters by the time of the next meeting, shortly before noon, conducted by managing editor Mary Ellen Donovan in the middle of the station's busy newsroom. She supervised all of Channel 4's news reporting, but not the presentation of the stories on the air, which was the job of executive producer Caskin and the producer of each newscast. No one in the newsroom had yet found an official to confirm the Rock Creek contamination warning, so Donovan decided to send Salinas, who had been at the dentist, out to Rock Creek Park with a camera crew to find something.

Unlike newspaper reporters, who spend most of their time reporting a story by interviewing as many people as possible, often on the telephone, and then piecing the story together, local television reporters spend most of their time traveling to and from locations for one or two on-camera interviews and a "live shot" at the scene of the story.

While Salinas and her camera crew were still on their way to Rock Creek Park, a competing station broadcast the first sketchy version of the contamination story, accompanied by live video of dead fish.

"We're still behind," Jack Heinbrow, the producer of WRC's 4 p.m. newscast, said as he moved into his chair in the station's state-of-the-art control room at 3:45. "Any Salinas sighting?"

"No, we're still waiting for a signal," answered the voice of one of the technical directors. Salinas was nowhere to be seen on the wall of television screens covering the front of the control room. Many of the more than fifty monitors flickered with images of what was being broadcast on competing stations and networks. Others showed available video "feeds" from various sources, including NBC News; locations where WRC reporters would show up in live shots from remote units; and the anchor desk in the adjacent studio, where the 4 o'clock anchors could be seen chatting as they prepared to go on the air.

Technicians who managed the complicated strands of sights and sounds woven into each hour of news were scattered around the control room. The newscast's director—who cued each of dozens of rapid-fire switches of studio camera views, videotape segments and fades into and out of commercials—sat at the front, headset on, ready to follow a second-by-second script supplied by Heinbrow. Several rows back, Heinbrow sat at a computer, still reworking that script, rearranging stories and rewriting the words the anchors would read from the TelePrompTer when the newscast went on the air.

He had planned to open the newscast with a live NBC feed from New York of Mayor Rudy Giuliani announcing that he was dropping out of the race against Hillary Rodham Clinton for the U.S. Senate. That was to be followed by a live report from Salinas in Rock Creek Park. But Giuliani's announcement had been delayed, and Salinas had not yet been found. So Heinbrow quickly substituted weatherman Bob Ryan, appearing coatless at his computerized "Storm Center" weather set in the newsroom, to report on the severe thunderstorm warnings for the region.

Caskin rushed into the control room to tell Heinbrow to "stretch Ryan" while they waited for Giuliani. "I *did*, Frank," Heinbrow answered testily. Just as Ryan finished his forecast, Giuliani appeared on the monitor.

Minutes later, as reporter I. J. Hudson came on live from the newsroom upstairs to report on a new computer virus, Salinas showed up on a monitor in the control room. She was standing under an umbrella in Rock Creek Park, rehearsing in front of the camera. Salinas went on the air next, reporting little more than the National Park Service warning, while the camera focused on the creek behind her. There was no close-up of dead fish.

Heinbrow next put on the story about the recreational pier collapse from the NBC station in Philadelphia. The reporter, broadcasting live with the pier in the background many hours after it had collapsed, kept talking and talking beyond her allotted time. "Can you wrap her up, please?" Caskin pleaded.

Now the entire newscast was off schedule. "We're blowing the show up," Heinbrow told everyone in the control room. "I have to kill a lot."

As weatherman Ryan gave another update from the newsroom on the expected thunderstorms, Heinbrow told everyone, including the anchors through their earpieces, about the changes he was making.

"We're going to do weather until we drop," Caskin ordered from behind Heinbrow in the control room. "Keep Bob on as long as the warnings are up."

The thunderstorm forecast had preoccupied the Channel 4 newsroom since it first came up at the 9 a.m. assignment meeting in Bob Long's office. Weather follows crime and disaster news on the list of subjects given the most time in local newscasts. Its popularity shows up in audience surveys and the minute-by-minute daily ratings available to stations in many cities. Television stations spend a lot of money on their own weather radar, high-powered computers to analyze data from the National Weather Service and private forecast services, and fancy newsroom sets like Channel 4's "Storm Center" to show off all this technology to viewers. They pay high salaries to weather anchors like Bob Ryan. He and his meteorological assistants operate the computers and prepare their weather reports and graphics themselves. A weather anchor as popular as Ryan constituted an independent power center in the newsroom, largely outside the control of individual newscast producers.

As Ryan finished his thunderstorm update, the control room stirred. Heinbrow spoke again to anchor Pat Lawson in the studio: "There is a breaking news story in the TelePrompTer for you to read."

On cue, Lawson told viewers that "a serious collision" between a school bus and a truck had occurred within the hour just outside Washington in suburban Montgomery County, Maryland. "News 4 crews are on the way."

Upstairs in the newsroom, everyone was scrambling. A reporter and camera crew were sent to the accident scene in a microwave truck, which transmits video and audio relatively inexpensively via a direct, line-of-sight signal to the station rather than bouncing it off satellites orbiting the earth. Dramatic, visual breaking stories like this are the holy grail of local television news. News directors hope that viewers will be drawn in to watch developments unfold in real time, many hours before the first newspaper accounts can reach their homes. Covering breaking news costs television stations big money, beginning with the millions of dollars they spend on satellite trucks and helicopters.

Even routine live coverage with one reporter, camera crew and micro-wave truck requires an investment of more than half a million dollars, according to Long. Satellite trucks and transmission cost even more. "To outfit a microwave truck is just under $200,000," Long told us. "The cam-eraman is $100,000 a year, not counting pension and welfare benefits. The technician at the other end who brings the signal back is another $100,000 item," plus the reporter and video editor. "It takes a lot of hands to make a television news piece."

As she hurried from the newsroom to take command in the control room downstairs, Brenda Mallory, the producer of WRC's 5 o'clock news, real-ized that she would have to reconstruct her newscast on the run. "Mary Alice hasn't landed," she said, referring to Salinas, who was on the move and out of touch again.

By the end of the 4 p.m. newscast, the threat of severe thunderstorms had passed and the weather was fizzling out as a story. "No more weather watches or warnings," Ryan told viewers in yet another update.

But no one in the newsroom, now frantic with activity, would miss the weather story. The school bus accident had blown it away—along with everything else on the agenda. "I certainly hope we can lead at 5 with [the bus]," Mallory said.

The control room was chaotic as the 5 o'clock news opened with anchor Doug McKelway interviewing an emergency room physician on the telephone about schoolchildren injured in the accident whom he had treated. On the monitors, competing Channel 9 had only a bulletin about the accident at the beginning of its 5 p.m. news, but Channel 7 already had a reporter on the air from the scene, with the wreckage visible behind her. And Channel 9 had both video of dead fish in Rock Creek and a reporter live from an industrial park near Rock Creek Park, where officials were looking for the source of the toxic discharge. Police and emergency vehi-cles were visible in the background.

Mallory knew her newscast was in trouble. Falling behind the other stations on breaking stories risked losing viewers who switch from one channel to another. She kept scanning the monitors, looking for a Chan-nel 4 reporter at the scene of the school bus accident or Salinas anywhere for the Rock Creek story. "I want a picture," she moaned to no one in par-ticular. "It's TV. I want a picture."

By 5:12 p.m., all she had to put on their air was another telephone interview with a county police spokesman about the school bus accident. He at least provided some needed details: one fatality, believed to be the bus driver, and three seriously injured children.

Then came more stories about disasters: another live report on the pier collapse from Philadelphia and dramatic video from a television news service of a fire in Tampa. After a commercial, there was an update on the school bus accident, still without video or a Channel 4 reporter at the scene. Its microwave truck had not yet gotten there.

To make room for coverage of the accident, Mallory dropped a scheduled story about the city budget. It is difficult for television stations to cover their local governments beyond press conferences staged for television. Most stations do not have enough reporters to spend time looking for stories at City Hall, and government stories usually do not produce good visuals for television. Given a choice between a news story without video and vivid video that might not be particularly newsworthy, most producers put the video on the air.

Earlier in the day, Mallory had said that her mission for the 5 o'clock news was to update local news and provide something special between the 4 and 6 p.m. newscasts for people just getting home from work or from picking up their children at school. "We do as much local news as possible. The 5 o'clock show is the metro section," Mallory said. "We try to go live whenever possible."

Most producers and news directors fervently believe that viewers want the sense of immediacy conveyed by a live report from the scene of a story, even many hours after the action has ended and the courthouse is closed, the police station quiet, the fire out or the accident cleared away. Whether a story can be reported live from the scene often determines the prominence it gets in a newscast, so more effort often goes into getting the right expensive equipment to the right place for a "live shot" than into finding out as much as possible about the story itself.

On this day, Mallory had difficulty going live when and where she wanted. And she threw local stories out of the broadcast while keeping the distant disaster stories like the Philadelphia pier collapse and the Tampa fire with their dramatic video. She had to cut still more after weatherman Ryan ran a minute long with his regular weather update at 5:25. A story about motorists running red lights that had been cut out of the 4 o'clock newscast was cut again.

On the monitors in the control room, Channel 9 was now reporting live from the scene of the school bus accident and cross-cutting to live interviews with children from the bus outside a local hospital where they had been taken, examined, treated and released. Minutes later, Channel 7 was also reporting live from both the accident scene and the hospital.

As Mallory fretted, Salinas popped up on another monitor. She had reached the industrial park where Channel 9 had been a half hour earlier. Salinas gave a brief live update about investigators searching there for the source of Rock Creek contamination. Her crew had finally found dead fish in the creek, and their video accompanied her report.

During the next commercial break, Channel 4's Tony Dorsey appeared on a monitor standing at the scene of the school bus accident after finally arriving there in one of the station's microwave trucks. He hurriedly adjusted his remote microphone pack and fixed the camera angle, finishing just in time to go live as the commercial ended at 5:40. Most of Dorsey's information came from a police public information officer sent to the scene to brief reporters on what was going on several hundred yards up the road, where the aftermath of the accident was visible over Dorsey's shoulder in the live camera shot.

As often happens with news reports broadcast so soon after an accident or crime has occurred, Dorsey's first account was incomplete and misleading. He and all the other reporters for local stations who appeared live from the scene initially gave viewers partially inaccurate and conflicting accounts of how the bus-truck accident occurred, what kind of truck was involved and what had happened to most of the children on the bus. Some of the first reports said it was a farm truck that might, or might not, have been pulling a trailer. The reporters didn't know which vehicle hit the other, which driver had been killed and whether the children on the bus had been taken to one or two local hospitals.

Only in later newscasts and the next morning's newspaper was it clear that a small truck towing a flatbed trailer with landscaping equipment had jackknifed on the wet, hilly and narrow road, colliding with the school bus, killing its driver and seriously injuring three of the thirty-six children on the bus. The other children were found to be fine after precautionary examinations. This was an example of what happens when getting to the scene and getting on camera quickly take precedence over the patient reporting from many sources in many locations that is usually necessary to piece together a fuller and more accurate account of a news event. The producers at WRC were more interested in getting the story on the air as soon as possible than in making sure they had the story straight. The primary focus in a television newsroom is less on content than on the technical quality of a story—its video, audio and timing and how it fits into the newscast.

After some confusion in Channel 4's control room over whether to keep Dorsey on the air or to put on the scheduled sports report, Dorsey gave way at 5:54 to the sports anchor in the studio. Like the weather anchors, most sports anchors, who have their own producers, operate independently of each newscast's producer. While WRC did sports, Channel 9 continued to broadcast more details and dramatic video of the bus accident scene from both the ground and a helicopter overhead. Channel 7 also stayed with the accident story. Channel 4 was getting clobbered.

By that time, Margie Ruttenberg, the producer of the 6 o'clock newscast, was hurrying into the control room to take over from Mallory. Hers was the top-rated early-evening newscast in Washington, an important advertising draw and moneymaker for Channel 4. Ruttenberg, in her mid-thirties, is a child of television who first worked as a summer intern for the producer of the 6 o'clock news at a Pittsburgh television station when she was just a nineteen-year-old college student. She learned her trade in control rooms and newsrooms, quickly working her way up to the job of producer herself, running newscasts without ever having worked as a full-time reporter. She had become the star of Long's "divas," the name he coined for the producers of his 4, 5, 6 and 11 p.m. newscasts when they were all women, though now one was a man. "We *are* divas," Ruttenberg said, "because you can't be passive in that job. You have to be tough. You have to be a bitch. You have to make sure it's happening to get it on the air in time."

Cocooned in the control room, she was dependent on what she could see on her computer screen and the wall of monitors in front of her and what she was told by the technicians around her and by reporters and assignment editors outside during frequent, terse telephone conversations. She sifted it all for the makings of dramatic television, relying on instincts developed during her lifetime in local television news.

Ruttenberg knew she was starting from behind this evening, and she was determined to catch up. She also knew that she would have to throw out most of what had already been scripted for her newscast and make up the new script as she went along. She talked into telephones, shouted commands around the control room, cooed instructions into the ears of the anchors in the studio and steadily rewrote the script on the computer in front of her. The more frantic the hour got, the more she appeared to be in her element.

"We were reacting to news—that school bus accident," Ruttenberg said later. "As a producer, you think this is spot news. It's great pictures. Children are involved. This is scary for people. This is spot news that has impact. It has legs. It's not a drug bust from overnight or an apartment fire caused by careless cooking. It's spot news that has an impact on the community. We could all tell that that story was going to be important. The daily challenge we face is how to blow up something that you have been working on all day to bring something like that to the viewer."

She said she wanted her newscast to be "the most informative, most impactful capsule of the day's news." The popular longtime anchors of the 6 and 11 p.m. newscasts, Jim Vance and Doreen Gentzler, "are real professionals who want to keep the quality bar as high as we can in this day of sensational television news," she said. "But we also have to give people a reason to look at you every once in a while. We need to use pictures effectively because we are a visual medium."

As the 6 o'clock newscast began, she broadcast live reports both from Dorsey at the scene of the school bus accident and from WRC reporters at two hospitals where children from the bus had been taken. To make more time for the accident story, Ruttenberg killed the rush hour traffic updates. But she fit in another live report from Salinas on the contamination of Rock Creek, brief video snippets of Giuliani's withdrawal from the New York Senate race and Hillary Clinton's reaction, a controversy between Washington's city council and the police chief over street patrols, a story on running red lights, the computer virus story, the Tampa fire and the Philadelphia pier collapse.

The scheduled live report from the military air show at Andrews Air Force Base was finally dropped, disappointing reporter Chris Gordon, who had spent the entire day there with a crew and truck. "Tell Chris Gordon he's dead," Ruttenberg instructed. On a monitor, Gordon could be seen shrugging and walking away from the camera.

But Ruttenberg kept a featured ten-minute special report by anchor Vance about a training program for young African-American children in Washington. It was the only piece of original enterprise journalism on WRC's evening newscasts that day. On the studio monitor, Vance contentedly smoked a cigarette as he watched the unusually long, nicely produced piece with obvious satisfaction. Ruttenberg told Vance through his earpiece how much she liked the story, repeating compliments she had been giving him about it all day.

The care and feeding of attractive, top-rated anchors is an important part of a producer's job. As Ruttenberg watched them on the wall of monitors facing her in the control room, Vance and Gentzler, sitting in a studio a few yards away, read on the air from a TelePrompTer the words she had written for them on her computer and followed the directions she soothingly spoke into their earpieces. "I do a lot of yelling and screaming in the control room," Ruttenberg said later, "but not when I'm talking to Jim and Doreen in their ears. When I'm talking to them, I'm calm, I'm cool, I'm confident—even when I'm not. . . . If they think the producer is nervous, they'll be nervous on the air, and the viewers will feel it. So much of what we do is presentation, and the presenters have to be at their best."

Finally, Ruttenberg had to kill a story about the local lottery to clear still more time for the school bus story, which, with trimmed-down weather and sports reports, filled the rest of the newscast. As she argued with executive producer Frank Caskin about which reporters to put on live from which locations for the accident story, Ruttenberg could see on the control room monitors that she had finally caught up with Channels 7 and 9. She could relax, giving everyone final instructions as the show wrapped up.

"Unfortunately, when you're dealing with television" when news breaks, Ruttenberg said at the end of her tense but exhilarating day, "you either get it on or you don't."


Watching the staff of WRC cover a big, breaking local story and produce a typical evening of news shows is a good introduction to the factors that drive and circumscribe local television news: the constraints of time and staffing, the costs and temptations of technology, the dramatic power of video, the competition for viewers' attention and the pressure from owners to make extraordinarily large profit margins. All those elements—plus the peculiar isolation of the television studio, control room and even newsroom from the world just outside them—too often combine to distort reality.

Local television does little original reporting of significant community issues, because news directors and producers doubt that viewers have the interest or patience to watch longer, more complicated stories, especially if they lack vivid video. Instead, event-driven crime and disaster coverage—with weather, sports, health, consumer and entertainment news—dominates their newscasts. News directors believe these subjects attract the most viewers, who in turn attract the advertisers needed to produce profit margins (the percentage of total revenues retained as profit) of 40 to 50 percent or more. Completing a vicious circle, maintaining those profit margins means keeping news staffs small, which leaves the handful of reporters on duty each day little, if any, time to cover local government or politics, business, education, environment or social issues that most affect people living in the communities they serve. At most stations, these subjects just aren't taken seriously anyway—they aren't part of the accepted formula for local television news.

WRC's news operation is among the best in the country. Its staff of anchors and reporters is remarkably stable by industry standards; most have been at the station for years, and know the community well. Several were former beat reporters at newspapers and had developed good sources in local governments, schools and police and fire departments—rare for television journalists. On occasion WRC reporters beat the local newspapers to good stories in the city of Washington. The station ran more stories than most do on local government and politics, schools and other aspects of civic life.

But WRC remains in the mainstream of local television news, as that day in its hectic life attests. Crime and disaster fill much of WRC's newscasts, especially the half-hour late-evening news at 11 p.m., an audience-ratings monster for WRC that made $120 million profit in 2000, according to news director Long. The first five stories on a typical 11 p.m. newscast on Channel 4 one summer evening were a "fatal" elevator accident, a "deadly" small plane crash many miles away in Virginia, a "deadly" shark attack in Florida, a big fire in New Jersey and details of the charges lodged against a suspect in the rape of a local seventy-five-year-old woman several weeks earlier. News directors and producers believe these melodramatic stories keep viewers from changing the channel. They echo the prime-time entertainment dramas that usually precede the late-evening news each night. And their well-edited video images and vivid language involve viewers emotionally.

"What makes a great newspaper headline doesn't always fly at the top of a newscast," said Long, a colorful, gruff-spoken veteran of local television news on both coasts who sported a mustache and goatee and stood out amid his casually dressed staff with his formal suits, bow ties and suspenders.

"We have an obligation to do news," Long said, but then he explained that he cannot pass up a "wonderful piece of video" when one comes along. He cited an example, a fistfight on camera between the new and old managers of a Taiwan television station after a change of ownership. "We have this video and we have to put it on television," he said. "It's just fascinating. Doesn't mean a damn thing. And we don't need more than twenty seconds of it. But we will suck that out of the sky, bounce it off three satellites, spend a ton of money on it."

Long said he has high aspirations for WRC, but he made it clear that the resources available to pursue them are strictly limited by the need to provide the extraordinary profits that NBC, the station's owner, demands. Partly because his newsroom is a small fraction of the size of the reporting staff of any big city newspaper, WRC's news programs produced most of the station's profit margins, which he hinted could well exceed 50 percent. Long did have a four-person consumer news unit and a medical news producer to provide the "news-you-can-use" features that many stations think will attract viewers, but he had no dedicated investigative reporters. "I'd love to add a three-man investigation team. But it's the most expensive kind of reporting to do. And if I have to take away from my infantry," Long said, referring to the bulk of his staff, the general-assignment reporters who produced one or two stories each day on whatever subject came up, "I'm resistant to it."

"We all have boundaries we have to work inside of. We have to make choices," said Ruttenberg, the producer of the 6 o'clock newscast. "You can't give viewers everything you want to. You hope that it is not the only news they get. You hope they read the morning paper and listen to the radio. We pick the stories that have the most impact and we make them the best they can get. If this is the only news they get, they aren't getting enough."

There is a gap between the stated aspirations of Long and Ruttenberg and the reality of the evening newscasts broadcast by a station regarded by their peers as one of the best in the business, and that gap is typical of television news today. News directors regularly espouse high journalistic ideals, Santa Clara media scholar John H. McManus found in studying television newsrooms in the western United States, but their newscasts show that their primary motivation is to attract the largest possible audience at the lowest possible cost. That means doing the least news gathering possible to get a passable story on the air. It means relying on visual images and emotion more than complex facts, abstract ideas or analysis in telling the story. And it means making the story as dramatic and entertaining as possible, even when that requires exaggeration, trivializing or the imposition on events of an artificial melodramatic narrative.

On the day we spent at WRC, the station's three hours of evening newscasts and the half-hour 11 p.m. newscast contained only about a dozen different news stories, many of which were repeated again and again—slightly altered and sometimes updated—throughout the evening. All were reported briefly. The next morning's *Washington Post* contained more than two dozen stories in its Metro news section alone, every one of them more detailed than the WRC reports. The whole newspaper contained scores of stories. And any single page in the newspaper contained about 40 percent more words than an entire half-hour newscast.

Half a dozen reporters worked on the local news stories that WRC broadcast that evening. Just as many covered the school bus accident for the *Post*, which had nearly a hundred local news reporters working that day, and many more covering local business, sports and cultural life.

Without a similar legion of reporters regularly trolling for news on a variety of beats around its communities, WRC depends largely on police scanners, press releases, press conferences, news services and newspapers to find out what's happening. Assigning editors and producers usually send their reporters to cover scheduled events (particularly events staged for television, such as media day at the air show), emergencies to which local public safety agencies are responding and other stories that most of the news media already are covering. And even then there aren't enough reporters to cover the obvious bases. Long said he and his colleagues often leave their morning story meeting "feeling bad about what we can't cover. There is stuff we do see, important public hearings, process stuff where I just don't have the resources to put a reporter."

"We don't have enough reporters," Ruttenberg agreed. "We wake up the next morning and read the *Washington Post* and see that they have a better story, because they have more reporters and sometimes better reporters. Each of our reporters has to do a story every day. They don't have time to develop stories with phone calls and beat checks."

An exhaustive 1999 study of 590 local newscasts on fifty-nine stations in nineteen cities across the country by Columbia University's Project for Excellence in Journalism found that nine of every ten local stories on those newscasts came "from either the police scanner or scheduled events." Fewer than one in ten stories came from the reporter's own initiative, which leaves uncovered most of what really goes on in the local community that is not a crime, a disaster or a staged event. Surprisingly the study found that even "coverage of breaking news, a staple of local TV that requires a lesser but still notable level of effort, is also dropping." Instead, local stations filled out their newscasts with more "out-of-town feeds"—video reports the stations buy inexpensively from the national networks or television news services, reports such as the Tampa fire and the Philadelphia pier collapse stories on the WRC newscasts we watched being put together.

Like many other local stations, WRC has been unable to cover much of what is happening in the suburbs, where most of its viewers now live. "Limited resources" is one reason, Long said, and "part of our problem is moving the equipment around" miles away from the station to get the video for a primarily visual medium and to put reporters on the air live. "We have to do our reporting with large amounts of equipment. We can't do it over the telephone," he said. "We can't sit in a newsroom and report a story. We have to physically go there with a lot of technology and technicians to operate it. And then get back somehow."

Some of Long's reporters do have responsibility for beats like local governments, but they can spend only a fraction of their time checking on them, because they are needed for daily assignments and breaking news. "The disadvantage to the television reporter," Long said, "is that he is always, even if that's his beat, plugging in at a point of crisis. He isn't there every day." Reporters who don't immerse themselves in the subjects they cover, and who have little time to research and report their stories, inevitably produce journalism that is sketchy and shallow.

The owners and managers of local television stations feel little obligation to provide coverage of government, politics or civic affairs in return for the free airwaves they use, or the First Amendment protections they enjoy. Most local stations offer so little coverage of election campaigns, for example, that viewers looking for information before voting most often find it in the tendentious paid political advertising that enriches the stations in election years. During New Jersey's hotly contested 2000 primary for a U.S. Senate seat, television stations in New York and Philadelphia (New Jersey has no commercial stations) took in $21 million in campaign advertising. But the top-rated stations devoted an average of only thirteen seconds a day in news time to what the candidates themselves were saying, according to one study. A University of Southern California study of television coverage of the 1998 gubernatorial election found that less than half of one percent (.45 percent) of the local news on the stations in California's five largest cities during the twelve weeks of the campaign was devoted to the governor's race, and very little of that coverage was about the issues.

A similar national study of coverage of the last thirty days of the 2000 election campaign by seventy-four broadcast television stations in fifty-eight cities found they devoted an average of seventy-four seconds of airtime on newscasts between 5 and 11:30 each evening to what national and local candidates actually said or did during the campaign. And they provided almost no coverage examining the accuracy and fairness of the candidates' television advertising that poured so much money into those stations during the campaign.

Americans who depend on local television news get little meaningful information—much less in-depth explanations or exposés—on what is going on in the world around them. Instead, they get a distorted caricature of their communities, a daily drama of crime, accidents, traffic tie-ups, stormy weather and other calamities, leavened by cheerful video of photogenic events like parades, charity walks and county fairs. Morning, evening or late at night, they can watch scenes that may resemble real life but actually depict a world that only exists on their television screens.

And the audience for this kind of news is shrinking. The ratings for local television newscasts have been declining steadily, and at a more rapid rate than the parallel decline in newspaper readership. At WRC, for example, the audience for its financially important 11 p.m. newscast has fallen from 224,000 Washington area households in November 1995 to 157,000 households in November 2000, even as it maintained its ratings lead over rival stations. The total audience for the late-evening newscasts on Washington's four broadcast stations fell from nearly 700,000 households in November 1995 to just over 500,000 households in November 2000. The numbers come from Nielsen ratings.

This reflects a national trend. A study by the Pew Research Center for the People and the Press found that only 56 percent of Americans were watching local television news regularly in 2000, down from 77 percent in 1993. Columbia University's Project for Excellence in Journalism concluded in its 2000 study of the content and viewership of local television newscasts across the nation that the stations are "driving Americans away from what was long the most popular and trusted source of information in the country."

The biggest story in many years—terrorist attacks on the United States and an aggressive American response—arrested this trend, at least temporarily. "A whole bunch of young people who haven't been watching TV news are sampling us now," Long said in October 2001. "They had only been interested in entertainment before, but they're coming to TV for public affairs now that public affairs are affecting their lives."

With their relatively small news staffs, local television stations could do little more than present summaries of the terrorism news produced by their network owners or partners, adding on-location stories about possible local targets for terrorists and steps being taken to protect them. With the September 11 attack on the Pentagon and threats to other institutions in Washington, WRC had more local angles to cover than most stations. Long also created a new two-person "tolerance beat" to report on "what is Islam" and what was happening in the Washington area's sizable Islamic communities. But he had to do this without increasing his news staff. WRC's owner, NBC, had forced a number of budget cuts on the station when advertising revenue began falling in 2001.

Long cautioned that the new television news viewers were flipping around among broadcast and cable channels looking for relevant news about terrorism. They wouldn't stay with local newscasts if stations couldn't satisfy that appetite, he thought. WRC's 11 p.m. newscast had stopped losing viewers, he said, but its audience ratings were only "flat or a little up" from a year earlier. "We're doing well, but not as well as you would think," he said. "These people are watching everything. They're going all through the dial."

Local stations began broadcasting news in the early days of television in the late 1940s, when the Federal Communications Commission required stations to devote some of their programming to the public interest. For years, local newscasts were only fifteen minutes long; then they grew to half an hour. They covered much the same news that local newspapers did but more briefly, and their reporters, many of whom worked first for newspapers, tended to cover the same beats, including local government and politics. Many stations, then mostly owned by local families and newspapers or by the national networks, tried to make their newscasts respectable enough to enhance their images in their communities and the industry.

The big news stories of the 1960s and 1970s—assassinations, riots, civil rights revolution, war and protest—proved to be a boon for local television news, as it was for the networks. The audience for local news burgeoned, surprising many people in the television industry itself. With those viewers came more advertisers, increased advertising revenue and unexpected profits for local stations.

Station owners came to realize that local news, which was relatively inexpensive to produce, attracted more viewers and made more money than other locally produced television. So they expanded local newscasts, first to an hour, beginning in Los Angeles in the early 1960s, and later to ninety minutes, then to two hours, and then—in the biggest markets—to three hours, plus late news at 10 or 11 p.m. More newscasts were added early in the morning, with weather and traffic reports and short recaps of the news ("sports in a minute") from the night before, recycled to catch people waking and getting ready for work or school. Noontime news shows were added, too.

As business boomed in the seventies and eighties, a culture of local television news evolved that still dominates the country's airwaves. It is the culture reflected in WRC's instincts and choices, at the higher-quality end, but also in the newscasts of broadcast outlets in Los Angeles, notorious for providing their viewers some of the most melodramatic and entertaining but least intelligent and least informative news in the country. That culture has several important aspects:

- *News is the most important profit center for local stations, and profit is more important than news.*

Local television is a huge business in America. Stations in big markets are now worth nearly a billion dollars, because of their ability to generate huge profits year after year. But as their value has risen and increasing numbers of stations have been absorbed into giant corporations—the equivalent of the newspaper chains—the pressure to preserve and increase those profit margins has intensified.

In 2001, twenty-five corporate owners controlled nearly half of the commercial television stations in the United States. Among the largest were two companies specializing in television properties and little known to the public: Paxson, which was partially owned by NBC, with sixty-nine stations, and Sinclair Television, with sixty-two stations. Several multimedia behemoths also owned dozens of stations. Viacom had thirty-eight in addition to the CBS television network and many other media, entertainment and publishing holdings. Rupert Murdoch's Fox owned thirty-three local stations, plus various Fox television and cable networks and production studios. General Electric's NBC, with its television and cable networks, owned thirteen TV stations, plus a third of Paxson, with an option to take complete control of its sixty-nine stations in 2002. Hearst-Argyle, owner of newspapers, magazines and television interests, had thirty-three stations.

In recent years the economics of the local television business have gotten tougher. The major networks had paid their affiliated stations to broadcast network programming, but the networks have begun to reverse that relationship, and they demand payment from the local stations. The stations' principal source of revenue is the advertising they can sell during the broadcast time they control. News shows are far and away the most important source of that advertising revenue.

So profitability is at the center of every decision stations make about news coverage. Ratings and the revenue they generate are the coin of the realm. Bob Long of WRC mentioned the huge profits made by his news programs in the first minutes of our first conversation. Long's future at WRC depends on his ability to preserve or improve those profits; nothing is more important to his bosses. News directors aren't fired for putting on lousy news programs, they're fired for getting lower ratings than their competitors—and in the television business, they are fired regularly. In 2001 the average news director had been in his or her job for less than two years.

"The day management recognized the fact that news can make money, things changed," said the legendary Hal Fishman of KTLA in Los Angeles, who has been a local news anchor there for four decades. "Rather than what could improve the station's image, the emphasis was on ratings to get more commercial money."

"We had a party today," Fishman told us at the end of a crucial ratings sweeps month in late 1999, "not because we had the most credible news, or for excellence, but because we were number one in the ratings."

As local news grew in importance to the stations, which devoted more and more time to news programming, news staffs hardly grew at all. In annual surveys by the Radio and Television News Directors Association and Ball State University, local television news directors reported doubling the amount of news they broadcast during the 1990s while adding only a few more people to their newsrooms. When asked in these other surveys why they couldn't do a better job covering their communities, the news directors cited insufficient staff, inadequate staff skills and time pressures as the primary obstacles to better journalism. All of those can be related to the amount of money a station spends on its news operation.

"Perhaps the best explanation for why local news looks the way it does is money," concluded the 1999 Project for Excellence in Journalism study of local television news. "News executives . . . say the biggest obstacle to quality is a 'lack of staff' at a time when they are being asked to fill an expanding news hole. Indeed, those station executives who provided an answer acknowledged that they require reporters to produce at least one story a day, a demand that precludes most in-depth or enterprise reporting. The reason for these demands has to do with the extraordinary profit expectations that permeate local news organizations and Wall Street. Of those stations that provided answers to the question, the average pre-tax profit margin expected of local news was 40 per cent. This suggests it is a misconception to assume that local TV news merely reflects what viewers want. Local TV news gives viewers what the resources allow."

"The business of television is not independent of the newsroom. It is absolutely part of the newsroom," John Lansing, news director of WCCO in Minneapolis, said at a Poynter Institute for Media Studies conference in New York in 1996. "So the people in charge of newsrooms realize that they are going to be judged every day on their ability to turn that [ratings] number up and win the game. That, by itself, I think, describes the dilemma of local TV news."

Bob Long of WRC allowed himself a moment of candor during a panel discussion among television journalists in November 1999. When a participant mentioned the estimate that local stations typically make 40 percent profit margins, Long offered a correction. "I guarantee you that 60 to 70 percent is not uncommon in major markets," he said. "We make a ton of money. You can't make the kind of money we make legally in any other way."

Because news is the most profitable product of local television, newsroom obligations to the station's business can go considerably beyond just winning high ratings. At many stations the news is part of the overall marketing effort, often in ways that raise ethical questions and undermine the newscasts' credibility. Some stations sell advertising tie-ins on news programs; others use news broadcasts and personalities to promote the station, its programs and its network's programs.

Stations have been caught doing some outrageous things. On its evening newscasts in January 2000, network-owned WCBS in New York broadcast a weeklong series of reports about tourism in Arizona that were produced by an advertising agency for the Arizona Office of Tourism, which bought advertising adjacent to the reports. Tampa's WTSP, a CBS affiliate, broadcast an unusual twenty-one minutes of enthusiastic news coverage about the local aquarium over two days in the spring of 1998, at the same time that the aquarium, seeking to improve attendance, spent nearly $100,000 in advertising on the station.

Some stations have launched new lifestyle news segments on their evening newscasts, sold sponsorships of the segments to local companies and then featured those businesses in the "news" stories. Philadelphia's KYW broadcast "Eye on Beauty" reports sponsored by a local hair salon and interviewed workers at the salon for some of the stories. New York's

WCBS broadcast a news story about laser eye surgery on its 5 p.m. newscast in March 2000 after being paid $300,000 by the TLC Laser Eye Centers to put a live webcast of laser eye surgery at one of its clinics on the station's Internet site on the same day. The news story included interviews with the same doctor and patient who appeared on the webcast. The lines between news and advertising—between independent journalism and paid promotion—should never be obliterated in this way.

It has become routine for local stations to promote their networks' entertainment programs as news stories during their evening newscasts. On one evening in spring 2000, Jacksonville's WJXT promoted two CBS programs in a single half-hour newscast at 5:30 p.m. First, one of the station's reporters interviewed a Jacksonville man featured in a *60 Minutes II* segment about the Persian Gulf War. Then, about fifteen minutes later in the newscast, a promotional preview of the Academy of Country Music Awards on CBS, sent to the station by the network, was broadcast as a news story.

WRC news director Long said his station receives "from the network promotion machine" a steady stream of memos "for everything from teases to [Tom] Brokaw [on the *NBC Nightly News*] to tie-ins to network entertainment shows." WRC has frequently included in its newscasts interviews with actors on NBC's hit hospital emergency room drama *ER* and stories about NBC's *West Wing* when scenes for the television drama about life inside the White House were being filmed in Washington. "If it's our product," Long said, referring to NBC shows, "we'll probably do it to a fare-thee-well. We have access to the actors, and we are not unhappy if we have something good to say about our own product."

- *When profits, and thus ratings, matter most, the temptation to woo bigger audiences with crime, violence, disasters and celebrities is overwhelming.*

Television is a visual entertainment medium. Making the news on television fun to look at and entertaining has always been relatively easy, and one way to draw a crowd of viewers. This begins with crime coverage, an echo of the crime shows that have been successful on television since Jack Webb and *Dragnet*. "Crime and violence became staples during the very rapid expansion of TV news because they were easy to do," recalled Long, who watched this happen in Los Angeles local news in the seventies and eighties. "All you had to do was point a camera at a crime scene and you could do several of those in a day with one camera. So crime was terribly seductive. It was easy to do. It required no real journalism. We'd gotten rid of the reporters and we got microphone holders."

Excluding weather and sports, news about crime and violence accounts for 25 percent or more of the content of local television newscasts, as measured by study after study over many years. " 'If it bleeds, it leads,' remains a truism on local TV news because crime events are dramatic and gain people's attention," a Colorado watchdog group, Rocky Mountain Media Watch, reported after studying 102 newscasts in fifty-two cities on a single night, March 28, 1998. "Many crime stories produce an intense emotional response in viewers, such as fear, alienation or excitement; these are highly prized reactions by news departments and advertisers. Crimes predictably occur every day and crime reporting has become routine, a lazy habit, for news departments." Heavy coverage of crime also leaves viewers with the impression that crime is rampant all around them, an impression that became increasingly misleading through the 1990s as crime rates fell.

Los Angeles is America's capital of tabloid TV. Competition among local stations there has been ferocious for years, and every one of them has used crime, disaster and celebrity coverage as a competitive tool. All of them slight coverage of government, politics and other community news.

The tabloidization of television news in Los Angeles began in the 1970s, after the network-owned stations there had pioneered longer local newscasts that focused more on community news. The turning point came, according to Pete Noyes, a longtime Los Angeles TV reporter and news executive who has now retired, when the city's stations closed down their state capitol bureaus in Sacramento, beginning in 1977, "to pay for the increased use of helicopters . . . for transportation to news events and coverage of disasters" like fires, mud slides and earthquakes. Later, helicopter-borne cameras could provide live video of freeway accidents, crime scenes and police chases. By the nineties, car chases on the city's freeways became a staple feature of Los Angeles television news. Everyone knows why.

"We in the TV news business simply never attempted to cover a freeway chase prior to 1994 and O. J. Simpson," Noyes recalled several years later. "As a TV news executive, I just didn't consider such events newsworthy. Such coverage would have been impossible anyway, because TV lacked the technology to rig helicopters with cameras that could get close-up shots from the skies. But now the choppers have camera stabilizers and powerful lenses that zoom in on targets from thousands of feet away. The Simpson chase in 1994—a helicopter-trailed odyssey winding around the

Los Angeles freeway system—was the spark for a whole new TV news genre. It was then that TV news brass discovered the ratings potential in such pursuits. And there's been no stopping it. The tabloid philosophy behind the chase coverage has done incredible damage to real news coverage."

Jeff Wald, the KTLA news director, believes in covering chases from the air, but told us, "I shudder every time we go live. I mean, it doesn't make me feel very comfortable, and the car chases, for example, that have become so commonplace worry me."

Wald's station was one of several that transmitted live pictures from helicopters of the April 1998 freeway pursuit of a despondent, terminally ill man unhappy about his medical treatment. The police chase ended when the man stopped at the intersection of two freeways, set his truck afire and shot himself. "We had the tightest close-up and just didn't expect it," Wald said. "You know, our critics will say, 'Oh, you wanted the money shot, you wanted him to blow his head off.' I say, My God, how could anybody want to put something like that in somebody's living room? There were no indications in my mind, and the people I've talked to since, that that was going to happen. I saw it as a protest. I saw it as affecting thousands of people on two major freeways at rush hour. I saw it as a traffic story. We saw him on the telephone and figured he was negotiating with the police and it was going to be over with."

That incident provoked public debate in Los Angeles. Local news directors, including Wald, promised to use more restraint in the future. Then, on the morning after Thanksgiving in 1999, KTLA was again drawn into aerial coverage of a freeway chase. Wald said he was able to resist this story for the first hour of the 200-mile police pursuit of a man in a white Datsun who had fled from a routine traffic stop for expired license plates at about 7 a.m., in the middle of KTLA's Friday-morning newscast. But after the man continued to elude police, Wald told us, he decided, "He's on three freeways. We've got to go with it." He then described how he made his decisions on coverage, talking by telephone from his home on the holiday weekend to producers at the station.

"I told my executive producer, and she said, 'I hate to ruin the show. We've got a great show planned.' And I said, 'So do I, but people have got to know about this.' So we continued with it. And then, not only did it fill our eight o'clock to nine o'clock hour, we extended and went past that. It went on for another hour after that, and we stayed with it.

"As soon as he pulled over, after running over a spike strip, we had a very close tight shot of him sitting at the wheel and we saw that he had a gun. At that point, I said, 'Pull out, pull back, get a wide shot.' I was afraid we would have to push the button real quick and get out of this.

"And sure enough, he got out, he pointed the gun at the cops, and they shot him. We saw it from a distance, saw him fall, and we immediately cut back to our anchors, who said, 'We're sorry we showed you those pictures.' But my feeling is there has to be a resolution to a story, and this is where we get into that difficult decision-making process. Other channels were tighter on it. Other channels stayed with it longer. As soon as he was shot, we went back to the anchors, and were off the air.

"I also think in a way that if you continue to show these things, it's got to act as a deterrent because nine out of ten of these people get arrested. Thank God, very few of them have ended in violence. Most of them have ended in the guy being arrested and put into handcuffs and put away in a squad car."

> • *High-tech gadgets and low-tech gimmicks appeal to local*
> *station managers more than spending money on deeper,*
> *more thorough news coverage.*

When stations in Los Angeles cut back coverage of state government to invest heavily in helicopters and airborne cameras, they joined a trend in the local television news business. To begin with, spending on equipment allowed stations to reduce labor costs. Handheld cameras, computerized robot cameras and editing machines allowed local news operations to cut their human production staff to a minimum. Perhaps more important, technology gave local news broadcasts the immediacy and entertainment value that station managers thought gave them the best competitive edge. Stations spend huge sums building high-tech studio sets and computer-ized graphics. Trucks and helicopters able to transmit live pictures by microwave over land and satellite links from farther afield provide the "live" coverage so important in the local TV news culture.

Beginning in the 1970s, another popular way for local stations to invest in news was to hire consultants to help them cope with the intense com-petition that became typical in every American city. The first television consultants had backgrounds in behavioral research and marketing, and had advised other businesses, from banks to motorcycle manufacturers, on how to market their products and services. Using extensive market surveys of each station's actual and potential viewers, they focused on ways to make local television news more entertaining for viewers rather than more informative.

Acting on the consultants' advice, local television news directors shortened most stories to one or two minutes at most, and moved coverage away from less visual and more abstract subjects like government and politics to more melodramatic and visually exciting news like crime, calamity and weather. Frank Magid, founder of Frank Magid Associates and one of the most successful and best-known consultants, advised stations to de-emphasize political and government news as early as the mid-1970s. He said he had concluded from his market surveys that viewers were not interested in political campaigns or what candidates and government officials had to say.

Consultants packaged the fast-paced, action-packed local television newscasts with brassy studio sets, stirring music and slogans like "Action News" and "Eyewitness News" to label and promote the newscasts. "If it bleeds, it leads" grew out of the consultant-driven efforts to grab viewers with crime and disaster stories in the opening minutes of these newscasts, when competition for viewers tuning in from entertainment programs was most intense. Consultants also told news directors that their viewers wanted more stories containing humor, sex, entertainment and human interest.

When satellite and microwave technology made it possible for reporters to appear on newscasts live from almost anywhere, consultants pushed news directors to put as many live reports on the air as possible. Big stations used this technology to showcase their anchors and reporters appearing live from distant places against the backdrop of big national stories—political conventions, major sports events, hurricanes and earthquakes, and from outside the courthouse in Los Angeles during the O. J. Simpson trial. Most local television anchors and reporters did little more than make "live" appearances at these stories.

The newscasts of Miami's WPLG, the longtime ratings leader in one of the most competitive local television news cities, are labeled and promoted as "Live, Local, Late-breaking." This slogan—another of those suggested to stations by consultants—is repeated over and over on WPLG newscasts and on-air promotions. "We live by 'Live, Local, Late-breaking,'" WPLG news director Bill Pohovey told us. He said he could see high ratings spikes "when a big breaking story is going on. People tune in when news is breaking."

At Jacksonville's WJXT, news director Skip Valet said he brought in

Broadcast Image Group consultant Larry Rickett because, as remote-control devices have established "viewer control" over television news choices, he needed to keep up with the latest trends. Rickett, a veteran of big-city television news wars who now worked as a consultant advising stations in smaller cities, insisted to us that "research shows that content is still king and the quality of content matters." But after watching WJXT's newscasts in Valet's office one evening in the spring of 2000, Rickett focused on the details of presentation, not news content: camera angles that could be improved, a sports anchor moving around the news set awkwardly, a five-day-forecast weather graphic that appeared in the wrong place on the screen.

When consultants turn to content, they offer stations tailored formulas for what they say their research shows viewers most want: information about weather, traffic, health, safety, shopping and spending money that affects their daily lives. For a fee, consultants create story packages consisting of a story line, background reporting and video clips that stations either could replicate or put right on the air. Stations receive scripts for voice-over narration by their anchors or reporters, encouraging viewers to think this material was news produced by the station rather than canned goods bought from a consultant. Consultants offer special packages for ratings sweeps periods that have been tested with viewer focus groups. Many stations jump at the opportunity to try new ways to improve their ratings while spending less of their own resources.

In 1999 NewsProNet of Atlanta offered client stations "SweepsFeed" packages—eight "high-impact" stories a month that they could "plug into key newscasts" and use to "build a loyal audience through topical news promotion." A sales video promised stations that "you can do more for less" and "you can have a new angle for your market" with prepackaged "investigations, health probes, consumer alerts, new trends" and other "hot topics." Each package contained a complete video story several minutes long, a full script, tips on how to localize the story, sources to contact and scripts for promotional spots for the story. Sample story topics included contamination of drinking water by leaks from gas storage tanks, avoiding flammable furniture, detecting cancer with lasers, measuring the impact of weather on traffic and putting fiber optics into the fabric of undershirts to monitor the vital signs of babies, athletes and the elderly.

The investigative reporting suggested or prepackaged by consultants tended to be small-bore, look-alike consumer-protection stories rather than real digging that could hold government, business or other powerful people and institutions accountable to local citizens. But stations could buy these stories and put them right on the air for a small fraction of what it would cost in the salaries and resources needed for real investigative reporting.

News directors told us they are not overly influenced by consultants, especially in actually covering the news. But with notable exceptions, most news directors have spent only a few years at any one station, while each station has often kept the same consultant on contract for years or decades, as news directors came and went. WRC's Long, an elder states-man in the industry, said that "news directors who are twenty-five years old in a competitive market being squeezed for another rating point" must be influenced by the consultants' wares and the fads of the industry. "TV," he told us, "is all about marketing."

From the beginning, consultants emphasized the personality of a newscast. They pushed local stations to hire more attractive anchors with pleasing on-camera personalities, even advising them on what clothes to wear and what color to tint their hair. Eventually, consultants screened the "on-air talent" for the stations.

Consultants convinced television news directors to encourage anchors and reporters to add light banter to the news—"happy talk." For a while the banter seemed to bury the news. That fashion changed, but chatting and joking at the anchor desk has remained a staple of local television news, because it makes the highly paid anchors appear more accessible to viewers and encourages the idea that local anchors, like Brokaw, Rather and Jennings on the networks, are celebrities, too. Stations further pro-moted this idea by featuring the anchors in feel-good video promotions for their newscasts, sending them to community events and using them to raise money for charities.

"The audience bases its view of the station on the anchors," said Alan Frank, president of Post-Newsweek Stations, a highly profitable sub-sidiary of the Washington Post Company that owns stations in Detroit, Houston, San Antonio and three Florida cities. "People relate to stations through newscasters. They enter people's living rooms night after night." The anchors embody the franchise.

The consultant-driven emphasis on anchors led to another spending habit that colors local television news. As anchormen and women came to appreciate their importance to the ratings of their stations, they were able to negotiate for higher and higher salaries. Today there are more than a few million-dollar-a-year anchors, and many more earning in the high six figures. Many stations balance the huge salaries they pay anchors with relatively paltry pay for the reporters and producers who do the hard work on the street. In smaller markets, reporters and producers can earn as little as $20,000 to $30,000 a year.

If anchors—glamorized newsreaders who occasionally get involved in reporting stories themselves—are paid for their good looks and manner, and reporters are often paid poorly, it's not surprising that local television fails to produce many marvelous journalists. Long said that too many of the people who came into local news operations during the expansion years came directly from college, with no background in news. Former NBC News president Andrew Lack said that when he searched for news-people to hire for the network, "I looked at a lot of local news and I was profoundly disappointed with the level of talent. I was shocked at how little they read," he said. "I had the feeling they just sort of listened to the radio and watched TV."

Frank Magid, who for three decades has been paid by hundreds of stations to analyze and advise their news operations, came to the same conclusion. "While they may be trained to write and while they may be trained to articulate what is written, the fact remains that many who call themselves journalists and are employed in local stations have no notion whatsoever about history, geography, political science, economics and other things about which an informed individual should have some grasp," he said at a 1997 Committee of Concerned Journalists forum in Chicago. "Unless and until the people in the profession come to grips with that, there will never be a change."

But the truth is that the industry doesn't want fundamental change. The culture of local television news is now deeply entrenched. Owners and managers are locked into doing whatever they consider necessary to try to drive up ratings and profits.

Nevertheless, all local stations' news operations are not the same. For Columbia University's Project for Excellence in Journalism, a group of television journalists, university scholars and professional researchers evaluated local newscasts in several dozen cities and found significant differences between the best and worst. "There is a wider range of quality out there than many critics might think," the group reported in 1999. "The best stations in the study scored twice as high in quality as the worst stations." The top-scoring station in 1999, WHET in Evansville, Indiana, covered "more of its own community, including the local schools, the environment and business, than any other station examined," the report said.

All three stations in Minneapolis have devoted five to six minutes of each evening newscast—an eternity in local television news—to special reports on significant people, activities and issues in their community. Louisville's WLKY, which has also covered more community issues at greater length than most stations, has had a reporter regularly covering the Kentucky state capitol in Frankfort, a local TV rarity. New York's award-winning WWOR, with one of the largest investigating reporting teams in local television, is credited with covering the city better than three larger network-owned stations, whose newscasts are dominated by crime and violence. Boston's WBZ won a 1999 Edward R. Murrow award from the Radio and Television News Directors Association for its extensive coverage of politics and government at a time, the judges said, "when political coverage seems to be declining in local TV news." The news director of KVUE in Austin, Texas, decided in the late 1990s to keep off the air coverage of crime that did not have a significant impact on the community.

The best local television news can make a difference. KTVX in Salt Lake City won a Murrow award in 1999 for its investigative reporting of evidence of corruption in the bidding process that won Salt Lake City the 2002 Winter Olympics. Detroit's WXYZ revealed that the state of Michigan had forcibly sterilized thousands of men, women and children institutionalized as mentally retarded before World War II. WANE in Fort Wayne, Indiana, used the emotional power of television to educate viewers about organ donations through the powerfully told story of two children's lives saved with organs donated by the family of an Indiana boy. Houston's KHOU first reported that Firestone tires on Ford Explorer sport utility vehicles were involved in dozens of fatal accidents across the country.

Yet even news directors who are able to get better coverage on the air mix good journalism with mayhem and frivolity to hold viewers' attention. The three major local stations in Minneapolis, for example, which have won awards and national attention for the noteworthy quantity and quality of their community coverage, featured rapes and drive-by shootings, bear wrestling and dolphin slaughters, along with good local stories about schools, the environment, highways and the homeless on their evening newscasts during several weeks we sampled in September and October of 1999.

WPLG in Miami maintains a relatively large news operation for a city of its size, and provides more complete coverage of its community than many stations. Veteran reporters regularly cover politics, government and important local issues, in the suburbs as well as the city. Bill Pohovey, the news director, told us he tried "to break out of the pack and be different from the other stations" in a highly competitive market with "thought-provoking" enterprise reporting, including stories produced by two full-time investigative reporters. WPLG had resisted moving away from this kind of coverage when other Miami stations tried tabloid news formats in unsuccessful efforts to overtake WPLG in audience ratings.

Yet many WPLG newscasts open with shootings and other crimes, fires and accidents that are dispensed with in short stories in Miami newspapers the next day. And many of the "live" appearances by reporters on newscasts seemed contrived to make news that had taken place much earlier look late-breaking. For a story about an accidental shooting of a teenager that had occurred almost a day earlier, a reporter appeared live in front of a police station where nothing more was happening. For a story about drunk driving, a reporter appeared live on a freeway overpass.

Many local broadcasters now take it as a matter of faith that those live, on-scene appearances by reporters are critical, especially on 11 p.m. newscasts, to make the day's stories look new and different, even if they had been reported on earlier newscasts. "The 11 o'clock news has to be made substantially different from the 6 o'clock news," said Alan Frank, the president of Post-Newsweek Stations, which owns WPLG. "That same story has to be made fresh, new and different. Otherwise, people won't watch it. They'll just go to sleep. And the best indication that it's fresh is the reporter being live."

But news director Dan Bradley is defying this conventional wisdom at WFLA, the NBC affiliate in Tampa. Bradley has built the largest audience for news of any single station in Florida, which has given him unusually long tenure at the station and the backing of the station's owner, Media General, to try to make his station's news coverage more comprehensive. "TV news is still young, really just coming into its adolescence or teenhood now," Bradley told us. "We are slowly getting away from 'drive-by TV.'"

Two years ago, he said, the station's audience research showed that "our viewership was softening up" because there were too many formulaic light features and not enough real news in WFLA's newscasts. "We took a look at our shows," Bradley said, "and saw that there was not enough time for the news of the day. So we decided to focus more on what was important, relevant and urgent."

And he said viewers were not fooled when reporters appeared live at locations long after the story there was over. "The audience knows when you are live and they expect you to be live when big news breaks," Bradley said, "but to be there live at the cemetery when the funeral was eight hours ago, you are stretching it and the viewers know it." WFLA now skips "on-scene" reports most of the time. Chris Gegg, producer of WFLA's 11 p.m. newscast, told us in July 2000, "We only went live once so far this week. And we are still ahead of the competition here in the ratings."

The 11 o'clock WFLA newscast that night contained much more community coverage of both the city and the suburbs than most local television news, including important, nonvisual stories about school budgets and teacher shortages. Yet in a typical contradiction between a news director's stated goals and the reality of catering to the late-news audience's baser instincts, the newscast began with a tawdry story about nude dancers and some of their customers being arrested for lewd behavior at a local adult club. And it included a story, labeled "health news," about a state senator in faraway Virginia who happened to be the sister of NBC's *Today* show anchor, Katie Couric, dropping out of politics after she was diagnosed with cancer.

The dominant station in Jacksonsville, Florida, WJXT, a CBS-affiliated Post-Newsweek station, boasts one of the most ambitious local television news operations for its size. With a staff of just fourteen reporters and anchors, it has covered its community comprehensively and won a wall full of awards, including two Murrow awards from the Radio and Television News Directors Association for the best newscast and best continuing coverage of any "small market" station in the country. "We are lean and mean," news director Skip Valet told us, "which means that each person does a lot. We grow monsters."

At the end of 2000 all the reporters and anchors had multiple beat responsibilities for everything from city hall to consumer and investigative reporting. They also had to be ready to cover breaking news and to produce longer projects. Deborah Gianoulis, a WJXT anchor for two decades, also covered education and Jacksonville-area military bases. In the spring of 2000 she was working on a long report about women in local shelters who had been repeatedly abused by men. She acknowledged then that there was a lot on her plate because the station had limited resources, but she was proud of what it was trying to accomplish.

WJXT supplemented the efforts of its busy journalists with stories, video and graphics it bought from television news services and received from CBS over the Internet. Years ago, the station took the lead in creating the Florida News Network with stations in Miami, Orlando and Tampa to share stories and video produced by the other stations and to cover jointly the state government and legislature. An unusually long and well-reported story from the Florida News Network about the state budget, complete with debate on the floor of the legislature and interviews with key officials, was broadcast on WJXT's evening newscasts the night we visited.

Those newscasts contained significant community news produced by the WJXT staff. But they also were larded with two promotional stories about programs upcoming on CBS and trivialities like video of a donkey-riding contest in Mexico. Its investigative reporting was similarly para-doxical. WJXT has had a reputation for investigative reporting since its revelations of local corruption in the late 1960s led to a complete reorga-nization of Jacksonville's government. But much of its recent investigative reporting bore the stamp of consultant-led local television trends: items past their sell-by dates found on local grocery store shelves, managed care "horror stories" and X-ray machines that can see through clothing that may be installed at airport security checkpoints.

It was clear that the ambition, energy and good intentions of WJXT's dedicated staff, many of whom, including news director Valet, had been at the station for most of their careers, could benefit from increased investment by Post-Newsweek Stations. Valet told us that the six-station group emphasized good local news coverage and allowed each station considerable leeway in accomplishing that mission. But he was trying to accomplish his ambitious news mission with only ten reporters and four anchors, about half the number of reporters and anchors at Post-Newsweek station WPLG in the much larger media market of Miami.

"We have invested" in WJXT, said Post-Newsweek president Frank. "They have a new building and all the [technological] bells and whistles. They are treated like a first-class station" despite the relatively small size of their market. Nevertheless, Frank added, the station could not spend more of its revenues on covering the news, because its profit margin had to be maintained. That profit margin is more than double that of the *Washington Post*, which invests a much larger proportion of its revenue in its newsroom.

We asked Frank why television stations were expected to maintain profit margins two to three times larger than those of most newspapers, even when that meant settling for much smaller news staffs and inferior news coverage. "There is a different tradition in our industry about what profit margins should be versus newspapers," he replied. Should that tradition be reconsidered to improve local television news coverage? "No," Frank answered. "The viewers are not unhappy."

Is Alan Frank right? Are viewers getting what they want from local television news?

The answer is, Not exactly, if one is to judge by the sharp decline in the measured audience for local news during the late 1990s. But it is harder to know why the viewers aren't watching as much, partly because the stations that broadcast the worst television news can do as well in audience ratings—or in some cases, as badly—as the best. In its attempt to measure the impact of quality on the popularity of local news broadcasts, the Project for Excellence in Journalism found that the stations broadcasting what the study ranked as the best news (about 10 percent of all stations surveyed) have the highest audience ratings, but the stations ranked lowest in quality—those featuring tabloid news, crime and mayhem—follow close behind. Interestingly the stations considered to be average in quality for television news—the vast majority of the total, which combine tabloid features and better stories—have markedly lower audience ratings than the best and worst stations.

A public television documentary filmed in 1999 captured the struggle of a local station news director to both produce better newscasts and attract more viewers. The station, WCNC in Charlotte, North Carolina, had been bought in the late 1990s by Belo, which owns the *Dallas Morning News* and other newspapers and television stations. Belo recruited news director Keith Connors from one of its other stations to improve the quality of WCNC's newscasts while also increasing their audience ratings, which distantly trailed those of Charlotte's other two local stations. In the documentary, Connors could be seen ignoring the advice of consultants to feature more lurid crime stories to attract viewers. Instead, he decided to increase thoughtful coverage of serious local issues like school desegregation. At first, audience ratings remained low. By the time the five-part documentary about the station, *Local News,* was broadcast on PBS in the autumn of 2001, WCNC's ratings had improved and its journalism had won more awards than any other station in its region. Yet it was still behind its two competitors in the ratings.

The Project for Excellence surveys have shown that many of the fea-

tures of good television news have been disappearing regardless of viewers' needs. For example, "the amount of enterprise [reporting that is initi-
ated by the station like investigations or explanatory features that are not
dictated by the day's events] . . . is withering to almost nothing" on local
television. One study found that viewers responded most positively to
broadcasts that featured strong coverage of breaking news and well-
reported stories on a wide variety of subjects, but also found that very few
stations were trying to produce that kind of news broadcast. This study
concluded that "the industry's refusal to provide its viewers with well-
researched stories will lead it down a suicidal path."

Yet it is also clear from American viewing habits a half century into the
television age that many of the people who watch local television news
expect it to be entertaining, and react negatively when it isn't. What the
television industry sees as a cautionary tale played out in Chicago over
nine months in 2000.

Chicago's CBS-owned WBBM, which had been suffering from low ratings, took the drastic step in early 2000 of completely transforming its
10 p.m. newscast, the Central Time zone equivalent of the 11 p.m. local
news on the East or West Coast, from the traditional melodramatic sensationalism to a no-frills, serious news report. It focused on in-depth stories
on topics such as city government and environmental problems while
competing stations featured shootings and water-main breaks. Its
weather and sports reports were shortened, scripted anchor banter was
banned, celebrity features were replaced by interviews with local officials,
and health reports once devoted to food scares became instead serious
examinations of issues like prostate-cancer screening. The changes drew
attention to WBBM from the national news media but attracted few additional viewers in Chicago.

"The ratings aren't good," acknowledged the newscast's architect and
anchor, Carol Marin, a popular Chicago television journalist, when we
talked to her while the show was still on the air. "What we are doing may
still be too radical. We have less mayhem, less traffic fatalities, less fires. We
have more cultural things, more religion and more investigative reporting. Our mantra is public accountability for the politicians here." She said
she was especially proud on the many days when the station reported significant local news before the *Chicago Tribune* did.

The new format was not accompanied by any change in WBBM's news
staff, so it was unable to cover much more news or cover it in much more
depth than it had previously. Mostly what Marin gave her viewers was
more talk—from her, from reporters, from people interviewed on the

newscast and a couple of new commentators—albeit talk about more serious news topics. After months of falling ratings and complaints from some viewers, local newspaper columnists and editorial writers that Marin's news was too dull and talky, the experiment was killed at the end of October 2000. WBBM's late-evening news once again looked and sounded just like most of the other newscasts at stations around the country.

"It wasn't given enough time to build back the audience," Marin said after the demise of the newscast, which she believed had slowly begun to attract viewers who had given up on television news. "I still think it was a good, enterprising newscast," she said, disputing critics who thought it was too dull visually to compete with other Chicago news shows. "You need to have both good production values and serious content. Otherwise, you're just like everyone else."

Viewers have also stayed away from a relatively new alternative to traditional local television news, the twenty-four-hour, all-news channels on cable television systems in several dozen American cities. Some were launched by the cable companies as a service to subscribers, others by newspapers and large media companies, including the owners of local television stations, to gain viewers who want access to the news around the clock. Some have had relationships with local newspapers—including the *New York Times,* the *Washington Post,* the *Boston Globe* and the *Chicago Tribune*—whose reporters appear on the cable news channels to discuss stories they are working on.

These stations present local news straight, without gimmicks. Television critics have complained that they are dull. Viewers have mostly ignored them, leaving the cable news channels with tiny audiences, much smaller than the broadcast stations' in the same cities. Small audiences mean small revenues.

The all-news outlets can be invigorating for the people who work for them, including refugees from local broadcast television. "I'm reporting things I never had a chance to before, that we would talk about at story meetings and couldn't report because of the time factor," Robin Smythe, news director of Central Florida News 13, said at the 1999 convention of the Radio and Television News Directors Association. "For the first time in my career, the only thing I'm worried about is journalism. The only thing I'm doing is news."

Scott Hallowell, director of news and programming for the Orange County NewsChannel near Los Angeles, said, "We did 100 hours of political coverage outside our regular news coverage for the elections last year. I would never get to do that at a broadcast station. I don't have to worry about 'Oh, my God, if we bump Oprah, what are the financial consequences of that?' "

But the local cable news channels have even smaller news staffs than the broadcast stations. They have held costs down by keeping out unions and hiring inexperienced young reporters and anchors at very low salaries. Many reporters are expected to shoot their own video and write and produce their own news stories without the supporting cast of camera operators, writers, editors and producers at bigger broadcast stations. Most of the cable operations recycle a limited number of fresh newscasts throughout the day to fill all twenty-four hours. So just like the broadcast stations, the all-news local cable channels are able to cover little more than breaking news and scheduled events, and their reporting has usually been superficial.

A notable exception is New England Cable News, the most successful of these channels, which broadcasts on cable throughout New England. It features longer, more thoroughly reported stories than competing local television stations and much more analysis, but it does not have a large or deep enough staff to do much investigative reporting. Phil Balboni, its founder and president, said New England Cable News is profitable, paying its reporters about two-thirds of the salaries for reporters at network-affiliate stations or Boston newspapers. Its audience is larger than those for the national cable networks in New England but significantly smaller than those for the network-affiliate stations.

Congress has given every local broadcast station the right to create four new channels when it converts to broadcasting a digital signal. This free gift could theoretically enable local stations to provide around-the-clock newscasts from the same newsrooms they now use for their broadcast news programs. But more quantity would not guarantee any improvement in quality, and it would undermine quality if the stations tried to expand news programming without spending more money on news staff, and without changing their news values.

"We need the fiery pictures and the prurient story, we used to say in broadcast journalism, because that was the hook, the hook that got 'em in the tent. And if we could hook the audience, they could follow with the dull stuff, with the experts and the talking heads, and offer some solutions to the problems we wanted to report," then NBC News president Andrew Lack told the Radio and Television News Directors Association at its 1995 convention, before local television ratings began sliding downward. "Unfortunately, it seems to me, we got too good at producing hooks, and more and more of the audience has taken the bait, and television news seems to have convinced itself that that's what it does best—tap the emotions. Someone else can tap their brains. And as a result, much of our news was never more shallow or more successful."

Does the mediocrity of local television news reflect what viewers want? Or have they merely become complacent about what they are given? Would better news coverage by larger and better local television news staffs, presented in a more compelling way than Carol Marin managed to do in Chicago, attract more viewers?

"Local television journalists and editors present their work to viewers and to themselves as a public service that serves the market," the University of Santa Clara researcher John H. McManus concluded in his study of local television news. "But their actions demonstrate daily the fundamental contradiction between serving the marketplace of viewers and serving the public. . . . They tell each other they would create better journalism if the public would pay attention; or if television weren't inherently better suited to entertaining than informing; or if television weren't so visually oriented that ideas and abstractions are technologically inappropriate; or if television could handle enough complexity for people to really learn from it; or if television generated enough money to support a serious news operation. Or they say television's role is only to pique people's interest so they can read about it or listen to it elsewhere. Or they say the public ought to choose what's news by its viewing decisions and journalists should simply follow the common taste."

While each of these rationalizations has some merit, McManus wrote, none justified what television journalists were putting on the air. "But they do succeed," he added, "in masking the subordination of the public's interest to the short-term interest of investors."

What is clear is that the values of local television news have reflected the relatively satisfied state of the industry, at least before the terrorist attacks and economic downturn that began in 2001. Although audiences had been declining, business was good before the downturn, and the market value of stations had remained high. Rich corporate owners, including the big broadcast networks, kept buying up more of them.

These owners and the managers of their local stations were generally comfortable with the local television news culture created during the last quarter of the twentieth century. Their interest in each station's news was focused primarily on audience ratings, which they tracked minute by minute, day by day, and on the profits dependent on those ratings. Except for rare occasions when local stations had become clearinghouses of vital community information during times of crisis, including the aftermath of the terrorist attacks in 2001, few of these local television executives saw themselves as providers of an important public service beyond promotional charitable activities and local boosterism.

Yet the warning signs were unmistakable, if still largely unrecognized in the industry. The local television news audience had been shrinking steadily before the terrorist attacks in 2001. And advertising revenue fell quickly and sharply during the economic downturn.

Swimming against the tide, news director Long in Washington expressed hope, near the end of 2001, that the war against terrorism might prompt real change in the industry. He argued in budget discussions with his owners at NBC that "we are entering a new cycle" in which local television should concentrate on more serious news coverage. "We have new eyeballs watching," he said. "We have to offer news that is relevant to these newcomers." Whether or not station owners seize an opportunity to be more public service–minded, Long argued they should at least recognize the business necessity of taking advantage of renewed public interest in serious news. "This might be the last chance," he said, "for growth in a mature if not moribund industry."

# Chapter Seven

# THE NEW NEWS

Building 25—three floors of look-alike little offices—is identical to all the other sterile steel-and-glass warrens for high-tech workers on the leafy Microsoft corporate campus just northwest of Seattle, with one exception: a sprawling, cluttered, open room on the second floor filled with rows of computers and walls of television monitors. Here, in the center of the futuristic computer software universe, is a familiar sight—an old-fashioned newsroom, albeit one equipped with the latest technology, filled with energetic young journalists busy producing a new form of news for the Internet site called MSNBC.com.

Microsoft originally built the newsroom for a news service of its own for users of its MSN network on the Internet. But when Microsoft executives realized how difficult it would be to assemble and run a news operation, they abandoned that idea and struck a deal with NBC News at the end of 1995 to create MSNBC.com and the MSNBC cable news network. MSNBC.com quickly became one of the most popular news sites on the World Wide Web.

The MSNBC.com newsroom is dominated by a wall of monitors displaying numerous network, cable and local television channels and the home pages of MSNBC.com and competing Internet sites. A door in the wall of monitors leads to a conference room, where Merrill Brown, the editor in chief of MSNBC.com, was conducting his daily news meeting on a summery day in June 2000.

"The Supreme Court just ruled on Elián," announced executive producer Bob Aglow.

"What did they do?" Brown asked, as he fingered the keyboard of a computer on the table in front of him, searching the Internet on a huge screen at the opposite end of the room.

"I'll know in a minute," Aglow said. As if on cue, a colleague stuck his head in the door to say the court was allowing the father of Elián González to take the boy home to Cuba, the denouement of a news melodrama that had captivated much of the country and the news media.

Brown tapped on his keyboard to check out the competition. He went first to rival CNN.com, whose front page soon appeared on the big screen at the end of the room. CNN.com, created by the cable news network, relied on CNN's news-gathering and video resources in addition to news services like the Associated Press and Reuters, just as MSNBC.com relied on NBC News and the news services.

Brown saw that CNN.com had already posted news of the Supreme Court decision. It took a few more minutes for an MSNBC producer to process a news service story on his computer in the newsroom just outside the conference room and post it on the MSNBC.com home page. Meanwhile, the editors and producers in the conference room, and others at NBC and MSNBC offices in Washington, New York and London, who could be heard on a speakerphone in the middle of the table, fired questions and suggestions back and forth about what to do next.

A compelling feature of Internet news sites is the speed with which they can produce and deliver news. Web users don't have to wait for the radio news on the hour, or the television news at 6 or 7, or the next morning's newspaper; they can find the news online whenever they want it, and can learn about breaking events moments after the fact. Measurements of Internet traffic—the "ratings" for this new medium—have shown that big, breaking news stories draw the largest audiences to news sites. So when the Elián story broke, MSNBC.com journalists rushed to put as much coverage on its site as they could.

And they sought to exploit other features of the Internet: infinite "space" for words, photos, video and audio; multimedia capability; and interactivity. The headline about Elián on the MSNBC.com home page was linked to the main story, written by a Web site producer, and to other stories from the news services and from the *Washington Post*, which has a partnership arrangement with MSNBC and NBC. Besides the print stories, MSNBC.com offered video clips from NBC and MSNBC television, and unedited, continuous streaming video from NBC cameras at various locations. MSNBC.com also invited readers to comment on the story in its discussion areas and offered the opportunity to participate in a "Live Vote" survey on the subject.

The Supreme Court decision had been anticipated for days, but MSNBC.com editors and producers clearly were scrambling that morning. A producer in NBC's Washington bureau could be heard on the speakerphone reporting that the story would lead the *NBC Nightly News* broadcast and its *Dateline* newsmagazine show later that night. Another producer, in the Secaucus, New Jersey, newsroom of the MSNBC cable network, described plans to cover the Elián story on news shows all afternoon and evening. MSNBC.com asked NBC television producers in Havana to provide telephone and video interviews.

Brown did not hide his frustration over his staff's apparent failure to anticipate the Supreme Court decision and plan how to cover it. "There should have been a plan in place for what has been coming for days," he said. But after the meeting, one of Brown's deputies, executive editor Michael Silberman, expressed optimism that "in a couple of hours we will have a huge package."

Out in the newsroom, Mike Moran, an MSNBC.com producer who specialized in breaking stories, rewrote the main story on the Elián case from AP and Reuters wire stories and information from NBC producers in Havana. A story from washingtonpost.com about the reaction of Elián's relatives and other Cuban exiles in Miami was added to the package, along with background stories from news services.

Before long, users could also find video reports from NBC and MSNBC, including a helicopter shot of the car carrying the father and son to Dulles International Airport outside Washington. The really curious could also find live streaming video from MSNBC.com's own cameras. One was in the Cuban neighborhood in Miami, where Cuban exiles were protesting in the streets. Another was on the sidewalk in front of the Supreme Court in Washington, where lawyers were holding press conferences. And still another was on the street outside the house in an affluent Washington neighborhood where Elián and his father had been staying while awaiting the court's decision. For most of the day, that camera showed little more than joggers running by.

"Breaking news is our traffic driver," Silberman said. "If we put a lot of energy into covering the big breaking story of the day, and pull out all the bells and whistles of video and nontraditional storytelling, not just text, people will come to us. It's one reason we are number one."

MSNBC was one of the most popular Web sites specializing in news on the Internet, visited by about 10 million people each month, including repeat users. Half of this audience came from Internet users on MSN, the Microsoft portal, which competed with AOL and Yahoo! as a principal highway into cyberspace. MSN featured MSNBC headlines, and a reader who clicked on one of the news stories from MSNBC would be counted as an MSNBC visitor. Much of the MSNBC audience is also drawn to the site by plugs for it on NBC's television networks. On-air promotions by their networks also drew large audiences to the CNN and ABC News sites on the Internet. The most popular news sites not affiliated with a television network were those of the *New York Times,* the *Washington Post* and *USA Today.* Because Internet users paid nothing to visit MSNBC.com (and nearly all other news sites on the Web), most of its revenue came from the advertising that appeared on the site. Ads appeared on the screen above, below and alongside headlines and news stories and sometimes popped up in ways that forced users to pay attention to them.

But revenue from advertising didn't yet cover the costs of most Internet news sites, let alone contribute to the costs their parent organizations incurred to cover the news. MSNBC.com was heavily subsidized by its prosperous parents.

The way MSNBC.com spent money and man-hours was revealing. Besides people, its biggest cost item was the technology needed to support the site and its content. Most of the staff spent most of its time operating the technology or gathering visual material for the site. Only a couple of dozen members of an editorial staff of 110 actually produced news stories. Most of them had once been newspaper or television journalists, but they did little or no original reporting or writing for MSNBC.com. Instead, working in shifts around the clock, they rapidly rewrote and updated stories from wire service and NBC News reports, adding headlines, summaries of the stories, graphics and video, plus material from partner news organizations.

This was the pattern MSNBC.com followed in covering the biggest story of recent years, the terrorist attacks on New York and Washington on September 11, 2001. The site relied almost entirely on wire service reports, stories from the *Washington Post* and *Newsweek* and video from NBC's broadcast and cable networks. One of its few pieces of original journalism was a first-person account by Martin Wolk, a reporter for MSNBC cable, describing his escape from the World Trade Center's Marriott Hotel. The most popular feature on MSNBC.com that day was continuous live video from NBC and MSNBC cameras covering the story in New York and Washington. These attracted 6 million viewers on September 11, Brown said.

Brown, Silberman and others at MSNBC.com said they would like to do more original work in the future, especially investigative and explanatory reporting projects that could exploit the Web's capability to provide multimedia presentations. But they acknowledged that most investment in the near future would be spent on still more advanced technology, rather than on additional staff to produce original reporting. They hoped that new technology would mix text, photography, graphics and video seamlessly and more creatively, and put MSNBC.com into more homes through cable television and into people's hands wherever they were, through wireless telephones and other portable devices.

Brian Storm, the energetic and visionary young "director of multimedia" in the MSNBC.com newsroom, said that eventually the new medium should emulate the in-depth reporting of newspapers rather than the "shallow" journalism of television news. The fact that webcasting would eventually provide sound and pictures as vivid as television's should not mean that Web news sites would mimic television news, he thought. He saw no reason to dumb down online news; on the contrary, the Web's technological capacities lent themselves most logically to high-quality news products emphasizing depth, interactivity and customized editing for different audiences. But he acknowledged that in the first years of MSNBC.com's existence, developing the necessary technology had proved to be expensive, time-consuming and sometimes distracting from the news itself.

"Everything is an experiment right now," Storm said. "Newspapers just focus on what is in the story. We get distracted from the storytelling by the technology, its possibilities, limitations and decisions" about how to use it.

This is a time of experimentation for all news media as they try to adapt to revolutionary new technology. Newspapers, magazines and television networks and stations repackage their news daily on their Internet sites. Some newspapers and newsmagazines cooperate on news coverage with television networks, and put some of their reporters and editors on network news shows to talk about their stories. The *New York Times* and its Web site shared stories and reporters with ABC News and its Web site. In the new AOL Time Warner empire, magazines, broadcast and cable networks and AOL itself were all trying to cross-promote and share content. The *Washington Post* and *Newsweek*, also owned by the Washington Post Company, were partners with NBC News and MSNBC. These arrangements have given new exposure on television to print reporters, their publications and their Web sites.

Some newspapers and local television stations are working together on news stories. Several newspapers and television stations owned by the same media corporation share multimedia newsrooms. Many newspapers have put video cameras and fully equipped television studios into their newsrooms to make it easier for their reporters to appear on television or to tape video reports for the newspapers' Web sites.

Collaborations like these exemplify an industry catchword, *synergy*, that implies the combining of old and new media resources and technologies to create something bigger and better and more profitable than the component parts. The search for synergy has significantly changed many newsrooms.

Reporters at large newspapers with active Internet news sites and radio and television relationships can produce news for four different media in the same day. They report and write stories for their newspapers; they prepare separate, often earlier, versions of the same stories in text or on video for the newspapers' Web sites; and they appear on television or on radio to talk about the stories.

Much of this news sharing amounts to little more than cross-promotion among co-owned or cooperating media. For example, in Tampa, the *Tampa Tribune* newspaper, television station WFLA and their Web site, TBO.com (originally Tampa Bay Online), are all owned by the Media General corporation of Richmond, Virginia. They share a new building on the bank of the Hillsborough River. Each of the three regularly promotes the others. On its 11 p.m. newscast, WFLA previews a story in the next morning's *Tribune* and refers viewers interested in still more information to TBO.com. The *Tribune's* weather page features forecasts by WFLA's Storm Team 8 illustrated by a photograph of the television station's four on-air meteorologists. And the TBO.com Web site has repackaged content from both the *Tribune* and WFLA. While this kind of cross-promotion has clearly increased traffic on their Web sites, it does not appear to have increased the audiences of newspapers and television stations.

With a few exceptions, attempts at synergy have produced relatively little additional original or improved journalism or new revenue. They mostly have "repurposed" (another news term) journalism already being produced by one news medium for use by another. In practice, this usually has meant repackaging newspaper journalism on television and the Internet, because newspapers continue to have by far the largest and most talented news-gathering staffs.

Still, there are obvious benefits from multimedia collaboration. Cooperation between newspaper and television news operations, even on a relatively small scale, offers viewers of network and local television additional news they might not otherwise see. It can expose wider audiences to significant enterprise and investigative reporting. And the cooperating news organizations can benefit from one another's news-gathering resources.

Evidence of these benefits can be seen in Media General's ultramodern News Center in Tampa, where the newsrooms of the *Tribune,* WFLA and TBO.com are stacked one on top of the other on two floors above the television station's studios. Hollowed out of the middle of the two floors is an atrium that allows everyone to hear and see what is happening in the newsrooms above and below. In the middle of it all, at the bottom of the atrium, is a multitiered "superdesk" where *Tribune,* WFLA and TBO.com assignment editors work side by side on telephones and computers to monitor breaking news and the movements of their reporters, photographers and video technicians.

After conferring with one another during the course of each day, editors of the newspaper and producers of the television newscasts meet in their separate conference rooms to plan that evening's news broadcasts and the next morning's newspaper. On the day we visited, they agreed that a *Tribune* story on a projected teacher shortage in a local county school system would be featured both on the *Tribune's* front page and on WFLA's 11 p.m. newscast. "The *Tampa Tribune* has discovered alarming information about the hiring of teachers," began the story on WFLA that night.

WFLA is the Tampa Bay area's dominant television station. The *Tribune* is the second-largest-circulation newspaper in the region, behind the *St. Petersburg Times,* but it still has a much larger news staff than WFLA. So the television station has benefited from the newspaper's beat coverage and investigative reporting and the sheer number of reporters it could send out on a big breaking story, while the *Tribune* has been able to present and promote its news reporting to a larger audience on WFLA.

"Today, the *Tribune* was at a city council meeting and we weren't," Susan DeFraties, WFLA's managing editor, said on the day we visited. A *Tribune* editor alerted her to an important vote by the council, "so we can catch up later." WFLA had 6 to 8 reporters working on an average day, while the *Tribune* had 125, she said, "so who is going to know more?"

When a big fire caused extensive damage in Tampa a few months earlier, WFLA news director Dan Bradley said, the newspaper sent six reporters to cover it, while he could send only two. So he put the paper's reporters on the air, along with his own, to tell viewers what they could see and find out from their various vantage points and news sources. "They all want to be on TV," Bradley said of the newspaper reporters. "We tell them that while a lot of people are reading your newspaper, there are lots of people watching us on TV who are not reading your newspaper."

Gil Thelan, executive editor of the *Tribune,* said the newspaper in turn benefited from the television station's faster start and greater urgency on breaking stories. "There is a lot more energy in the building from being around broadcasters," he said. "The newspaper is moving faster."

But most of the reporters at the *Tribune* and WFLA have continued to do most of their work only for the newspaper or the station. And very few of them produced original journalism for the TBO.com Web site. Despite being in such close proximity, they tended to stick to working in their own newsrooms and had little meaningful contact with the others. Both Bradley and Thelan, who expressed strong belief in the future of what they called "convergence" of the television, newspaper and Internet news operations, acknowledged that the Tampa News Center still housed three quite different and often conflicting news cultures. "This is an experiment," Thelan said.

Perhaps the best-known and most closely watched experiment in multimedia convergence, or synergy, has been at Chicago's Tribune Company. Tribune owns the venerable newspaper from which it takes its name, the top-rated WGN television and radio stations, the CLTV (Chicagoland Television) all-news cable station and the chicagotribune.com news Web site. The newspaper's main newsroom in the Tribune Tower on Michigan Avenue downtown is dominated by "the stage," a spacious, open studio with three television cameras where reporters are interviewed for Tribune's television outlets. Nearby, at the city desk, representatives of the television outlets and the Web site work side by side with the newspaper's local news editors. The *Tribune*'s largest suburban news bureau west of Chicago shares a former warehouse with CLTV's studios and newsroom, where newspaper editors and CLTV producers also work together at the same news operations desk, trading information about what they are covering.

Tribune executives said their long-term goal was to make the news-gathering operations of its newspaper, television, radio and Internet outlets in Chicago virtually interchangeable, with reporters for any one of them gathering news for use by all. They even created a news synergy staff in the Tribune Tower to move toward that goal by encouraging more cooperation among the Tribune news organizations. But progress has been slow. While many *Tribune* reporters appeared on CLTV, a typically low-budget, low-audience cable news channel that welcomed their contributions, they were mostly shunned by WGN, Chicago's dominant television station, which preferred its own highly paid broadcast professionals. And Tribune's news Web site could not always count on *Tribune* reporters to produce around-the-clock updates on developing local stories, so it had to hire its own reporters.

"We preach synergy, but we don't *do* synergy," said Mark Hinojosa, who ran Tribune's synergy staff. "We don't have shared cultures." Asked specifically what multimedia cooperation he had been able to achieve in his first half year on the job, Hinojosa said, "Nothing. Really almost nothing." A year later, Hinojosa said he was making some progress, but reiterated that real synergy remains a hope for the future.

So in the first years of experimentation, hopes for a creative, fruitful convergence of traditional news media have not been realized. New technologies and new attitudes have allowed new kinds of collaboration, and online journalism has created a new medium. Some old ways of doing things have been displaced by new ones. But nothing has yet challenged the pre-eminence of broadcast and cable television, and ink-on-paper newspapers and magazines.

This lack of synergy should not be confused with a prognosis about the future, however. The stunning growth of the online world since the early nineties and the rapid evolution of new technologies obscure the fact that we are still in the infancy of this new medium. The greatest potential of the Internet may be its capacity to combine many of the advantages of television, radio and newspapers in ways that *could* make it much more powerful than all three. As Internet technology improves and the "picture" on a computer screen becomes as good as on TV, users will be able to "watch television" on their computer screens while retaining control over what they watch and when. They should be able to skip around from item to item as and when they like, the same way they now read a newspaper. When they find a subject or story that interests them, users will have the option of stopping to read about it in detail. Technologically, this capability isn't far off. If and how it will be exploited, and by whom, remain to be seen.

Everyone in the news business has become aware that the Internet can change everything we do, but we don't yet know how or when this may happen. Already, news is everywhere on the Internet. But none of the first experiments with news on the Web has been commercially successful or particularly innovative journalistically. They have taught interesting lessons without yet demonstrating how journalism on the Web can thrive.

Many Internet pioneers hoped that this new medium would enable the creation of new news outlets independent of the established media. Starting a newspaper is enormously expensive; a new television or radio station requires an impossible-to-acquire broadcasting license; launching a cable channel is plausible only for those who can negotiate deals with cable systems to carry it. Buying an existing news organization requires outbidding the huge conglomerates that now own most of the news media. But anyone with a personal computer big and fast enough to be used as a Web "server" can host a news site on the Internet. Here is technology, like the printing press earlier in American history, that can make a free press a meaningful concept, and not just for the wealthy.

On the most superficial level this potential has been exploited by the proprietors of countless Internet sites. But the provenance of the information they provide is often obscure, and its reliability often dubious. And the Internet's cacophony has overwhelmed most information providers on the Web. Only a tiny handful of independent sites have attracted many readers.

For those that have reached larger audiences, the journalistic and financial results have been less than exhilarating. Many have been overwhelmed by the costs of staff, increased technological capacity and marketing required to reach and reliably serve large numbers of users. Only a handful have managed to break through to sustainable profitability, and even fewer have been able to provide original, informative journalism.

Two of the first news sites to develop significant readerships on the Internet were Web magazines, Slate.com and Salon.com. They both combined opinion journalism with a limited amount of original reporting, a lot of chat and some breaking news from wire services.

Salon.com was started independently by journalist David Talbot. It attracted readers and attention in the national media with gossipy stories and cheeky commentary during President Clinton's Monica Lewinsky scandal. It held the interest of loyal readers with literate journalism about politics, religion, sex, books, movies and the arts. Capitalizing on the Internet investment craze in the late 1990s, Salon raised a lot of money with a successful stock offering that funded a large writing and editing staff and offices in New York and San Francisco. But when the Internet investment bubble burst in 2000 and Salon had difficulty attracting enough advertising or other revenue to cover costs, its stock price plummeted and it began cutting back on staff.

Slate.com, started by magazine editor Michael Kinsley, had more financial security because it was owned by Microsoft and was available on, and promoted by, its MSN Internet gateway. Kinsley said he originally intended Slate.com to be a weekly magazine of news and opinion, the Internet equivalent of a print magazine like *The New Republic,* which he had edited. But he quickly learned that Internet readers expected Slate's content to be updated constantly. So the Web site's contributors, many of them successful magazine journalists, wrote and posted articles and commentary whenever events or their whim dictated.

Slate devised one popular innovation that was widely copied on the Web. It encouraged its contributors to write personal commentary about news being reported in newspapers and on television, and accompanied their comments with hypertext links to the full stories on the Web sites of traditional media organizations that originated them. Slate's single most popular regular feature during the 2000 election campaign was a daily summary of various newspapers' political stories called "Today's Papers."

Slate invented e-mail dialogues between well-known writers on the hot topics of the day, which Kinsley said have established "e-mail as a form of journalism." E-mail is "just a wonderful medium for exchange of ideas," he said, "and when it works it's like the best of talking and the best of writing. The spontaneity of talking but the reflectiveness of writing."

But most of Slate.com's content remained traditional opinion-magazine journalism, supplemented by numerous links to news stories, opinion columns, editorial pages and literary and arts criticism on news-media Web sites. Slate also provided links to the Web sites of newspapers in other countries and to transcripts of network and cable television talk and opinion shows. While much of Slate's writing was original, very little of its reporting was. Most of the news it presented came from the Web sites of established media organizations with large news-gathering staffs. Kinsley said it was easier for Slate.com to exploit "information that already exists on the Web" than to amass the resources to do its own reporting.

Slate.com has not been a lavish operation. Kinsley kept a few writers and editors on the staff and relied mostly on freelance contributors. But even with low costs, Slate struggled unsuccessfully to break even. It did sell some advertising, but not enough. When Microsoft tried for a year to charge readers for access to Slate.com, traffic fell off dramatically. Only about 30,000 readers agreed to pay the $19.95 subscription fee, so it was dropped in 1999, and Slate became free again. Kinsley told us he hoped to break even during 2002.

One of the very few people to exploit the publishing power of the Web successfully as an individual entrepreneur has been an online chat room gadfly named Matt Drudge. Beginning in the mid-1990s in Los Angeles, where he traded show business gossip in chat rooms and through e-mail, Drudge gained a growing Internet readership and e-mail source network, especially among journalists and political operatives. The scoop that got him the most attention came from a source at *Newsweek* magazine, who told Drudge in January 1998 about a story *Newsweek*'s editors had held out of the magazine at the last minute—a story that opened the floodgates to what became the Clinton-Lewinsky scandal.

But for every Drudge "exclusive" that contained a germ of truth, another proved to be wildly wrong. "Like reporters, he disseminates what he finds out, but he does not necessarily take pains to verify his items, and he operates without an editor or other gatekeeper," Tom Goldstein, dean of Columbia University's Graduate School of Journalism, wrote about Drudge. "He has had his scoops and he has made his mistakes." He's made many, but hides them from readers by refusing to keep an archive on his Web site of exclusive stories that "stayed exclusive," as reporters like to say of rivals' scoops that don't pan out. Even the editor of the supermarket tabloid newspaper the *Star* accused Drudge of "dealing mostly in barroom gossip and wild speculation."

Drudge brushes off such criticism, contending that the great popularity of The Drudge Report on the Web, where it has been visited by millions of Americans each month, has shown "there is a hunger for unedited information, absent corporate considerations." But he also realized early on that he could attract more people to his site by showing them other interesting news on the Internet. So he put on the Drudge Report headlined links to news stories on the Web sites of newspapers and other news organizations. This quickly made Drudge an important source of traffic for newspaper sites on the Internet. In 2001 Drudge sent more readers to washingtonpost.com than did any other Web site that linked to the *Post*.

The established news media that Drudge loved to lambaste in interviews were critical to his own success. He couldn't provide a sustained diet of exclusive stories of his own, and relied on traditional media sources to keep his site lively and interesting. For all his talk about how "now, with a modem, anyone . . . can report on the world," much of Drudge's Web site merely listed what traditional news organizations were reporting on their sites.

Drudge may have lived up to the romantic notion that the Web would produce new Ben Franklins and Tom Paines, electronic pamphleteers or news-site proprietors who could break the hold of big media companies on the information reaching the American public. But if he did, his personalized site has turned out to be *sui generis*. As befits the times, commercial interests dominated the early years of the Internet, not resourceful individuals eager to crusade for truth and justice.

The most typical Internet news sites were launched by entrepreneurs targeting specialized audiences, and hoping to make money. These offerings, products of the Internet bubble of the late 1990s, were often lavishly backed by wealthy investors and money raised from public stock offerings. They focused narrowly on news about subjects like business and finance, politics, women, minority groups, sports, crime, health or the weather. APBnews.com hired veteran reporters to chase down stories about crime. Drkoop.com was started by C. Everett Koop, the former U.S. surgeon general, and investors to provide health news and advice. Voter.com collected veteran political journalists and campaign workers to present election and other political news. Women.com, whose investors included the Hearst media corporation, specialized in news and features for women.

These and other "stand-alone" Internet news sites mirrored on the Web the proliferation of magazines, newsletters and other print publications that similarly targeted specialized audiences. They hired their own editors and reporters and produced their own journalism. They spent a lot of money promoting themselves and initially attracted large and enthusiastic audiences. But their readers were all freeloaders; none of these sites could charge their readers a fee. Long before the World Wide Web simplified access to the Internet for millions of citizens, an Internet culture had evolved, which decreed that information on the Net should be free. In this first phase of the Web's history, that culture proved very strong. Only specialized providers targeting specialized, eager audiences succeeded in charging for information on the Internet.

The backers of most new information and news sites on the Internet counted on advertising revenue to earn them profits. But after healthy growth in online advertising for several years, the demand for it fell abruptly in the second half of 2000, largely because many Web advertisers were new Internet start-ups, which themselves fell on hard times after their stock prices collapsed. By the end of 2000, many of the stand-alone Web news sites were hemorrhaging money. Those that did not go out of business altogether were forced to cut costs and staff drastically, seek new investors or sell their content to more successful Web sites.

Voter.com got more attention than most of these start-ups. A young venture capitalist, Justin Dangel, launched the site. He hired as his executive editor former *Washington Post* reporter Carl Bernstein of Watergate fame. They hoped to use media and public interest in the 2000 presidential election to gain a large audience rapidly. They tried to attract attention with expensive publicity campaigns, beginning with lavish parties and prominently placed work spaces at the Democratic and Republican national conventions in the summer of 2000. The parties were fine, but the site flopped. Voter.com went out of business early in 2001.

The news and information sites that survived focused on subjects best suited to continuous updating on the Internet: business and financial markets, sports and the weather. But even these were not guaranteed success.

The popularity of financial news sites was linked to the personal-investing and new-technology booms of the late 1990s, which played out in part on the Internet. Day traders bought and sold the stocks of online entrepreneurs through online trading houses, and relied on online information to make decisions about what to buy or sell. According to one survey, active stock traders were relying more on Internet-based financial information than on traditional news media in the spring of 2000. But the bubble burst that spring.

In the months that followed, many of the most successful online publishers had to relinquish their ambitions, face painful adjustments or go out of business. One was Fool.com, a Web site full of news and advice for individual investors started by brothers David and Tom Gardner and their friend Erik Rydholm. They began in 1993 as an iconoclastic newsletter, *The Motley Fool*. They moved onto America Online in 1994, then launched their Web site in 1997. By the end of the nineties, after years of bull markets and an ever-expanding number of individual stock traders, several million people were visiting Fool.com each month. Exploiting a talent for self-promotion, the three founders, often wearing court jester hats, became a kind of multimedia conglomerate. They launched a radio show heard on 130 stations and a newspaper column that appeared in 170 papers. They added chat rooms to their Web site. When Internet business dropped dramatically at the end of 2000, this diversification helped The

Motley Fool struggle to stay afloat. But it didn't prevent layoffs and cutbacks of content when advertising revenue fell in 2001.

Two other business news Web sites, TheStreet.com and MarketWatch.com, quickly gained large audiences in the late nineties. They used money from sales of their stock to hire reporters and editors who produced original business journalism. But their stock values tumbled in the 2000 sell-off of Internet issues. MarketWatch.com depended for its financial health on partial ownership by CBS. TheStreet.com shrank its news operations and ended a joint newsroom-operating agreement with the *New York Times.*

By 2001 the common missing ingredient for these enterprises was profit, regardless of the size of their audience. Those owned wholly or in part by established media companies were subsidized by their parents. The CNBC.com and CNNfn.com financial news sites were subsidiaries of cable news networks. Weather.com was run by cable television's Weather Channel. And the three most popular sports news sites were owned by CBS, the sports cable channel ESPN and a combination of the CNN cable network and *Sports Illustrated* magazine.

After the shakeout of 2000 to 2001, the Web outlets of old-media organizations were indisputably the dominant news sites on the Internet. Not only did the networks and major newspapers draw big audiences, their material also became ubiquitous on other sites as a result of content-sharing agreements and the free links from one site to another that are a unique feature of the Web.

But even the most popular news sites had many fewer visitors than the major "portals"—Yahoo!, AOL and Microsoft's MSN, among others—that many people used as gateways to the Web. The portals offer easy access to the Internet, e-mail, Web searches, chat, online auctions and shopping, entertainment—and news.

The portals do not create any journalism of their own. They buy standardized news summaries and stories from the Associated Press and Reuters wire services, and they provide links to stories on the news sites of newspapers, magazines and television networks. They treat news as a commodity.

As a result, one of America's oldest news organizations, the Associated Press, has become a ubiquitous news provider for the newest news medium, the Internet. The AP supplies most of the news displayed by the portals. Even the major newspapers and television networks, which produce fresh news stories for their Internet sites all day long, use the AP for breaking news bulletins and updates on their sites. Many newspaper and television news sites use only the AP for the latest news. The more ambitious sites use AP dispatches until they can complete their own stories and "put them up" on the Web.

With 2,700 reporters, photographers and editors in 146 bureaus in the United States, including all fifty state capitals, and ninety-five more bureaus around the world, the AP has more journalists in more places ready to report breaking news than any other news organization. More than 1,500 member newspapers are the primary clients and cooperative owners of the 152-year-old news service. The AP also sells selections from its daily output of more than 20 million words and 1,000 pictures to 5,000 American radio and television stations and nearly 9,000 newspaper and broadcast customers in other countries. And now it sells around-the-clock news reports to a number of Internet sites besides those operated by its newspaper and broadcast clients.

The AP delivers a basic and bland diet of news bulletins that Internet news consumers will find almost wherever they roam on the Web. The AP emphasizes speed, accuracy and fairness in its reporting. In the words of the AP's chief executive, Lou Boccardi, the goal is to produce "a dispassionate account of news across the country and around the world." As new technology creates "many new voices [with] a point of view," Boccardi said, "the AP keeps its objective tradition."

The AP provides journalistic meat and potatoes, a diet that satisfies a wide variety of customers. It distributes concise, straightforward accounts of the big national and international stories, local news from every state in the union, sports news and business news. The AP's reporting reflects the abilities and experience of many AP correspondents, who tend to start their journalism careers at the news service and move on after a few years. AP pays mediocre wages, but it gives young journalists intense and extensive experience in busy bureaus with large workloads that keep all hands running all the time. With some notable exceptions, the AP does not produce much investigative or interpretative reporting that goes beyond or behind the events of the day. But it stays on top of those events, updating them all the time. The news bulletins heard on the hour on American radio stations come predominantly from the AP.

The fact that the Associated Press and its main competitor, the British news service Reuters, are the principal providers of news on the Internet suggests that, so far, consumers see the Web more like a user-friendly radio station than a serious provider of in-depth news. But there is also a strong and growing demand for more serious journalism on the Internet. The links offered by most of the portals to stories on the sites of major newspapers and television networks draw thousands of readers to those news sites. And of course Web surfers can go directly to the sites of the *New York Times,* the *Los Angeles Times* and the *Washington Post* to read the entire contents of those papers, plus stories and features specially produced for the Internet. The *Wall Street Journal* also has a good Web site, but, uniquely, it is only available to paid subscribers. *Journal* readers need the information their paper provides for business purposes, so they can treat its cost as a business expense, which may explain why the *Journal* has been able to attract hundreds of thousands of paid online readers.

The *Times* and the *Post* have vast armies of new readers, hundreds of thousands daily, who read *Post* and *Times* journalism on their computer screens from every corner of the globe. Anyone with access to a computer and modem can read the country's—and many of the world's—leading newspapers whenever they like.

The *Post*'s experience has demonstrated the power of big news events to drive up the online audience. As the number of Internet users grew by leaps in the late 1990s, usage of washingtonpost.com jumped every time a big story broke. The first of these was the death of Princess Diana in August 1997. Later, each big development of the Lewinsky scandal and the impeachment of President Clinton drove readership up. Yet every time a new record for "page views" was set, that became a new level of everyday readership. Then the next big news event drove the audience up again. One surprising example was the sinking of the *Kursk,* the Russian submarine, which drew a huge readership in the days when the fate of its crew was still uncertain. Then the 2000 presidential election and, especially, its suspenseful aftermath set more new records. Then all records were shattered on September 11 and 12, 2001, when a huge audience, three times larger than the one that read about the presidential election, visited washingtonpost.com's coverage of the terrorist attacks on Washington and New York. On each of those days, washingtonpost.com recorded more than 28 million page views, indicating that millions of people had visited the site.

If charted as a graph line, washingtonpost.com's readership grew like a staircase, sharply up with a big new story, then leveling off until the next one. Clearly, readers who found the site liked it enough to return, even when there wasn't a dramatic new development. But breaking news is always the most popular feature on washingtonpost.com.

When the owners and managers of the established news organizations began to grasp the potential of the World Wide Web in the mid-1990s, they first saw a mortal danger. Newspapers were particularly worried that online competition would draw away a large portion of classified advertising, unprepossessing little advertisements that make up 20 to 50 percent of all revenues of most newspapers. The theory was that the Web was an ideal classified-ad environment that would enable consumers to search easily for exactly what they wanted in a car, job or apartment. This proved true, but not devastating. After several years of anxiety, the consequences have been significant but not yet dire. The economic slowdown at the end of 2000 hurt classified advertising considerably more than Internet competition had up to that point.

Confronted by dramatic technological change, hundreds of newspapers, television stations and the networks all came to the same conclusion: They had to defend their own interests by staking a claim to a piece of cyberspace. So they launched Web sites, sometimes with ambitious and creative plans for how to use them, sometimes without much thought at all.

Some newspapers have added newsroom staff or created new subsidiaries to work on their Web sites and invested many millions of dollars in Internet publishing ventures. But many others are struggling with tiny Web staffs that do little more than dump the contents of their papers onto the Internet each day. Newspaper chains like Gannett and Knight Ridder appear to be undecided about whether they should emphasize collective, corporate Web news strategies or let their individual papers go their own ways. Some have debated whether their papers' Web sites should be built primarily around news or become multipurpose local portal sites, on which the news plays a much smaller role.

Most local television stations have also starved their Internet sites of money and staff until recently, and the audiences for these bare-bones sites have been tiny. The networks are now investing in the sites of stations they own, and dozens of other stations have banded together to put the operation of their sites under a consultant called Internet Broadcasting Systems, which began by improving their graphics, weather reports and promotion. The Internet sites of most television stations amount to little more than an alternative way to view the relatively limited news coverage the stations put on the air.

At the opposite extreme are the best sites, most of them belonging to the biggest newspapers and the networks, which combine breaking news, updated twenty-four hours a day, with the journalism published or broadcast by the parent organization. Besides news, these sites typically offer photographs and snippets of audio and video from news events, press conferences and interviews, which can make them look like combinations of newspapers and television on a computer screen. The best news sites also offer many of the services provided by the portals, including e-mail, online discussions, Web search engines, classified advertising and online shopping. Many newspaper sites offer extensive guides to their cities' dining, entertainment, cultural activities and community events. Some are sending e-mail newsletters to subscribers who want tailored packages of breaking news, sports highlights or movie and restaurant reviews. At first the big newspapers reacted fearfully to the Internet, seeing it as a destabilizing competitor, but by 2001 many of the major papers had decided it could be a means to strengthen their local franchises and expand their audiences into the regions around them and the rest of the country.

By 2001, about five years into the Web era, the more ambitious and better-funded news sites of major newspapers and television networks had attracted the great majority of readers and advertisers on the Web, while local newspaper and television station sites were struggling. But even the big national sites had to be subsidized by their old-media parents. Neither advertising nor other forms of revenue (mostly the resale of content for other purposes) produced enough money to fund an ambitious news site. As in the early years of radio and television, many advertisers are still uncertain about the effectiveness of advertising on the Internet. Yet the Internet built audience much faster than radio or television did, and it seems only logical that advertisers will find a way to exploit the eyeballs the Web attracts.

After Wall Street lost its enthusiasm for money-losing Internet businesses in 2000, a number of big media companies decided to reduce the red ink at their subsidized Web sites. The Tribune Company, Knight Ridder, the New York Times Company, NBC and CNN were among many that cut the staffs of their Web operations, even as they tried to increase their news content to attract larger audiences and more advertisers.

So the first period of journalism on the Internet was similar in many ways to the first period of "e-commerce," the selling of goods and services on the Web. Most Net-only enterprises failed, in retailing as in journalism. Once established brand names like Barnes & Noble and Wal-Mart learned how to use the Web to do business, they proved to be as strong in cyberspace as they were on land, while their Web-based competitors could not survive. Big news organizations also used the Web to defend their brand names and spread their journalism, although no old-media business made significant money from Internet operations.

. . .

Profits or no, the Internet is destined to remain a significant distribution channel for the country's biggest news organizations. Millions of people across the globe have already embraced the Web as a provider of journalism, and the number grows every day. As Internet service gets cheaper and faster and reaches more people, and reading devices become more portable and more sophisticated, use of the Web can only become more and more popular.

Web journalism has begun to alter the cultures of the big news organizations. Initially deep divisions were typical between the new staffs hired to launch Web sites and traditional newsrooms, where Web skepticism reigned. But these differences are disappearing. At the big news organizations, more and more reporters produce stories for the Internet and participate in online chats and Web videos. Traditional journalists have begun to see the Web as an opportunity to give readers background, details, graphics and photographs that won't fit into newspapers or television broadcasts, which now regularly inform readers that they can find additional information online.

The 2000 presidential election became an important laboratory for these changes. That something new was happening was evident at the party conventions, where Web sites took up positions on "Internet Avenues" in the work space for traditional journalists. Most noticeable were the futuristic news operations of MSNBC.com, CNN.com and ABCNews.com, which featured open TV studios in which network news personalities like Sam Donaldson and Cokie Roberts conducted panel discussions for video broadcasts on the Web. One of the webcasts that appeared regularly on the Internet during the conventions and then throughout the 2000 campaign was a *New York Times* discussion group featuring the newspaper's Washington bureau chief and political reporters, part of the *Times*'s Web and television partnership with ABC News.

During the election campaign and the month-long postelection recounts and court battles that followed, *Washington Post* political journalists produced up-to-the-minute coverage of breaking developments throughout each day for washingtonpost.com. They then wrote more in-depth stories and analyses for the next morning's newspaper, which were also put onto the Internet site overnight. They interviewed politicians in online forums and video webcasts and answered readers' questions themselves in online chats. Washingtonpost.com also featured live and recorded video, as well as full printed texts and transcripts, of candidates' speeches and press conferences. This blended the speed of broadcast news, the depth of print journalism and the limitless information capacity and interactivity of the Internet. Washingtonpost.com's audience on the Web tripled during the election. Its readers included hundreds of thousands of people around the world who would never be able to hold an ink-on-paper *Washington Post* in their hands. Research by the Pew Center showed that the number of Americans who used the Internet for election news grew dramatically during the 2000 campaign. According to the survey, 18 percent of Americans got political information from the Web, most of them from the sites of major old-media news organizations whose names and credibility they knew and trusted.

The success of the *Post*'s site altered the culture in our newsroom. By the morning of September 11, 2001, it was second nature for *Post* reporters to immediately start filing information to washingtonpost.com. "No one needed to be reminded that this story had to be covered on the Internet," said Tracy Grant, an editor responsible for rushing breaking news coverage to the Web site from the newspaper's downtown Washington newsroom.

*Post* reporters covering the White House, Congress, the Pentagon, the Justice Department, Wall Street and the air transportation system, among many others, wrote reports for the Internet throughout the day while also producing stories for the newspaper's "Extra" print edition that afternoon and its regular editions the next morning.

From the twelfth-floor offices of washingtonpost.com across the Potomac River in Arlington, Virginia, the Web site's executive editor, Doug Feaver, could see the smoke rising from the stricken Pentagon. Clearing everything else off the site's home page, he and his staff updated it around the clock with new information about the terrorist attacks from *Post* reporters and the wire services, plus video from the *Post*'s television partner, MSNBC.

Coverage of the terrorist attacks and subsequent war on terrorism demonstrated the Web's potential. The package of material available on washingtonpost.com resembled television coverage in some respects: it provided video of the big moments, and could be updated constantly. But consumers did not have to be watching all the time; they could view the video and other material at a time of their own choosing. The pictures were accompanied by written accounts much more detailed than any of the brief news reports broadcast on television. And the coverage was always available—no commercials or entertainment programming competed with it.

. . .

Trying to forecast the future of the Internet is probably futile. How predictable was the future of radio in 1921, or the future of television in 1951, comparable moments in the history of those two media? The Internet is just getting started.

Of the many unknowable facts about the future, perhaps one is most critical: what consumers will want and expect from the Internet five, ten or twenty years from now. Today using the Web is still pretty clumsy. The computers that provide access to it are much clunkier, harder to use and less portable than they will be soon. When your Internet "receiver" is as easy to use as your television today, when it provides moving pictures as vivid as a television's, when it can take oral orders from you and respond in kind, when you can easily take it anywhere, how will you use it?

It isn't difficult to imagine the Internet displacing television as we have known it. The evolution of both distribution technologies and receivers will quite soon give the Web all the advantages of television but none of the many disadvantages. Consumers will be able to watch whatever they want, whenever they want. Commercial interruptions will be easily avoided. Where television news is constricted by the relatively short time allotted to it, and by the fact that viewers can watch a news program only in exactly the order and form its producers choose, Web news will become a malleable product that can be shaped by every viewer to suit his or her tastes.

Such an evolution would wreak havoc with the economic model that prevails on television, which presumes viewers' willingness to sit still for some commercials if they want to watch whatever comes next. This is one of the ways in which television presumes the passivity of its audience. Another is the way news is presented on the tube, one item at a time. Of course this may be what many consumers want, even if they have an alternative. In modern America television has become an opiate as well as an entertainment medium.

The cardinal difference the Internet offers is the power to talk back— genuine interactivity. Choosing what to read or watch and when to read or watch it is the simplest form of compelling interaction. Internet users can also talk back to the news media, get answers to their own questions from newsmakers and journalists, participate in surveys, discuss the news with others online, take tours of remote places or assemble their own packages of information on various subjects. If a lot of them want to do this, traditional television will be in trouble.

These opportunities will threaten newspapers too. But the newspaper will retain many of its peculiar advantages, beginning with what may be the ideal way to put advertising in front of the public. It's already a simple matter to read a newspaper without looking at a single ad. Research has shown that almost nobody does that, however. And many newspaper readers say openly that they like the ads; some buy the paper *for* the ads. By contrast, early studies of the impact of "banner" ads on Internet sites suggest they are poorly read, and they don't appear to enjoy particular popularity with consumers.

Journalism won't exist without financial support—someone has to pay the journalists and the expenses of gathering news. National Public Radio has persuaded many of its listeners to pay for news through contributions to their local stations, and it augments this income with NPR's uniquely subtle commercials by businesses that want to reach its listeners. Perhaps a high-tech version of the NPR model will ultimately prevail on the Web. Tiny fees charged to Web readers could produce substantial revenues, assuming the number of readers keeps growing.

What has happened so far on the Internet has been a great giveaway of news content. Newspapers did it first, and television stations and networks followed. Advertising revenue has offset a fraction of the costs on the most popular news sites, but not yet enough to generate a profit. This can't go on indefinitely, especially if technological evolution makes the Web more user-friendly than the traditional media themselves. When a substantial proportion of NBC News viewers or *Los Angeles Times* readers are consuming those products on the Web, some way will be found to make the consumers pay, or make advertisers pay more to reach them.

No one yet knows definitively what Internet users ultimately want from news sites on the Web. The Pew Research Center's 2000 study showed that a growing number of better-educated Americans, who are generally more interested in the news, were watching television news less but reading news more often on the Internet. Perhaps, because these people regularly use computers both at work and at home, they find the Internet a more efficient way to catch up on the news whenever they want to.

Young adults aged eighteen to twenty-nine, who are generally less interested in the news, are the fastest-growing audience for news on the Internet. And they are watching news less on television and reading it less in newspapers. Perhaps they find it less demanding of their time and attention to skim headlines and news summaries while surfing the Web.

We know already that Web surfers like to use the Internet for headlines, quick updates on breaking news, stock quotes and sports scores. They like personalized news that delivers them headlines on subjects they have chosen. The popularity of the Internet sites of the *New York Times* and the *Washington Post* demonstrates that a market also exists for fuller news stories reported, written and edited by authoritative journalists. It's entirely possible, perhaps probable, that both appetites will survive into the unforeseeable future, but we can't be certain. Will tomorrow's Web readers be more interested in revelatory, original journalism? Or will they prefer raw information like texts, transcripts and unedited audio and video, or interactive features like online discussions and packages of news that cater to their individual needs and tastes, which are uniquely available on the Internet? Or might they just want headlines and brief bulletins?

The Internet sites of the major news organizations now offer all these and more. And they are working to create the kinds of mixed, interactive print, audio and video presentations of the news envisioned by MSNBC.com's Brian Storm and others. Internet users are beginning to migrate slowly from limited-capacity telephone lines to broadband fiber-optic cable being installed by both cable television and phone companies, which offers greater speed, more interactivity and better audio and video quality. Will Americans want to take advantage of these capabilities for higher-quality news coverage? Or will they prefer to use them primarily for entertainment, the way they use their televisions?

At least in its infancy, the Internet has disappointed those who predicted it would become a significant new source of original journalism. Instead, it has quickly become an important new means of distribution for the journalism produced by the established news media, giving more Americans access to the best journalism than ever before. This suggests to us that the work of the best news organizations, those with the strongest commitment to independent and original journalism, is most likely to find the largest audiences on the Web of tomorrow. But this prediction can only come true if the owners of those news organizations are willing to support the evolution of this new medium and take advantage of the opportunities it offers.

# Chapter Eight

# NEWS VALUES

The 1990s were not a happy decade for American journalism. A few fine news organizations continued to thrive, but many more suffered. The pressures from owners to make more profit undermined good journalism; frivolous subjects often displaced more important topics; celebrities became more important newsmakers than presidents and potentates. Many in the news business thought traditional news values were in grave jeopardy.

Then, on September 11, 2001, the news media were transformed. Confronted by a national catastrophe, reporters, editors and producers, columnists and anchors, even the proprietors, all knew what to do. They tossed aside commercial considerations to give Americans vivid, thorough, responsible and informative coverage of the biggest story of modern times. Readers and viewers devoured the coverage, watching and reading more news than they ever had before.

Those terrorist attacks had a profound effect on America's news organizations. Sandy Mims Rowe, editor of the *Portland Oregonian,* described it: "To have this affirmation of our importance to the democracy, and of our readers' need for detailed, comprehensive, intelligent information, will spur editors to do what we should have been doing all along. . . . We have blamed all of the trash that's been out there on our readers, and on our customers, and said that's what they want. But I don't buy that." Peter Jennings of ABC, heartened by the renewed interest in serious foreign news, said the coverage of the terrorist attacks and public reaction to it "should give us a new look at life."

Not surprisingly, the best news organizations did the best job covering this story, but nearly everyone in the news business made a memorable effort to serve readers and viewers. Seventy-five of the Gannett Company's ninety-seven daily newspapers published extra editions on the day of the terrorist attacks, and devoted many extra pages to the story in the days that followed. Network television showed no commercials for four days, an expensive decision. The journalism was not uniformly excellent, but the best news values did prevail.

The juxtaposition between alternative sets of values about journalism was stark. For much of the 1980s and 1990s, American news organizations had drifted toward softer, sillier, less significant journalism in a society that didn't seem to protest. Then an unanticipated national catastrophe reminded both the providers and consumers of news that good journalism was not just appealing, but absolutely necessary. Suddenly, the choices between soft and hard, silly and serious news values came into clear focus.

*News values:* the term isn't easily defined. Partly this is because values of all kinds are a slippery concept: it's much easier to proclaim the highest values than it is to uphold them by concrete actions. News values are also complicated because the meaning of the word *news* is not so obvious as it may seem.

When terrorists fly airplanes into skyscrapers, that's plainly news, but it is also a rare occurrence. In more ordinary times, Americans confront a bewildering array of information labeled news, from first light to lights out. Awakened by their clock radios, they can hear staccato headlines, last night's ball scores and the weather report. On an all-news commercial radio station they'll get a few more brief items, often rewritten from that morning's local newspaper, and the latest on traffic jams around town. The morning television news similarly consists of a few headlines and items revived from the previous night's late news. The networks' morning shows also provide a few headlines on the hour and interviews with people in the news. Before the war against terrorism began, these were more likely to be entertainers and other celebrities than government officials or experts on the news.

The local newspaper will provide more—a lot more local news, plus lifestyle, sports and financial news. In a relatively few cities the paper also contains significant national and foreign news. Most of the stories are about events—speeches, news conferences, court decisions, athletic contests. A good paper will also publish revelations, information discovered by good journalists that wasn't handed out in a press release or at a news conference. Some mornings good newspapers will surprise their readers with unexpected reports that are deep, thorough and engaging.

All day long the cable news networks—CNN, CNBC, ESPN, Fox Cable News and MSNBC—provide continuous headlines, live coverage of breaking stories and lots of chatter *about* the news, much of it mindless or tendentious. On the Internet, news sites also provide a vast quantity of information, from stock prices to serious, revelatory journalism. Many will send out e-mail news bulletins throughout the day to those who request them.

In the evening the local television news reports a few stories on the local events of the day, primarily those that are photogenic. The networks' evening news programs, which once emphasized hard news from Washington and overseas, became—before the terrorist attacks—steadily softer, more interested in health news and feature stories. Similarly, the prime-time newsmagazine shows like *Dateline* and *20/20* occasionally contained real news, but more often they were devoted to crime stories, celebrity interviews or both. After the terrorist attacks they began to pay more attention to more serious news topics.

Then just before bedtime the local stations return with the day's last news: usually a crime story to begin, then a recap of some of the day's news events, the ball scores, the next day's weather.

So much "news"—but is it really news? Are you watching news when you see stock quotes streaming across the bottom of the screen while commentators trade gossip about companies and markets on CNBC? Are the polemics hurled back and forth by politicians and pundits on CNN's *Crossfire* a form of news? Are the interviews with Hollywood personalities on *Good Morning America* or *Entertainment Tonight* news? Is that item about the eighteenth birthday of Britain's Prince William on the *CBS Evening News* a news story? What about the vivid video of a relatively harmless tornado on NBC's *Nightly News*? The melodramatic retelling of a sensational crime on prime-time *Dateline*? The local television reporter appearing "live" in front of police headquarters to say there were no new developments in the latest murder case? The political rumors on The Drudge Report on the Internet? What about the promotional special report on Keyport, New Jersey, in the *Asbury Park Press*—was that news?

There are so many pretenders, and so few clear standards. As news proliferated, its definition blurred. What really *mattered*? President Clinton, or one of his speechwriters, confronted that question in a speech to the annual convention of the American Society of Newspaper Editors in his last year in office: "I think it's hard to run a newspaper today in an environment in which you are competing with television news, Internet news sources, radio news and entertainment, which abuts on the news, and all the lines are being blurred. . . . The thing I worry most about is that people will have all the information in the world but won't have any way of evaluating it . . . [or know] how to put it in proper perspective. That's what I consider to be the single most significant challenge presented to all of you by the explosion of media outlets and competitive alternatives in the Information Age."

There is news as noise, news as wallpaper, news as spectacle, news as a constant drumbeat entering American minds through eyes and ears numbed by sensory overload. What indeed has news become, and how can the historic mission of informing the public be fulfilled? No editor listening to President Clinton could have stated the challenge any better.

A few weeks later Clinton did something unusual that proved his point, and compounded the problem. Speaking to the annual White House Correspondents Association dinner, he showed a very funny short documentary depicting, in *Saturday Night Live* style, his final months in office. In the video, made by Phil Rosenthal, director of the CBS sitcom *Everybody Loves Raymond,* Clinton was shown strolling and riding a bike through empty White House hallways, giving a press briefing to a single, sleeping reporter, and playing the board game Battleship with the chairman of the Joint Chiefs of Staff in the White House situation room. Wearing a casual shirt and trousers, the president surfed the Internet on a computer in the Oval Office, accompanied by a scruffy young actor familiar from television commercials. And as the nattily dressed senatorial candidate Hillary Clinton left the White House in a limousine, he chased after her, shouting and waving the brown-bag lunch she had forgotten.

Clinton's deadpan comic acting on the brief video created a sensation that itself became news. This was fiction; nothing real happened. But the video was the subject of numerous news stories. The evening news shows broadcast scenes from the tape. Pundits analyzed it for clues to Clinton's mood and the state of the country in the final year of his presidency.

This was not an isolated incident. Around the same time, ABC News hired the popular young actor Leonardo DiCaprio to interview President Clinton in the White House for a prime-time network news show about the environment. The interview and the show that would broadcast it were timed to coincide with the Earth Day 2000 rally on the National Mall in Washington. DiCaprio was the honorary chairman of this rally, and its emcee.

By traditional journalistic standards, this was a howler. Use a boyish actor to conduct an interview with the president of the United States? Make that a boyish actor who had openly, fervently taken sides on the issues that would be the subject of the interview? When word of this arrangement reached the news professionals in ABC's Washington bureau, they were livid. David Westin, the corporate lawyer whom ABC had cast as its president of news, responded to their anger with an e-mail to his troops in which he denied that DiCaprio had ever been expected to interview the president. "No one is that stupid," Westin wrote. "All roles of journalists must be played by journalists." But the White House undermined that assertion by disclosing that ABC had indeed requested a DiCaprio-Clinton interview. Westin then angrily accused his colleagues of leaking his e-mail to the press. But it turned out that Westin himself had orchestrated the leak, apparently thinking the e-mail would make him look better.

So how was this crisis resolved? ABC went ahead with the program, and with DiCaprio's interview—or conversation—with President Clinton, which ran on the air. And there was no great outcry from television viewers. Perhaps they understood better than the ABC journalists who had gotten so angry what to expect in 2000 from network television.

In the twenty years before the terrorist attacks, news values had changed, both for the American public and for many in the news media. The best news organizations tried to preserve traditions of seriousness and excellence, but many news media had turned in a different direction. They blurred once clear lines between news and entertainment, between serious news and the trivial, between news and opinion, between news that mattered and news shaped primarily to attract and entertain audiences to sell advertising and make money. Sometimes those lines disappeared entirely.

The national crisis that began in the fall of 2001 challenged proprietors and journalists to confront the choices they had made over the previous generation, to see their consequences and to try to return to a more rigorous definition of news. Would they? Could they? As we write, those questions cannot be answered.

The bad habits that developed over two decades would not be easily broken. But they *can* be broken: journalism is entirely the product of human beings who enjoy great discretion in deciding how to report and what to report—what to put on their news program or into their newspaper. The challenge will be to use that discretion to break the bad habits of two decades and alter the journalistic fashions they produced.

Those fashions—examples of late-twentieth-century news values—undermined good journalism. Half a dozen of them deserve elaboration, each one an unfortunate trend that took hold in the eighties and nineties.

The first was illustrated by the treatment of Clinton's White House video and DiCaprio's star turn as a reporter: *the rise of tabloid-style celebrity news.*

Americans have long been starstruck by celebrities. Our forebears loved Wild West heroes and villains and early Hollywood and radio entertainers, Roaring Twenties socialites and sports stars. Today the public is intrigued by high-tech billionaires, teenage entertainers, gun-toting rappers and almost anyone who appears on television or in *People* magazine. The electronic media have magnified celebrification, making nearly everyone we see in our homes on television or the computer screen appear to be both glamorous celebrities and people we know personally. That personal connection has created a powerful popular appetite for information about these celebrities, their lives and loves.

Appeasing that appetite was a cause that all the media embraced. Celebrity news filled newspaper lifestyle and entertainment news sections and increasingly turned up on the papers' front pages. *Time* and *Newsweek* put celebrities on their covers more often, and *People,* devoted entirely to celebrity news, became the most popular and profitable magazine in the country. Show business celebrity programs like *Access Hollywood, Entertainment Tonight* and *CNN Entertainment News* became fixtures on broadcast and cable television stations, usually appearing right after the local and network news each night. These programs looked and sounded a lot like the preceding newscasts, except that all the "news" was about entertainers and other show business celebrities, much of it staged to promote their movies, television shows and music.

News about celebrities also invaded the newscasts themselves. Rather described this as one of the biggest changes in the content of *CBS Evening News.* When he told us in 2000 that there was "more celebrity news on the broadcast than I would like to have," he acknowledged that he had been "slow to come to accept the view that public tastes have changed . . . what our expectation of news would be." The change was even clearer on the networks' morning news shows and their newsmagazine programs, including the venerable *60 Minutes* on CBS. Celebrity interviews and profiles proliferated on all of them.

Americans now have a closetful of shared experiences that came from the culture's preoccupation with celebrities during the 1990s: The O. J. Simpson murder case, the death of Britain's Princess Diana in an automobile crash in Paris, the Clinton-Lewinsky scandal and the death of John F. Kennedy Jr., his wife and her sister in the crash of a small plane he was piloting. Each was the subject of "wall-to-wall" saturation coverage on television, and filled acres of type in newspapers and magazines.

Events earlier in the television age had similarly captured the nation's rapt attention, including the assassinations of John F. Kennedy, his brother Robert and Dr. Martin Luther King Jr.; the Vietnam War; the Watergate scandal and the resignation of President Richard Nixon. But these were different—they all held real meaning for the well-being of the nation. And coverage of them consisted mostly of the reporting of significant facts without contrived drama or endless, uninformed commentary—like the coverage on and after September 11, 2001.

Robert MacNeil, former co-anchor of the *MacNeil-Lehrer NewsHour* on public television, watched old tapes of the coverage of President Kennedy's death and funeral after the 1999 death of John F. Kennedy Jr., and said he was struck by "how responsible and how careful and how dignified the coverage was. . . . [It] had a tone befitting a moment of national grief and it provided a vehicle for catharsis."

By contrast, "John Jr.'s accident was treated as though it had not only broken the nation's heart but scrambled its brains. Astonished, we watched an orgy of competitive gush and sentimentality that went on for hours and then for days, another installment in what is fast developing into a genre of its own: grief television, an unction machine ready to be switched on instantly and run until it has milked every tear in the nation and sucked up every fraction of an audience ratings point."

John F. Kennedy Jr. was the publisher of a struggling political magazine when he died. His celebrity came from memories of his father dying when John Jr. was a small boy living in the White House, his own rugged good looks and charismatic personality and his recent marriage to the fashionable Carolyn Bessette. Perhaps he might have played some important role in the republic had he lived, but at the time of his death, JFK Jr. embodied media-magnified fame without much underlying accomplishment. After he flew his small plane into the ocean off Martha's Vineyard late on a Friday night, television provided continuous coverage through the weekend, though there was little to report and, after the first few hours, little to say. So the cameras showed distant views of ships searching for wreckage, and anchorpersons conducted endless interviews with people who had nothing much to add.

The newsmagazines, with weekend deadlines, scrapped cover stories on other subjects (*U.S. News & World Report* had to throw away 1.8 million already-printed copies of its forthcoming issue) to rush JFK Jr. cover packages onto the newsstands the Monday after his Friday-night death. *Time* devoted thirty-seven pages to the tragedy; its Time Warner cousin, *People*, did even better: forty-one pages. Their publishers and editors knew this would be good for the magazines' circulation; *People* and *Newsweek* had each sold 2 million copies of issues devoted entirely to Princess Diana after her car-crash death two years earlier.

The *Washington Post* and other newspapers also gave the death of JFK Jr. the kind of coverage normally reserved for heads of state. Newspaper editors clearly were influenced by the saturation coverage on television, the enduring Kennedy mystique and their instinctive feeling that their readers were unusually interested in this story.

The news executives responsible for the coverage of young Kennedy's death compromised traditional news values to cater to popular tastes. Even the public seemed to think so. An interesting poll taken soon afterward found that 52 percent of Americans thought the coverage of Kennedy's accident was excessive, and 55 percent said they thought the news organizations that provided the excessive coverage did so to "attract large audiences," not because they thought it was an important story.

But wait. The public also devoured the coverage. It had high ratings on television. The same poll found that Kennedy's death was one of the most closely followed stories of the 1990s. Americans were as interested in it as they were in the death of Princess Diana; they paid more attention to Kennedy than to the O. J. Simpson case. The Monica Lewinsky scandal provided similarly conflicting evidence: Asked in polls if the coverage of it was excessive, majorities said it was. But when Lewinsky appeared on ABC with Barbara Walters, she drew one of the biggest audiences in television history. Lewinsky's thin memoir was a best-seller.

America is a big country; large numbers of Americans can hold, and act on, contradictory views of the same subject. But there is no doubt that a big audience developed for celebrity news, for salacious celebrity news, for stories that feature celebrity sex or scandal or both. Andrew Kohut, director of the Pew Research Center for the People and the Press and a pollster, told us in 2000 his surveys showed that about a third of the television-viewing audience was hungry for the big celebrity and scandal stories. In an era of fierce media competition for audience, advertisers and profits, that was a big pool of potential customers.

For the television networks, the O. J. Simpson case was an important turning point. From the beginning—the dramatic freeway chase of Simpson's white Bronco, captured by the airborne cameras of their Los Angeles affiliate stations—the networks jumped at the O.J. opportunity. NBC was the most aggressive, but all took part. For broadcast and cable television, the Simpson trial was huge, much bigger than for the country's newspapers.

"We did do more on O.J. and I wasn't completely comfortable with it at the time and I'm fully aware of that," *NBC Nightly News* anchor Tom Brokaw said when we asked about his show's Simpson coverage. "On the other hand, there wasn't a place that I went in America that people didn't have a huge appetite for a little more O.J., and when I look back over the long curve of our coverage during that time, I don't know of a story that we sacrificed just to get more O.J. on the air."

In fact, many important stories don't make the nineteen minutes of noncommercial time on evening news shows, so the minutes devoted to Simpson stories did crowd other subjects out. And Brokaw and his producers have complete editorial discretion over what appears on the *Nightly News.* Their decisions about how to use precious airtime convey to viewers and to their own colleagues at NBC what kinds of news they considered important. When NBC's *Nightly News* and *Today* gave the Simpson story so much coverage, proportionately far more than it deserved, that sent a powerful signal that the network's news values had changed. "We were trying to find our place" in dealing with that kind of story in a tight ratings race, Brokaw recalled.

When Peter Jennings of ABC talked about the impact of the Simpson case he portrayed himself as a protector of traditional news values against the O.J. onslaught. But in the end, he said, because of "a changing audience universe," his initial decision to try to hold down Simpson coverage had unwelcome consequences. "It was costing us to do what we thought was the right thing."

Although it isn't easy to say exactly how, tabloid values have changed many news professionals. Anna Deveare Smith, the playwright, captured this change in an interview with Walter Shapiro, a political columnist for *USA Today* whom Smith portrayed in her play, *House Arrest.* She got Shapiro talking about the impact of the Monica Lewinsky story, which first broke in January 1998. He said:

"I mean, there was a moment in December, January [1997], where I really was actively wondering whether I had made a totally wrong career choice. I mean here I am, growing up wanting to be a newspaper columnist, and I really thought that how come all the good stuff like the Cold War, Joseph McCarthy, Vietnam, happened on Walter Lippmann's watch, and I get Bill Clinton and the balanced budget? And then suddenly we had this [Lewinsky story]. And all of a sudden life changed. But let's make no bones about it. I mean, it doesn't get any better! I mean, this is life not only imitating art, it's doing better than art."

Shapiro wrote two columns a week for *USA Today* during the thirteen months of the Clinton-Lewinsky saga. Three-fourths of them were devoted to the story that changed his life.

Tabloidization reached a kind of apogee in the summer of 2001 in the matter of Representative Gary Condit (D.-California) and Chandra Levy, a young intern in Washington with whom Condit had an affair, and who disappeared at the end of April that year. Condit initially lied about his relations with Levy, so he was treated by many reporters and talk-show hosts as a suspect in her disappearance, though police repeatedly said he was not a suspect. By August Condit madness was ubiquitous, especially on the cable news networks, but also in other media.

"By my reckoning," said Rather later, this "was one of the worst hours [for the news business] in a lot of bad hours in recent history, of moving to the trivial at the expense of the important." Rather thought it was appropriately ironic that the terrorist attacks on the United States should follow so closely on the heels of the Condit frenzy. After September 11, he observed, "the center of gravity in American journalism shifted dramatically . . . back to serious news. . . . The question is whether this is a permanent shift."


Celebrity-consciousness contributed to a second important change in news values: *The rise of journalism about celebrities was accompanied by the rise of celebrity journalists.*

The network-news anchormen were leading examples. Added together, their three salaries totaled 150 percent of the entire cost of the *Raleigh News & Observer*'s news operation, including its staff of 260. In public the anchormen were treated like movie stars. Universities rained honorary degrees on them, their books were often best-sellers, young girls even screamed after spotting one of them on the street. These three men symbolized the fact that once-insignificant journalists had become some of the culture's most prominent and wealthiest celebrities.

Journalists contributed to confusion over where they stood in relation to the celebrities they covered. The big dinners that news-media groups held for themselves and politicians in Washington each year, and which were televised by C-SPAN on cable, became symbols of this. Washington correspondents for the television networks and major newspapers competed to attract the most prominent politicians and biggest Hollywood stars to their tables at the annual correspondents' dinners, and to the receptions their news organizations put on before and after the dinners. Warren Beatty, Annette Bening, Kevin Spacey, Michael Douglas, Sean Penn, Morgan Fairchild, Tom Selleck, Martin Sheen, Claire Danes and Kevin Costner were among those who socialized at dinners with congressmen, cabinet members and the journalists who covered them.

Michael Oreskes, who was then the Washington bureau chief of the *New York Times*, announced in 1999 that his newspaper would no longer buy tables at the White House Correspondents' dinner. "Partying in Washington with movie stars, celebrities and politicians is not the image of our profession that we should want projected to the country," Oreskes said afterward. But no other news organization followed the lead of the *Times*, and the soirees with the stars continued.

In turn, the news media gave accommodating coverage to Hollywood figures, like DiCaprio, who contributed their celebrity to various causes, from saving the environment and endangered species to campaigning for women's rights in Afghanistan and freedom from Chinese rule for Tibet. When these "cause celebs," as they were dubbed by *Washington Post* gossip columnist Lloyd Grove, were invited by Congress to testify at fact-finding congressional hearings, their views were dutifully reported by the media as though they were authoritative figures making news. After watching actress Goldie Hawn at a news conference where she called on Congress to defeat legislation liberalizing trade with China, the producer of *Hardball with Chris Matthews* brought her onto the CNBC news talk show to be interviewed by Matthews about the China trade bill.

But the most unfortunate trend was the conversion of working journalists into celebrities themselves. That anchors would become celebrities was probably inevitable, but it went far beyond that. Television news talk shows gave journalists the opportunity to become famous. Newspaper and newsmagazine writers and editors, previously unseen by their readers, became well-known personalities by going on the air to talk about the news.

This phenomenon reached a kind of apogee when a number of journalists who frequently appeared on the talk shows—including Paul Gigot of the *Wall Street Journal*, Eleanor Clift of *Newsweek*, E. J. Dionne of the *Washington Post*, James Warren of the *Chicago Tribune* and syndicated columnist Bob Novak—agreed to play themselves parodying their real-life roles in a television movie, *The Last Debate*, based on the novel of the same name by PBS news anchor Jim Lehrer. In the book, Lehrer savaged the Roman circus atmosphere of American political campaigns and much of the gladiator-style coverage of them by the media, including pundits very much like those playing themselves in the movie.

A more substantive manifestation of the impact of journalistic celebrity was visible in Buffalo, New York, in September 2000. Tim Russert of NBC was moderating a televised debate between the New York Senate candidates, Hillary Rodham Clinton and Rick Lazio. Russert came to journalism after a career in politics—he was press secretary to Senator Daniel Patrick Moynihan and Governor Mario Cuomo—and established a reputation as a rigorous, well-prepared cross-examiner in his role as host of NBC's *Meet the Press*. His continued success on that show made Russert a star; soon he was sitting beside Brokaw at big events as NBC's leading political analyst.

At the debate in Buffalo, two local journalists were invited to ask questions of the candidates, and Russert also joined in. Near the beginning of the hour-long program he told Mrs. Clinton he wanted to show a videotape. The MSNBC technical crew put on the tape of an interview with her in January 1998, on NBC's *Today*. The debate audience saw her denying that there had been any improper relationship between her husband and Monica Lewinsky. This was the same interview in which she said a "vast right-wing conspiracy" was out to get the president.

When the tape ended Russert asked, "Do you regret misleading the American people? . . . Would you now apologize for branding people as part of a vast right-wing conspiracy?"

Mrs. Clinton gave a flustered reply: "Well, you know, Tim, that was a very—a very painful time for me, for my family and for our country."

This was the most dramatic moment of the debate, more memorable than anything Lazio or Clinton themselves had to say. Russert's question had made him the center of attention. He took it upon himself to ask the candidate to apologize. A visitor from another planet would not have been able to distinguish the moderator from the two candidates—they seemed to be on an equal plane. That impression was reinforced by the fact that Russert and the candidates stood through the debate, while the two reporters sat behind a desk.

Such is the status of figures like Russert in American public life that almost no one criticized his performance in the debate. There was much comment about his question—how tough it was, how flustered Mrs. Clinton was in reply—but the reaction seemed to confirm that our most prominent television celebrities had moved well beyond the station of mere reporters, and were accepted as players in their own right. Only someone who saw himself as a player would bring, as "moderator," a provocative piece of videotape to show during the debate.

In the days that followed the terrorist attacks on New York and Washington, Russert again demonstrated his sense of his own status. When he interviewed Vice President Dick Cheney from Camp David on the Sunday after the attacks, he wore a large red, white and blue ribbon on his lapel. Two days after the attacks Russert held forth on *Today* in a discussion with host Matt Lauer. "Matt," he said, discussing public opinion, "the anger is just boiling over. You can feel it in every corner of this country. People want someone to pay a price for this, even if it means protracted war. And I believe that that only is going to build when we see the brothers and sisters of [the victims]. . . . We feel violated. We'll try to absorb it. . . . We'll do our best; we'll hold our flag high; we'll tell people—we'll be defiant, but we also know that we're going to be a lot more security-conscious and a lot more careful." Was this news analysis, or a political speech?

The status enjoyed by prominent television personalities may explain why careers in television have been so popular among former political figures. There's a revolving door now through which many of them have passed: George Stephanopoulos, David Gergen, Pat Buchanan, Jesse Jackson and Russert among them. Many elected officials have acted as though they considered prominent news-media personalities more important people than themselves. It's disturbing to think that in modern America, they may even be right.

Pontificating commentators symbolized another significant change in the news values of Americans and their media: *the substitution of talk, opinion and argument for news.*

Talk shows have become staples of public affairs programming on ABC, CBS and NBC, particularly on Sunday mornings. And they have helped fill the schedules on the twenty-four-hour cable news networks—CNN, MSNBC, CNBC and the Fox News Channel. They cost very little to produce because they do not require expensive news gathering, yet they create the impression that they are covering the news.

But the talking heads are not covering news, they are commenting on news. Early versions of these programs—the original *Meet the Press*, for example—used reporters to perform their proper role, asking questions. But the modern television talk show wants answers more than questions. So the reporters are expected to pass judgment. And to give the shows drama to attract viewers, the producers prod the participants to state strong opinions and make snap judgments. Many talk shows invite journalist guests for their ideologies, to be sure left will clash with right. Journalists who once were careful with facts often wind up performing like professional wrestlers, tossing around rumors, conjecture and opinions in verbal combat that amounts to playacting.

While the television talk shows give viewers the impression that they are engaging with the news, such shows seldom if ever produce new or reliable information. More often, participants mislead viewers with the sound and fury of their noisy arguments. "I'm still waiting for one of these Washington talk shows to deal with a fact," Brokaw said.

Trying to draw a meaningful conclusion from a talk-show argument is a daunting assignment, especially since none of the arguments are subjected to rigorous fact checking. In the era of talking—or shouting—heads, facts can lose significance altogether and be overwhelmed by emotionally expressed opinion. The ideologues who are often the stars of talk television regularly offer incompatible versions of "reality" as the basis for their opinions, but no effort is made to reconcile conflicting portrayals. Objective reality, once a goal for good journalists, becomes a meaningless category, lost in the heat of tendentious argument.

Opinion and argument posing as news coverage was pervasive during the long-running Clinton-Lewinsky scandal. A study of media coverage of the scandal found that about 40 percent of the coverage "in the first six days of the Clinton-Lewinsky story was not factual reporting at all . . . but was instead journalists offering their own analysis, opinion, speculation or judgments— essentially, commentary and punditry." At its worst, this commentary provided outright misinformation.

Both Russert, who also serves as the Washington bureau chief of NBC News, and Sam Donaldson, Washington correspondent for ABC and co-host of *This Week with Sam Donaldson and Cokie Roberts,* raised the possibility right after the Lewinsky-Clinton story broke that if the president was lying (as he later admitted he was), he might resign within days, which of course he never did. A few days later, Russert invited the notoriously inaccurate and cheekily irresponsible Internet gossip columnist Matt Drudge onto *Meet the Press.* The two of them discussed in all seriousness what Russert called "reports" and Drudge called "talk all over this town" that Lewinsky said Clinton had been involved with other White House staffers, an assertion for which no evidence ever appeared.

The Clinton-Lewinsky scandal, like the O. J. Simpson trial before it, became the sole subject of new talk shows on cable like *The White House in Crisis* on MSNBC. And it filled hour after hour of such established shows as NBC's *Today* and *Meet the Press* and CNN's *Larry King Live.* Round-the-clock talk about the scandal, whether or not there were new developments, attracted many new viewers to the twenty-four-hour cable news networks, including CNN, CNBC, MSNBC and the Fox News Channel. Chris Matthews, the former aide to House Speaker Tip O'Neill, author, journalist and loudly aggressive impresario of his own CNBC talk show, *Hardball with Chris Matthews,* exploited the Lewinsky scandal to build an audience for his show, and to win a multimillion-dollar long-term contract from NBC.

Matthews understood that he was in show business. This was clear from the way he explained his frequent use of the left-wing British expatriate journalist Christopher Hitchens on his program. Hitchens was "probably our most successful guest just in terms of his ability to be an incredible raconteur and all attitude about the Clintons, and fun," Matthews said. "Although he approaches the Clintons from the left, I think our viewers from the right appreciate his attack because it's more sophisticated than their attack, and they find it exciting."

Joining the journalists on many of these talk shows were nonjournalist talking heads, apparently chosen for some connection to the story, or their ability to argue, or just their good looks. President Clinton's critics were usually pitted against his defenders in animated verbal combat that grew ever more shrill as the scandal wore on.

A regular conservative critic of the president on many of the talk shows was Ann Coulter, a lawyer and formerly obscure legislative researcher in Congress. She parlayed her increasingly frequent and strident appearances as a Clinton attacker on cable television talk shows into a best-selling book about the scandal, *High Crimes and Misdemeanors.* Right from the start, Coulter added to the misinformation rampant on the talk shows by stating as a fact to talkmeister Geraldo Rivera that Clinton, in addition to Lewinsky, had had sex "with four other interns." On various shows, Coulter called Clinton "crazy," "a horny hick" and "creepier and slimier than Kennedy."

Coulter at least knew something about the Lewinsky scandal from her involvement with right-wing lawyers working against Clinton. Heather Nauert had only her blond, youthful good looks and a sincere desire to become a television star when she joined the world of talkers on the Fox News Channel. She had worked in her family insurance company and appeared occasionally on local television stations and a conservative cable network before popping up first on Fox, then on ABC, PBS, CNBC and

MSNBC. With no expertise whatsoever, she offered her views on every-thing from the Lewinsky scandal to national tax policy and student shoot-ings in high schools.

What were the thirty-year-old's qualifications? "When I first saw her I thought Heather was our demographic, that she could bring in younger people," Fox News executive producer Bill Shine said. "When you have a pundit who is young, and knows what they're talking about, they exude more energy. . . . If you've got a debate show, you want that energy."

All this talk, opinion and argument may not amount to much as news, but millions of Americans lumped it together with traditional news cov-erage. Matthews insisted that it really *was* news, provided by the reporters who appear on his show to talk. "We are a conversation which is occurring based upon all the reporting that people who are really reporters have had the benefit of before they get in the conversation," Matthews said. "So it would be like if you had a meeting in Washington in somebody's house and everybody had read all the papers that day, everybody had been reporting all day, and they all came together and talked about it and argued.

"In the course of the argument," Matthews said, "the facts would be presented, not necessarily in a sort of disciplined fashion, but the facts would be presented. They [viewers] would get a lot of information." He thought a regular viewer of his show would say, "I know what they're arguing about in Washington. I know what the issues are that seem hot. I'll probably know a few details."

Glib repartee and sharply partisan debate oversimplify the news, and render the issues of the day in stark black-and-white terms. This is the opposite of the effect created by a well-reported and carefully written news story, which is likely to feature the many shades of gray in which human reality is usually best painted. Reducing it to fodder for argument can also make the news seem more alarming, and public debate of the issues of the day less enlightening and civil. This not only can confuse Americans; it can discourage them from participating as citizens. Yet for the producers of talk shows, clashing views are not just desirable but essential to their art form. It's the clash that attracts talk-show audiences, because a good clash is entertaining.

That was another hallmark of late-twentieth-century news values: *news treated as entertainment, and entertainment treated as news.*

Entertainment has always been part of the news. Newspapers have published comics for nearly a century. The penny press of the nineteenth century and the tabloid papers of the modern era have emphasized entertainment value over serious journalism. The early days of the otherwise news-packed *Today* show featured the antics of a chimpanzee named J. Fred Muggs. But the balance between news and entertainment in the media, especially on television, changed dramatically in a very short time.

By the summer of 2000, CBS News executives thought it was appropriate for their struggling morning news program, *The Early Show,* to report regularly, as news, what was happening on the network's two popular prime-time "reality" entertainment shows, *Survivor* and *Big Brother.* Contestants on the shows competed for large cash prizes awarded to the last one remaining on a tropical island in *Survivor* or a group house in *Big Brother.* Each contestant voted off the island by the others or out of the house by the television audience was interviewed the next morning on *The Early Show.* The newsreader on *The Early Show,* Joyce Chen, also played the role of the commentator on *Big Brother,* and she hosted a prime-time program devoted to each week's developments on the "reality entertainment" show.

Was this appropriate behavior for a network news division? When a *New York Times* reporter asked the president of CBS News, Andrew Heyward, exactly that, he replied, "It's an experiment well worth taking on." Steve Friedman, producer of *The Early Show,* was blunter: "All I can say is: Thank God for *Survivor,*" adding that exploiting developments on the show as though they were news had significantly helped the *Early Show* ratings. He insisted it was not crowding any real news off *The Early Show.* "It's not like there's been a lot of news," Friedman said. "If I see one more story on gasoline prices, I'll choke."

For local stations, using local news shows to promote their network's entertainment programs has become routine, most often through interviews of the stars of the entertainment shows.

The 2000 presidential campaign provided a new lesson in the extent to which "news" and "entertainment" have merged. An extensive survey of voters during the campaign found that half of all Americans aged eighteen to twenty-nine said they got information on the presidential race from the late-night comedy shows. So Jay Leno and Dave Letterman had become political reporters. The candidates got the message too, and eagerly sought guest slots on entertainment programs, from Leno's and Letterman's to Oprah Winfrey's and Regis Philbin's.

If entertainment can make "news," so can news make entertainment. This is a lesson television mastered, most obviously on the networks'

magazine shows. These programs, which competed successfully with traditional entertainment shows in prime time, transformed the economics
of network news, and altered its aesthetics too.

The early models of news as entertainment were the "tabloid TV"
shows conceived in the late 1980s as television versions of tabloid newspapers. They featured stories of crime, sex and bizarre behavior, presented
in melodramatic narratives. The most popular of these pioneers were *A
Current Affair, Inside Edition* and *Hard Copy.* All were syndicated to local
stations. In an exhaustive study of their content in the mid-nineties, University of Illinois journalism professor Matthew C. Ehrlich found that
these shows' favorite subjects were the Mafia, sensational murders, prostitutes, deviant sex, celebrities behaving badly and exposés of fraud and
consumer abuse. "The formula is as old as tabloid journalism itself,"
Ehrlich concluded. "Crime, sex, gossip and human interest always have
been central to the genre."

MSNBC found that news alone did not attract the audience it hoped
for, so it added tabloid newsmagazines in prime-time hours to lure more
and younger viewers. Two of these shows, *Special Edition* and *Crime Files,*
featured crime, sex and other "real-life stories that are compelling, fascinating and somewhat sensational—if we're choosing them right, maybe
frequently sensational," MSNBC vice president Erik Sorenson told the
*Washington Post.* "On a slow news day, which most days are, it's a nice
alternative. To a younger news viewer, that generally is more appealing
than institutional news that is incremental and slow-moving."

The networks' hour-long newsmagazines—*Dateline, Prime Time Live,
48 Hours* and others—were the slickest, best-produced examples of the
genre. They often did stories like those that appeared on *Hard Copy* and *A
Current Affair,* but did them more professionally, using highly paid network anchors and correspondents. Soon they blew away the original
versions, which died or withered.

The model network magazine show had been *60 Minutes,* which presented serious investigative reporting in a dramatic narrative format for
several decades. The *60 Minutes* formula has always included celebrity
interviews and other lighter pieces, but the new generation of magazine
shows took them much further. They often tried to create a *60 Minutes*
feel, but their subject matter came mostly from the staples of tabloid journalism. Movie actors and rock stars, prostitutes, mass murderers, child
molesters, illicit lovers and victims of dread diseases paraded across the
television screen in what looked like news shows, presented by familiar
network news personalities. This was a little like printing the *National*

*Enquirer* in the format of the *New York Times*, with the bylines of *Times* reporters.

The newsmagazine shows did very well in the ratings and made a lot of money for the networks' news divisions during the late nineties. "It is not just that the programs are inexpensive to produce," noted Ehrlich. "It is also that the exposé, the staple of both tabloid and investigative news, is ideally suited for prime time. A dogged reporter digging up dirt on somebody or something, regardless of who or what it may be, makes great television similar to police or detective shows: good guys chasing bad guys."

We were reminded of the newsmagazine approach to journalism when the *Washington Post* and NBC agreed to collaborate on investigative projects that could appear in the newspaper, and on NBC's *Dateline*. At an early meeting, one of the NBC producers told *Post* editors what the ideal *Dateline* story should contain: "A villain, a victim and a confrontation."

These shows did occasionally present serious investigative reporting, particularly about consumer and medical subjects. But in Tom Brokaw's words, the magazine shows were too "down-market, because that's where they get their audience." The better journalism that sometimes appears on the magazine shows "just gets lost with the other shit that's on there," Brokaw said.

"I know that there's a lot of fussing over the magazine shows . . . and whether those are real shows or whether they're entertainments," Brokaw's boss, Andrew Lack, said. "They're produced by news divisions for a reason. They're full of information, they're usually pretty well written, and they're not full of shit, and if they were produced by an entertainment division, they would be. So whether you think they're too flashy, or they're too taken with themselves, or they self-promote, or are theatrical in ways that are not your cup of tea, all fair game, the fact of the matter is that those shows would be off the air if it weren't that the information they report is accurate, is very carefully looked at by serious journalists."

Peter Jennings said in 2000 that he sympathized with those at his network who insisted that ABC's *20/20* "does some very good things." But he added that "I'm not prepared to wade through all that stuff in order for you to come up with a piece of reporting that's really relevant or interesting to me. . . . They now do too much of the same thing. They're very serious bottom feeders, and therefore a whole chunk of the audience has just gone away and done other things." Jennings said he feared that many of those viewers also have "left the evening newscast because they're just fed up with television."

Dan Rather said that the profitability of the prime-time newsmagazines on CBS meant that his *Evening News,* with its more costly news gathering, had become "no better than the fifth priority" of CBS News. "The priorities are *60 Minutes, 60 Minutes II, 48 Hours, The Early Show* and the *Evening News,*" Rather said. "We have gone from being the number-one priority to being sort of a bastard child. We cost money; we don't make nearly as much money as the others."

One-fourth of the stories on the networks' prime-time newsmagazines were about crime and justice, according to a 1997 Project for Excellence in Journalism study, and half were "people stories, lifestyle/behavior, news you can use and celebrity entertainment." Only 8 percent of the prime-time newsmagazine stories were about education, economics, foreign affairs, the military, national security, politics or social welfare issues. Since "most of television's in-depth news coverage and the vast majority of its investigative reporting occur on these programs," the study concluded, "it means investigative work in network television today for the most part does not concern" such serious topics.

After September 11, 2001, the formula for the magazine shows abruptly changed. Initially they did stories only on the terrorist attacks and their impact. Many were human interest stories about survivors or the families of those killed; many others were stories about past terrorist acts, the career of Osama bin Laden and the new hunt for him and his associates. But there were also serious pieces of foreign reportage.

Peter Jennings worked on ABC's *Prime Time* and *20/20* in the days after September 11. "They are very set in their ways and their theories of what a prime-time audience wants," he told us in October 2001. Yet Jennings thought it was possible the magazine shows would become more interested in hard news subjects, including foreign news, as a result of the new war on terrorism. "I would look there for the first signs of change," he said.


The fact that hard news had become much harder to find on television before September 11, 2001, demonstrated another important change in late-twentieth-century news values: *Government, political, foreign and other news of importance to people's civic lives was largely supplanted by crime, weather, health, consumer, investor, entertainment and other news believed to be of more interest to viewers and readers in their personal lives.*

This was most obvious on television, beginning with the networks' evening news programs, which carried many fewer reports from foreign countries and from Washington than they had fifteen or twenty years earlier. By one careful count of the time devoted to foreign coverage, the three evening news programs broadcast 4,032 minutes of foreign reports in 1989 (a high point—the year the Berlin Wall fell), and 1,382 minutes in 2000. "We moved away from what we call 'process news' " about government, politics and foreign affairs, Lack explained in 2000. "It's easy news to report, but it isn't real news. We believe in health news, consumer news, the war on cancer, the war on drugs—a lot of domestic issues that I felt were under-covered."

In interviews in 2000, all three network news anchors described the latest fashions in news as adjustments to a prosperous, contented post–Cold War America. Brokaw said, for example, that there was "no return" for the network to put stories from Africa on "the number-one newscast in America"—his *Nightly News*. But NBC would broadcast stories from Africa anyway, he said, because "it's something that is important for them [his audience] to at least get exposed to, we think."

In interviews, each of the three anchors depicted himself as the protector of what remains of the traditional news values, occasionally able to perform the noble act of reporting stories from foreign lands despite the evisceration of the networks' foreign staffs. Brokaw and Jennings defended the new news values, arguing that they gave their viewers different kinds of information important to their daily lives.

Television executives like Lack believed that old-fashioned news could not succeed in the modern marketplace. So they largely abandoned it. This meant not just fewer stories from overseas but much less attention to national politics in this country as well. The First Amendment to the Constitution was written on the assumption that a free press would pay attention to politics, but the modern television networks moved beyond that idea. They let cable cover politics. A television viewer with cable could get extensive exposure to the candidates and hear quite a lot about the issues. But nearly a third of American households don't have cable, and cable programming remains much less popular than the shows on the major networks. At many times during the day, the audience watching CNN, Fox News or MSNBC is smaller than 100,000 people. In mid-2001, the average number of daily viewers of all three cable news networks (CNN, MSNBC and Fox) was 735,000.

Lack of interest in politics was even more obvious at local television stations, at least in their news departments. Local stations in battleground states enjoy windfalls every two years from political advertising, but few of them tried seriously to cover the campaigns. And local television stations outside state capitals rarely sent a reporter to the seat of state government or tried to cover the state legislature.

Declining television coverage of politics and government dragged down the country's civic life. Voters had less information when they went to the polls. National and local politicians complained bitterly that it was impossible to discuss important issues or launch serious new ideas on broadcast television, because the networks and stations had no vehicles other than Sunday-morning talk shows that permitted extended discussion of political or policy topics. When the medium that most Americans rely on for news reduces its coverage of government and politics, government officials and politicians can safely conclude that the country is paying less attention to them and to what they are doing. That can easily lead them to misbehave.

The weekly print newsmagazines, once a vibrant part of America's news culture, also followed the modern fashion away from political and policy subjects toward emphasis on celebrities and news you can use. A serious news story on the cover of *Time* or *Newsweek* became almost a surprise; the cover stories were much more likely to be on lighter subjects. The news-gathering organizations of both magazines have been significantly reduced over the last quarter century.

Newspapers have participated fully in this shift away from coverage of politics, government and the world. The viewer whom Walter Cronkite used to advise to consult his daily newspaper for a full account of world events couldn't do that today in most American towns and cities. A majority of newspapers of all sizes studied by the *American Journalism Review* in early 2000 printed less than a page of foreign news daily. Most papers printed only slightly more about the national government and politics. The sad truth is that only a handful of American papers give their readers enough news to make them well-informed citizens of the country and the world.

None of the fashionable experiments of the eighties and nineties to try to win new readers for papers included increasing the emphasis on foreign or national news. On the contrary, many editors and publishers shrank their national and foreign news coverage to make room for increased coverage of local, business and lifestyle news they considered more attractive to their readers. "Fewer and fewer newspapers carry significant national reports; some pretty major American dailies have just about eliminated them," said John Carroll, the executive editor of the *Los Angeles Times*.

When Linda Crist Cunningham, editor of the *Rockford (Illinois) Register Star*, was asked how much foreign news she published each day, her answer was, "Not enough." Yet "when I listen to readers," Cunningham said, the demand for world and national news "is second only to the demand for local news." She said her readers know that "manufacturing companies in Rockford have deep ties to the Far East, to Germany, to Australia and all around the globe." But her newspaper, owned by the high-profit Gannett chain, typically published barely a page and a half of national and foreign news each day.

Like Cunningham's readers in Rockford, newspaper readers generally rank national and foreign news right after local news in importance, ahead of sports, business or other subjects that appeal to devoted but narrower audiences. This was the common result of readership surveys long before the terrorist attacks of 2001. But editors and publishers looked elsewhere for readers. When in 1999 the Associated Press asked more than 150 of them about their future plans, very few mentioned foreign or national coverage. Many expected to increase their newspapers' coverage of business, technology, sports, entertainment, health and fitness news.

The existence of the global economy did not persuade many news organizations to spend money on correspondents abroad, or to cover the State Department and foreign affairs in Washington. A number of newspapers reduced or eliminated foreign correspondents and State Department reporters during the nineties. Only the *Washington Post,* the *New York Times,* the *Wall Street Journal* and *USA Today* increased the number of their foreign bureaus during that decade.

Before September 11, 2001, most of the American news media gave scant coverage to the fact that the United States was the key participant in an interdependent global society, or that our economic well-being depended on foreigners, or that our population included millions of people born in foreign lands, more every year. John Carroll of the *Los Angeles Times* observed that foreign coverage had been declining in many American newspapers for thirty years. "You don't have foreign correspondents or space in the paper, and you don't have editors and staff members who are conversant with the issues and with the world beyond our borders, so foreign news is easy to ignore a lot of the time."

This indifference—so exasperating to foreigners who thought the last superpower should be showing more interest in its global neighbors—was the subject of much discussion after the 2001 terrorist attacks, when foreign news suddenly became fashionable, and personally compelling too. "When people want it, they want it desperately," Carroll said. "The audience can't get enough" foreign news about the terrorists, their allies, their hiding places and so on, Rather said soon after September 11. Sandy Rowe of the *Portland Oregonian* said she thought how well a newspaper covered the foreign aspects of the terrorism story was a basic measure of its quality and usefulness to readers. Her paper published thousands of words from overseas in the weeks after September 11. But Linda Cunningham's *Rockford Register Star* published very few.

Coverage of the national government also did not improve in the nineties. Newspapers could not hold accountable agencies and departments they did not cover, and they covered fewer of them than in the recent past, according to a 1999 study by the Project on the State of the American Newspaper, a project sponsored by the Pew Charitable Trusts, whose results were printed in the *American Journalism Review* in 1998 and 1999.

The overwhelming majority of newspaper reporters posted in Washington reported on news of local interest to their readers, including their congressional delegations and actions by federal agencies that affected their communities. In 1999 only about a dozen newspapers still had beat reporters covering the Defense Department, the Justice Department and the U.S. Supreme Court, and only a handful regularly covered the Internal Revenue Service, the Social Security Administration, the Environmental Protection Agency, the Food and Drug Administration, the Federal Communications Commission or the Departments of Agriculture and Labor. No newspaper at the time of the survey had a beat reporter covering the Department of the Interior, which controls 500 million acres of federal land and runs the National Park System. Specialized publications and newsletters cover all the agencies, but usually for tiny audiences of concerned professionals, not for the general public.

The federal government is covered rigorously, however, compared with the way America's newspapers cover state governments. State government is an enormous enterprise in the United States: The states employed just under 4 million public officials in 1997 (a year later the federal government had 2.8 million employees), and spent (in 1999) about $904 billion (more than half the federal budget). State policies are more likely to affect the lives of Americans than federal policies in areas like health care, child care, welfare, education and support for the elderly. The states' importance in these fields has grown steadily since the early 1980s. Corporate America has noticed this change; corporations and interest groups have hired hundreds, probably thousands, of lobbyists in the state capitals in recent years. But the country's newspapers seem indifferent. Another State of the American Newspaper study found that papers cut back their coverage of state governments in the eighties and nineties, while the experience level of statehouse reporters declined. Even good papers often send only one or two reporters to the state capital; many papers send no one at all. This makes it unlikely that many state agencies are ever covered by a reporter. And quantity of coverage is less important than quality. In-depth coverage of state government by experienced reporters is actually rare in the United States. The majority of state governments is never subjected to such attention from a first-rate news organization.

The drift away from serious coverage of serious subjects was part of the most important change in American news values in the last years of the twentieth century: *Covering the news, once seen primarily as a public service that could also make a profit, became primarily a vehicle for attracting audiences and selling advertising, to make money.*

The big corporations that owned the television networks, most local television stations and the overwhelming majority of newspapers, with very few exceptions, cut back their news organizations, curtailed their ambitions for serious news coverage and tried to pander to perceived public tastes to build audience and thus attract more advertisers. They did these things with an aggressiveness that altered the rules of the game for American news professionals. Most newspaper editors and television news executives lost any sense of insulation from the economic pressures on their owners.

In many news organizations, once well-defined walls between news gathering and the selling of advertising eroded, risking a cynical response from news consumers who had increasing reason to wonder if news coverage had been corrupted by the influence of advertisers. Newspapers published special-interest news sections requested by, or entirely devoted to, groups of advertisers without labeling them as such. Some newspapers sponsored special events with advertisers, or published special sections with a sponsoring advertiser and shared the advertising revenues. Local television stations broadcast advertiser-generated news segments and covered events put on by advertisers in exchange for commitments to buy more commercials from the station. The television networks shaped the content of their newscasts and prime-time newsmagazines to attract the kind of audience by age, gender and interests that advertisers wanted to reach. Both the networks and their affiliated stations used their newscasts to promote their entertainment programs, and manipulated the news programs to try to increase their viewership.

Unannounced commercial relationships between television stations and advertisers who were also featured on news broadcasts were an especially insidious form of corruption. Consider the arrangement between Mercy Hospital and WBAL television in Baltimore, first struck in 1994. The hospital would buy advertising on the station to help launch its new women's health center. The station would broadcast a new regular feature called "The Woman's Doctor" during the 5 and 11 p.m. newscasts every Monday, and again on Tuesday and Saturday mornings. "The Woman's Doctor," produced by WBAL's news department, featured guests, both patients and doctors, from Mercy Hospital. At the end of every segment, WBAL's medical reporter referred viewers to a help line where they could get more information.

This worked beautifully for Mercy Hospital. According to polls of the Baltimore market, before the WBAL deal was launched, Mercy ranked seventh among Baltimore hospitals when people were asked what hospital they would recommend to a friend for women's care. A year into the new arrangement with WBAL, Mercy ranked fourth. Two years later it ranked first (in the hometown of one of America's finest hospitals, Johns Hopkins Medical Center). By 2000 "The Woman's Doctor" had been running on WBAL for seven years. Its title was copyrighted by Mercy Hospital, which used the name in its advertising.

Neither the hospital nor the station would say how much Mercy paid WBAL, but it must have been hundreds of thousands of dollars a year. Bill Fine, the general manager of the station, defended the arrangement adamantly. Did Mercy Hospital buy access on WBAL's news? "The answer is no," Fine said. "They buy advertising time. Separately from that, they help us provide information to our viewers." There's no question of selling content on the news, Fine said: "We retain total editorial control." This is Orwellian language. The station retained control, provided it met its contractual obligation to put Mercy doctors and patients on the air. WBAL's viewers were getting a weekly feature on women's health, always featuring Mercy and always referring them to Mercy's telephone number, not because any news producers or reporters decided this was the best way to use that airtime but because WBAL's advertising department had made a lucrative deal with Mercy Hospital. According to officials of other hospitals, such arrangements are now common around the country.

Viewers already suspected that their local news was not entirely pure. A

1998 poll conducted for the Radio and Television News Directors Association found that 84 percent of Americans believed that advertisers "sometimes" or "often" improperly influenced news content on the air. And 43 percent of television news directors, surveyed in a companion poll, agreed with them.

Newspaper industry surveys showed that the readers of American newspapers also suspected that advertisers influence news coverage. Sadly, they too had good reason for such suspicions. One such was the notorious deal struck between the *Los Angeles Times* and the Staples office supply company in 1999. The *Times* would become a sponsor of the new Staples Arena in downtown Los Angeles, and would publish a special section about the new arena, implicitly giving it a boost. The arena would help sell advertising for the special section to other sponsors, and would share advertising revenue with the newspaper. When some midlevel editors in the *Times* newsroom became aware of what was going on and raised questions, no one, including the then editor of the *Times,* stopped it. When an alternative paper in Los Angeles and then the *New York Times* wrote about the arrangement, a scandal erupted. But the deal seemed to follow the mandate of Mark H. Willes, who was then the CEO of the newspaper's parent company, Times Mirror, for "closer cooperation" between the news and business departments at the *Los Angeles Times.* After the Tribune Corporation bought Times Mirror in 2000, Willes, the publisher and the editor involved in the Staples controversy were all replaced.

That one of America's best papers would compromise itself in this way was sad enough. Worse were the results of a survey of newspaper publishers and editors conducted at the end of 1999 by the industry journal *Editor & Publisher.* Half of the sixty publishers responding to the survey found the Staples deal to be an "acceptable" practice for newspapers. One-fifth of the 105 editors responding to the survey agreed. Three of every four editors and publishers surveyed said they believed that the traditional separation of news from advertising was "sometimes" or "frequently" violated by newspapers. And four of every ten said their own papers had published special news sections to obtain certain kinds of advertising even when they knew the sections' content had "little reader interest." Perhaps these are the fruits of a system in which editors are paid handsomely when their newspapers meet the profit targets set by senior management.

Distorting the news to make money is corrupt in a straightforward sort of way. More subtle is using the news to promote a brand or a company.

Here the payoff is inexact, often immeasurable, but still sometimes irresistible. Local television stations report as news community promotional events featuring their anchors and other station personalities. Newspapers use their news columns to promote community events sponsored by the paper itself or to organize "civic journalism" events like candidate forums during election campaigns—both practices that give the paper a chance to promote its name and its community role.

When CNN staged and broadcast one of the 2000 campaign's debates between the Democratic presidential candidates, Al Gore and Bill Bradley, promotion of CNN and its parent company, the media and entertainment giant Time Warner (even before its merger with AOL), was ubiquitous. The logos of *Time* and CNN and their Web sites were visible in every camera shot inside New York's Apollo Theatre, where the debate was held. The theater itself, a historic landmark, is run by a board largely appointed by AOL Time Warner. The debate's moderator and journalistic questioners all worked for CNN and *Time*. Other Time Warner journalists had special access in the theater. Time Warner CEO Gerald Levin shook hands with the candidates and mingled with reporters after the debate. Was this a political debate, or an advertisement for Time Warner?

When George W. Bush tried to change the plans agreed to by both political parties for a series of three October 2000 debates with Gore, he suggested as an alternative that the two candidates appear on a special, prime-time edition of *Meet the Press,* moderated by Russert. This would have given a scoop to NBC, but it would have undermined the arrangements—negotiated over months by the nonpartisan Commission on Presidential Debates—for debates that all the television networks would broadcast simultaneously, ensuring a vastly bigger audience. NBC happily embraced Bush's idea, which network executives obviously saw as a boon to them, if not to the country. NBC News gave Gore a hard time for refusing to accept this idea. Later, after Bush agreed to take part in the originally planned debates, NBC announced it would offer its affiliates a baseball playoff game as an alternative to the first debate.

Many news media learned the arts of salesmanship and of pandering, and eagerly pursued both. But a successful pander is a two-party transaction. Our subject is the American news business, but the business doesn't operate in a vacuum. Its lifeblood is the audience, the American public, whose tastes and choices determine the success of any pitch made to it.

Traditional news providers operating before the era of celebrification and commercialization took for granted the public's interest in "the news." Partly this was a noble sentiment. Of course, citizens of a democratic republic would care about their communities, their government, their world. That assumption reflected in part an important fact: Until the modern era, "the news" was consistently the most entertaining aspect of everyday life that the mass audience of Americans could easily share. The crowds that went to hear Abraham Lincoln debate Stephen Douglas around Illinois in 1858 were there in large measure because Lincoln-Douglas was the best—and often probably the only—show in town.

Most modern news providers did not assume that the public was instinctively interested in their product. There were momentary exceptions—during the Gulf War, for example, or after the suspenseful 2000 presidential election, when the winner was not yet known. But the fashionable assumption among many news executives in the 1980s and 1990s was that Americans had lost interest in traditional hard news. And they had evidence. Opinion polls showed that droves of young adults (for advertisers, the most desirable demographic segment) just didn't care about government, politics, foreign countries or serious journalism. Surveys showed a steadily declining number of Americans who said they "enjoy keeping up with the news," down to 45 percent of all adults in 2000, and to 31 percent among eighteen- to twenty-nine-year-olds. Comparative surveys showed that Americans were, on average, much less knowledgeable about current affairs than the Germans, French or British, for example.

There was no consumer rebellion when the networks cut back on foreign coverage. No popular movement demanded more national news on television and in the newspapers, or better coverage of state and local governments, or less entertainment and celebrity-watching packaged as news. In a time of broad prosperity and relative tranquility, Americans happily consumed entertainment in countless packages, including packages labeled "news." And they happily bought the products advertisers tried to sell them while they consumed those entertainments.

On September 11, 2001, everything changed. In the course of a few hours the United States was transformed from a fat and happy enclave of peace and prosperity to the shaken victim of terrorist attacks. News organizations, from the best to the weakest, realized immediately that all previous assumptions had been overtaken by events, at least for a time.

In Los Angeles on the morning of September 11, the *Times* chartered a Gulfstream jet to take reporters and photographers to New York—an expensive gesture that didn't bear fruit until Thursday, when the plane was finally allowed to fly. In San Antonio, Bob Rivard, editor of the *Express-News,* put five photographers and reporters into two Jeep Chero-kees and pointed them at New York, where they arrived thirty hours later, in time to file for the paper of September 13. In Minneapolis, the *Star Trib-une* put twenty-one extra pages into its main news section for September 12 to cover the story. The networks began their four long days of uninter-rupted round-the-clock coverage that was thorough, compelling, digni-fied, intelligent and careful. Only two cable networks made serious mistakes: CNN, in misattributing the September 11 attack on Kabul, and Fox, by luridly holding its cameras on the spectacle of desperate people jumping to their death from the burning World Trade Center.

Throughout the news business, everyone understood they were partic-ipants in an event of transcending historic significance. Owners and man-agers, apparently without exception, told their news organizations to do whatever was necessary to cover this story. Unanticipated declines in advertising had already made 2001 a bad year for profits, and the terrorist attacks further eroded the bottom line for every news organization in America. Optimists hoped the investment would ultimately pay off. One was John Carroll of the *Los Angeles Times:* "I have a gut feeling that the bond we are building with readers [through aggressive coverage of the terrorist story] is going to be worth a lot of money over the long haul," he said three weeks after the attacks. "But in the short haul you lose a lot of money." Yet the Tribune Company, owner of the *Times,* had only encouraged the paper to do what it considered necessary, Carroll said. No one on the business side had complained.

Americans consumed this news coverage voraciously. The *San Antonio Express-News* printed 50,000 copies of an extra edition on September 11 and quickly sold them all. "We could have doubled it," said Rivard. Three weeks later the paper was still selling 10,000 copies more than its usual cir-culation of about 230,000. Papers all over the country had similar experi-ences. Most Americans watched television coverage of the disaster, which had the biggest audiences of any news broadcasts in American history. News executives across America reported enthusiasm among viewers and readers for their journalism. Sandy Rowe, editor of the *Portland Oregon-ian,* passed along what she called a typical e-mail message from a reader named William Fouste:

"Thank you for the fantastic amount of information you have been publishing about Islam, the Middle East, and Southeast Asia! I, and many other readers, have learned a great deal in the last few weeks. My wife, not a regular reader, has really worked hard to digest all the information about a part of the world most of us are so woefully uninformed about."

The same American public that seemed, a short time before, so willing to accept the pandering of many news media was suddenly hungry for hard facts about the threat to their country. Without doubt, the threat made an enormous difference in public attitudes.

In fact, though, there were already indications that Americans weren't as indifferent to news, and especially to big stories, as some insisted they were.

The same 2000 poll that reported declining enjoyment in keeping up with the news asked Americans if they agreed that "news is not as important today as it once was." Only one-fourth of respondents said they agreed with this statement, while three-fourths disagreed with it. News still mattered to Americans before September 11, 2001, or at least they said it did. Perhaps the sense of declining enjoyment from following the news had been more a reflection on the news than the citizenry.

Andrew Kohut, the pollster who found that a third of the public constituted an eager audience for celebrity-scandal coverage, pointed out that most other Americans actually disliked that journalism, especially when they saw a lot of it. Pandering to the eager third risks turning off everyone else, Kohut said.

The work of careful researchers like Kohut has demonstrated that sweeping generalizations about "what people want" from their newscasts or newspapers are invariably wrong. The real hallmark of our age is the fragmentation of the American public, typified by the 100-channel cable television systems that now come into most American homes. The proliferation of magazine titles is another indicator. In 1988 there were 13,541 magazines published in the United States; by 2000 there were 17,815. In a society whose members generally feel independent, empowered and entitled to pursue their own tastes and interests, we now have a fragmented media marketplace. But the fragments do not stand alone; they interact and overlap. Individual Americans can belong to many different fragments. It's complicated out there.

That complication had intimidated owners and managers of news organizations, whose goal had been to attract fragments into as big an audience as they could. Intimidated, uncertain executives hired "expert" consultants and market researchers, who, to earn their fees, came up with formulaic recommendations for how to build that big audience. Both newspapers and television succumbed to fashionable gimmicks—often promoted by those market researchers—for trying to hold or build audiences, despite the fact that the gimmickry rarely proved very successful.

Reliance on research and experts is characteristic of our times. Something very similar happened in politics, where pollsters and consultants largely took over the roles of candidates by determining, through modern market research, which issues would move voters, then concocting campaigns built around those issues. Douglas Bailey, a prophetic voice among political consultants, explained the consequences of sophisticated political technology back in 1988: "The biggest problem is that it's no longer necessary for a political candidate to guess what an audience thinks. He can do so with a nightly tracking poll. So it's no longer likely that political leaders are going to lead. Instead, they're going to follow."

Interestingly, the "audience" for politics shrank in the years that modern political technology ruled our campaigns; voter turnout in the United States became the lowest in the industrialized, democratic world. Similarly, the audience for news, especially television news but for many newspapers too, shrank during the age of market research and pandering to perceived public taste. We can't prove a causal relationship, but it's tempting to speculate.

What intimidated executives have feared is that their competitors would outpander them and win the contest for higher circulation or higher ratings, and thus higher profits, with sleazier programs and publications. This fear has also been characteristic of our times, which have been marked by a pervasive sleaziness in many realms: television, movies, popular music, popular literature and fashion among them. Compared with earlier eras in America's cultural and intellectual history, the end of the twentieth century was a decadent time. Decadence affected news just as it affected pop music and much else.

But decadence should also be seen as a consequence of social fragmentation. Most Americans have not covered themselves in tattoos or pierced their noses; most Americans get no kick out of misogynistic rap lyrics. The popular song may have gone to the dogs, but America has more symphony orchestras than ever before. It's complicated out there.

You have to wonder why more news-media owners and executives hadn't noticed the fact that the country's best news organizations are also enormously successful. No really fine news product has failed in the marketplace since the *New York Herald Tribune* went out of business in 1966. America's very best newspapers all have made handsome profits, and have steadily broadened the scope and improved the quality of their news coverage. *60 Minutes* has remained a huge commercial success, and the best magazine show on television. In many markets the leading local television news station has been the one offering the highest-quality news. National Public Radio is the favorite news source of millions of Americans. The Internet sites that offer the best news coverage—those of the television networks and the best newspapers—attract some of the biggest audiences on the Web.

But quality is hard. No market researcher or consultant can teach a news organization how to be good. That requires years of tradition, persistent high standards, intelligence and determined professionalism. Unfortunately, frivolous news values were easy to embrace, easy to pursue and easy to defend as the best way to cope with a competitive marketplace.

That last argument—always disputable—became much more dubious after September 11, 2001. In the words of Andrew Heyward, the president of CBS News, the terrorist attacks "showed the network news divisions something that we really knew in our heart of hearts all along, that you can do well by doing good. . . . It's almost as though this story was so big it kind of shocked everybody into focusing on what we do best and what we should be doing best."

Journalists in other news organizations that, like CBS, previously might have been "distracted" (Heyward's word) from the pursuit of serious journalism must have had similar reactions to the terrorists' attacks. Those terrorists issued an unmistakable warning to professional journalists to return home.

# Chapter Nine

# THE FUTURE OF NEWS

errorist attacks on the United States revived interest in serious journalism—a hopeful development for the news business, born in horror. But there is no guarantee that a brighter future lies ahead.

Economic forces have held the upper hand in American journalism for the last quarter century. Pressure to be more profitable blew like a gale through the country's news organizations, changing the personality, mission and ownership of all but a handful of the biggest news providers in the country. The CBS television network has had four different owners during the past quarter century, the venerable *Baltimore Sun* newspaper has had three. Some local television stations and smaller newspapers have changed hands half a dozen times. Different ownership has most often signaled different values for news organizations, changing the way they produce news. Too often the changes have been for the worse: smaller news staffs, and less ambitious coverage. The terrorist attacks did not remove those economic pressures, and the recession that began in 2001 aggravated them.

Many news people were caught off guard by the way economic forces blew through their business. By the second half of the 1990s—even before another damaging round of cuts in staffs and coverage in 2001—a crisis of confidence was evident in American journalism. Owners who had forced many news organizations to shrink in size and ambition, or to distort the news to pander to the basest perceived instincts of viewers and readers, were an important cause of that crisis. So was anxiety about adverse public reaction to journalistic overkill of stories like O. J. Simpson's arrest and trial. Journalists feared a general loss of their credibility. Opinion surveys showed declining public confidence in the news media. In the summer of 1997 a group of prominent journalists and former journalists issued a sort of manifesto, a "Statement of Concern," which said in part:

Many journalists feel a sense of lost purpose. There is even doubt about the meaning of news, doubt evident when serious journalistic organizations drift toward opinion, infotainment and sensation. . . . Journalism can entertain, amuse and lift our spirits, but news organizations also must cover the matters vital to the well-being of our increasingly diverse communities and foster the debate upon which democracy depends. The First Amendment implies obligation as well as freedom.

From this manifesto grew the Committee of Concerned Journalists, a group funded by the Pew Charitable Trusts that organized meetings around the country where journalists could vent their worries and discuss how best to shore up or restore the standards of their profession. In 1999 the committee published an extensive survey of opinion among journalists that confirmed the malaise in the profession.

A majority of those questioned said business pressures were hurting the quality of their news product. Business-side media executives who were questioned in the survey disagreed; most thought business pressures merely altered the way things were done in the newsroom, without affecting quality. Three-quarters of the journalists surveyed said the pressure to attract audiences had pushed the news industry too far toward entertainment. Just over half the business-side executives agreed.

Journalists were sharply self-critical. Large majorities said they and their colleagues had gone too far in blurring the distinction between news and commentary, and had become obsessed with "being first with the big story and impressing their colleagues." More than 70 percent agreed that the news media pay too little attention to complex issues. About half said the news media lack credibility with the public.

Three prominent social scientists who studied the attitudes of successful journalists in the late nineties found pervasive gloom. After interviewing their eighty-five subjects for hours, the authors concluded that these journalists were "almost twice as likely to characterize recent news media changes as negative than as positive." In discussing the trends in the business, they were "four times as likely" to evaluate them negatively. Specifically, "they decry a desperate clawing for market share that, they believe, is eroding the integrity of their domain."

The magazines devoted to the news business—especially the *American Journalism Review*, the *Columbia Journalism Review* and the *Nieman Reports*—published dozens of articles on the crises that beset the industry. All this soul-searching and self-examination was without precedent. And it was justified by the facts we have described in this book.

But we don't share all the pessimism. Even before the heartening response to the terrorist attacks of 2001, there were signs of good health in some provinces of the news media. America's best news organizations became stronger in the nineties than they had ever been. At the *Wall Street Journal*, the *New York Times* and the *Washington Post*, news staffs had never been more talented, and their journalism had never been more ambitious. Thanks to the Internet, their work was much more widely read than ever before.

A number of important regional papers improved significantly in recent years, including the *Dallas Morning News*, the *Portland Oregonian*, the *Raleigh News & Observer* and the *New Orleans Times-Picayune*. During the last quarter century a distinguished news organization has grown up, National Public Radio, which maintains a corps of talented foreign correspondents and covers Washington and the nation with a serious sense of purpose. C-SPAN, the cable network that brings congressional hearings and debates and many other public forums into America's living rooms, has given the public access to many events of public interest and importance previously unavailable to them.

Another sign of journalistic good health is the coverage given to business and finance. When we entered the news business thirty-five years ago, financial news coverage was minimal and deplorable in most general-interest publications. Today newspapers, magazines, television and Internet news sites are providing thorough, sophisticated and useful coverage of business and finance, subjects of great importance to the country.

Even the hand-wringing self-examination that beset journalism in recent years was a positive sign. It demonstrated that many men and women in the news business understood the difference between good and bad journalism, and believed that good journalism was crucial to the health of society. They saw themselves as professionals who embraced high professional standards, even when they weren't allowed to pursue them. High professional standards are relatively new in American journalism. They have evolved over the last century or so, and continued to develop even under the commercial pressures of recent years. Obviously, standards can still be raised much higher, but the professionalism of America's journalists has already become a defense against bad journalism. Professional journalists often serve as a kind of loyal opposition inside their own newsrooms when management tries to compromise standards to make more money. The resignation in 2001 of Jay T. Harris as publisher of the *San Jose Mercury News* in protest against budget cuts was the noble act of a very loyal professional whose self-sacrifice resonated throughout the newspaper business.

Good journalistic standards have also infected American society. The Supreme Court has repeatedly reinforced them in decisions affecting the press. Even Americans who don't like the news they're getting tell opinion pollsters that they believe in the value of a free press and its role as a watchdog in our democracy.

More watchdogs keep their eyes on the news media than at any previous time. Journalism reviews, alternative newspapers, magazines, Web sites and academic journals all publish regular critiques of local and national news outlets. A few newspapers and newsmagazines have assigned reporters to cover the news media as a full-time beat. The Pew Charitable Trusts has funded useful research that has held news organizations accountable for their work. A craven publisher or station manager who would like to kowtow to an advertiser has to fear exposure in one of these outlets, a welcome change.

The fact that some news organizations improved during the era of profit maximization is important. The high profitability of the best news organizations is even more important. It's conceivable that owners will come to realize that high-quality journalism and commercial success can coexist in the news business. Conceivable, however, does not mean inevitable, or even probable.


We've been around too long, and surprised too often, to make predictions about the future. But we can pose questions whose answers will determine what will happen to news in this new century:

> • *When most American households have high-speed, high-powered Internet connections that can bring video, sound and text into the home and onto electronic reading devices that are as easy to use as a television, a book or a magazine, how will that technology affect the way people get their news?*

Such fabulous devices and pathways are certainly in our future, perhaps just five or ten years away. Gurus of the new age have been predicting for years that when the whole country is wired with broadband Internet connections, and armed with amazing new portable reading devices, traditional news media will be blown away.

But we doubt it. The history of new media is instructive: radio did not eliminate newspapers; talking movies did not destroy radio or newspapers; television did not obliterate radio, newspapers or movies. For nearly a century, Americans have made room for and taken advantage of new technologies without turning away from old ones that are still useful or fun.

And new technologies are just delivery devices. What might actually *appear* on those whiz-bang new reading devices of the future? And who will provide that content?

News does not grow on trees, and raw data is not the same as journalism. Some bits of data—ball scores, stock prices, weather conditions—are interesting in their own right, but most data and facts become useful to people only when they are organized, put into context, evaluated and digested. And of course much important information is not readily available but must be dug up by resourceful investigators called reporters.

Improving technology has already made more and more information available to each of us, and will continue to do so. But more is not necessarily better. We think that the more raw information there is available, the more consumers will need professional journalists to sort through it for them, find the wheat and reject the chaff, organize the important information in an easily digestible form, check to be sure it's accurate and display it in a way that reflects its importance. Journalists make sense of things—that is their function. A data-rich world, all interconnected by the Internet, will generate a great deal of confusing information that won't be useful until someone makes sense of it.

In other words, even when amazing, still-unimagined new gizmos make the transfer of information fast, easy and fun, the art of journalism will still be necessary. We're convinced that people enjoy a news product that provides a coherent overview of what is happening in the world— like a good newspaper. A good newspaper is not just a random collection of news items but a carefully prepared package of stories, opinion pieces and columns, photographs and graphics, comics and television listings, well-written feature stories, entertaining sports reports and much more. It is produced by a large staff of smart, hardworking people who think carefully about what it should contain. Television newscasts are produced in the same way. Every commercially successful news product, even on the Internet, is edited and organized for the consumer.

We're even hopeful that the newspaper itself can survive the technological future. The humble ink-on-paper newspaper turns out to have been a technical marvel, far ahead of its time. It is shareable, easily portable, compact and clipable. It can be read nearly anywhere, at any time, now or later, all at once or in snatches. It is not just a conveyor of news and information but a physical package that offers tactile pleasures, and also the serendipity of bumping into a story or photograph that catches one's interest by surprise. A good newspaper has its own personality, with which readers identify, and brings many different personalities, from public officials to columnists and comic strip characters, into the lives of its readers. It combines news of the world with commercial information in the form of advertisements from merchants and manufacturers that appeal to numerous citizens. When well made and well sold, the newspaper can also be very profitable.

In the future, technology may provide better ways to sell ladies' dresses, men's shirts or cars than newspaper advertisements do today. Internet services are already taking away some of the classified ads that are so important in today's newspaper economics. If newspapers lose their economic viability, they won't be able to support the big staffs that are needed to cover the news well. Warren Buffett, the legendary investor, whom we have gotten to know from his service on the board of directors of the Washington Post Company, has declared that he is becoming more pessimistic about the future of newspapers simply because they have lost their monopoly on retail advertising. A big metropolitan paper once enjoyed "a bullet-proof franchise," he said in an interview, because merchants needed its readers to sell their goods. Now they have lots of alternatives, which in the long run will erode newspapers' position. At the same time, Buffett is buying new printing presses for the newspaper he owns, the *Buffalo News*. The erosion in newspaper franchises that he foresees "won't happen tomorrow . . . or next week or next month," he said, "but ten or fifteen years from now, it will look a lot different."

So far newspapers are holding on. They may prove to be the last real mass medium in America, as television channels continue to proliferate, dividing and subdividing the television audience into smaller and smaller slivers. Like a number of big-city newspapers, the *Washington Post* today reaches far more Washingtonians than any competing medium—any other publication, television network, local TV station or radio station. And as the Internet grows more popular, it appears to be taking audience away from television, not newspapers.

Still, there's no denying that the traditional ink-on-paper newspaper is at risk. The biggest immediate danger is the decline in the quality of many newspapers. If they fail to provide information that is important to their communities and their readers, their claim on those readers' loyalty will weaken. And this is now a real danger. Even good newspapers face new competitive challenges. They're not cheap to produce or deliver, whereas electronic news products are both. And a paper can't be read until many hours after it is produced, a definite drawback in an age of instant communications and gratification.

But the overriding importance of great newspapers to the health of American society remains indisputable. Today only great newspapers support big, ambitious news organizations committed to extensive coverage of American society, politics and government, the economy, sports and entertainment, and also to covering significant events in every country of the world. Only great newspapers systematically provide the factual information, interpretation and commentary that make the American system work. The journalism that the great newspapers produce is the basis of the shared knowledge and experiences that make us a relatively self-aware and cohesive society. If cultural and economic forces undermine newspapers' ability to play their historic role without creating a substitute for them, Americans will be woefully ill informed.

The automobile prevailed over the horse and buggy because it was so much more efficient at getting people from one place to another. When—if—the Internet and its offspring enjoy a similar advantage over newspapers in collecting, assembling and delivering the news, then Internet-based news products could prevail. But even then, they'll only be electrons on a screen, not something tangible that can be folded, carried around town, torn or clipped, saved or reused at the bottom of a birdcage. Already, the most successful newspapers are building complementary audiences for their printed editions and their Internet sites.

Conventional television news may actually be at a greater risk when high-speed connections allow computers, or handheld reading devices, to carry motion pictures that the consumer can select from a huge menu. Why worry about catching Tom Brokaw at 6:30 when your computer or two-way wrist television will give you a Brokaw-like experience whenever you want it?

- *If the twenty-first century is to be an information age, what does that mean for journalism? Specifically, what will the inhabitants of an information age want or need in the way of news?*

We would like to think that Americans will want more and better journalism to help them survive and thrive in an information-heavy world, where knowledge provides a competitive edge. If they do, the demand for better journalism could increase the supply.

Arguably this has already been happening. Over the last several decades, the best newspapers have moved from a somewhat stenographic and narrow approach to reporting the news to a much richer diet of sophisticated stories about complicated subjects. As American society and the American economy have gotten more complex, so has the best journalism about them. The same is true of foreign reporting. American correspondents for the best news organizations are much more likely than a generation ago to speak the language of the country they are in, to know its history and culture and to spend a prolonged period of time there developing expertise. Newspapers that have made these improvements— including the *Wall Street Journal,* the *New York Times* and the *Washington Post*—have been rewarded by their readers with continued loyalty. All three have many more readers than they did a generation ago, including an expansion of their audiences via the Internet.

Still, large segments of American society remained indifferent to good journalism about the world they lived in, though their number appeared to decline sharply after the terrorist attacks of 2001. Before the attacks, young people seemed particularly disinclined to pay attention to what was happening outside their private worlds. On the eve of the 2000 presidential election, the MTV network released polls showing that a quarter of eighteen- to twenty-four-year-olds didn't know who was running for president. Seventy percent could not name the vice presidential candidates. The threat of war got young America's attention in late 2001, but those earlier findings suggested that the civic education of young Americans would take a lot of effort.

The reaction of young people to the war on terrorism was instructive. As soon as they saw a threat to themselves, they flocked to the news—like most Americans. Suddenly the emerging generation looked like a market for journalism.

This great interest in news about the struggle against terrorism was one powerful reason to be optimistic about the future demand for good journalism. Terrorism is one of many difficult challenges that lie ahead, all of them complicated and hard to understand. Americans will also need good information to monitor and understand the changing environment of the earth; to master a competitive global economy; to keep watch on governments at all levels as political power is diffused to states and localities; to closely observe the publicly owned corporations that we now realize are so important in our lives. The demand for good journalism *should* increase in the future; the need for it certainly will.

- *Will economic pressures continue to push down the quality of journalism?*

So far the record is not encouraging. As we've discussed, the news organizations most fully exposed to the raw power of the modern marketplace generally have not improved in quality, although many of them thrived economically under managements that mastered the art of squeezing profits from newspapers and television stations. Those that have gotten better generally enjoyed some protection from the power of the marketplace, usually in the form of family control or venerable tradition.

The basic pattern is now painfully familiar: Managers in search of higher profits insist on reduced costs. In journalism, the most malleable cost item is people—reporters, editors, newscast producers. It's also tempting, at a newspaper, to reduce its consumption of expensive newsprint by cutting the space for news; or, at a television station, to eliminate all original, innovative and time-consuming reporting by requiring all correspondents to put one or two stories on the air every day. This is how news quality was reduced at countless papers and television stations, and at the networks, during the 1990s. At most papers and television stations, the process recommenced in 2001, when advertising revenue dropped off suddenly.

John Morton, the country's leading financial analyst of newspaper companies for many years, has accused owners who curtail news coverage to cut costs of "eating their seed corn." In an interview, Morton told us that some managements are undermining their own interests by weakening newspaper franchises for the future. Like many of the editors we interviewed, Morton said he believes that the papers that will thrive in the long run are the ones whose readers find them the most interesting, most compelling. Yet today's corporate owners often aren't thinking about a long term at all. As a result, they may not have one, or it may be much less profitable than today.

- *Can America's finest news organizations survive?*

The concept of a great news organization is an important part of our view of journalism. We have tried to illuminate some of the differences between the very best organizations and others that are less ambitious, less committed. Like a great university or a great company, a great news organization has its own culture of excellence, a sense of its place in the world, a set of reflexes that govern its behavior in moments of crisis. Its traditions dictate an overriding concern for getting the story, giving the reader or viewer the best possible report on what is happening around them. Its journalists absorb the organization's standards and expectations, and act on them by instinct.

Most important, a great news organization can count on wonderful people who are committed to it, and are willing to sacrifice personal comfort and well-being to carry out its commitment to inform Americans. In the best newsrooms reporters and editors really do talk about their responsibilities to readers or viewers, and about their First Amendment obligations. There is a powerful streak of idealism in the best news organizations.

American society has benefited greatly from the traditions of the great news organizations. They have helped us through great national traumas, taught us unpleasant truths about ourselves, forced us to confront ugly realities many would have preferred to avoid. Yet there is no law that guarantees their good health or survival. The existence of great news organizations depends on their owners. Ownership can change. Even well-intentioned ownership can fail, as when, for example, the Bingham family failed to successfully manage and protect the *Louisville Courier-Journal*. Blessed are those media executives who have learned how to make the money needed to support the newsroom *and* report a healthy profit.

The best newsrooms are supported by big businesses that generate a lot of cash. They are all publications with vast audiences. The *Wall Street Journal* and *New York Times* have specialized, elite readerships across the entire country, but the *Washington Post, Los Angeles Times* and *Dallas Morning News*, to name some of the best, are mass media in their home communities, supermarkets of news and features that appeal to a wide range of people. One question for the future is whether such broadly targeted, general-interest publications will be undermined by new niche products aimed directly at specific subgroups of their readership.

Even the best owners and the happiest economic circumstances cannot guarantee the good health of a news organization. Good newspapers will have to be steadily more authoritative on a growing number of subjects to protect their place in the world. To do that, they must attract bright, dedicated men and women who think news is a calling that deserves their very best energies. Will some of the best and brightest young people continue to be attracted to high-quality journalism? Can an industry whose entry-level positions exist mostly in small cities and towns, in newsrooms that pay low salaries and often do mediocre work, compete against much higher-paying employers for the best talent? Good newspaper journalism has always depended on the idealism of talented people willing to pursue news careers for their intangible rewards.

A great news organization is difficult to build, and tragically easy to disassemble. CBS News was a great (and extravagant) news organization until the mid-1980s; now it is the least ambitious of the three networks, a fallen star. The *Philadelphia Inquirer* has been deeply shaken by a steady drumbeat of cost cutting, upheavals in its newsroom management and the departures of dozens of talented staff members. Bad things can happen to good newsrooms.

The biggest practical issue for the future is how to maintain thriving businesses that can pay for great news organizations. It's impossible to imagine the economics of news-delivery systems that haven't been invented, but there are grounds for hope that today's great newspaper organizations could survive as the leading news providers in whatever medium shares or takes the newspaper's place. Already, the Web sites of the *New York Times* and the *Washington Post* are among the most popular for news on the Internet, and the *Wall Street Journal*'s is supported by subscription revenue. We expect such news organizations to find their place in an electronic future.

- *Might the corporate owners of news organizations eventually decide that their best interests are served by encouraging better journalism and spending more money on covering the news?*

This just might happen, in one of several ways.

The first is straightforward: High-quality journalism does make money, and in competitive markets, higher-quality news products generally win out over lesser ones. America's finest news organizations are among its most profitable.

"Journalistic excellence and profitability go hand in hand," wrote Katharine Graham, the late publisher of the *Washington Post,* whose paper became vastly more profitable after its reputation was transformed by the Watergate story.

Gannett, Knight Ridder and other newspaper owners found ways in the 1990s to ratchet up the profit margins of their monopoly newspapers, but they did so at the expense of quality and ambition. They raised advertising rates and subscription prices while cutting costs, including newsroom costs, but rarely if ever sold more newspapers. Many local television stations followed similar tactics, increasing profits while watering down the news, but losing audiences as measured by steadily plummeting ratings. These owners demonstrated that profits can rise even when quality doesn't. But will ordinary newspapers with declining readership be able to extract steadily rising revenues from advertisers? Or will the improving papers—the *Raleigh News & Observer*, the *Portland Oregonian*, the *Dallas Morning News*—be more successful over time?

Even if the improving papers do better than the declining ones, Gannett, Knight Ridder and the other chains so focused on short-term profits may be trapped in a downward spiral. They have continued to encourage Wall Street analysts to expect steady growth of their profits, which over time they may not be able to provide. Wall Street will then push down the value of their shares. And the owners may then desperately seek still more short-term profits. This is what happened in 2001, when a sudden economic downturn and sharp declines in their stock prices prompted Gannett, Knight Ridder and other news providers to again cut costs—and news coverage—to try to preserve or increase profit margins.

If, five years from now, it is obvious that the news organizations that continue to invest in the news, improve their coverage and make it more important to their readers and viewers are the most commercially successful, surely that will have an impact on the owners of other properties. Or so we can hope.

Another way that owners could be convinced to invest in better journalism was suggested to us by Richard Leibner, an engaging, emotional man who has made a handsome living as the agent for numerous television news personalities. It was Leibner who in 1980 negotiated Dan Rather's ten-year, $22 million contract, which changed television news forever. "The competition for a broad audience has brought journalistic standards down" on network television, Leibner said in 2000. The fundamental change has been going on for forty years—a slow, steady shift in television's journalistic standards that accelerated in the last twenty years—from "what does the public *need* to know to what does the public *want* to know." This, Leibner said, is what caused the tabloidization of so much TV news.

Yet Leibner described himself as "hopeful" about the future of network news even before the terrorist attacks of 2001. In 2000 he connected his hopes to the process of consolidation that was steadily reducing the media and entertainment industries to a handful of huge corporations. "When you end up with four or five companies dominating the culture of the universe," Leibner told us, "commanding the public's respect" will become much more important to those four or five companies. Partly this will be commercial pressure, a need to maintain a quality brand name in a competitive environment. Partly it will be public relations—a perceived need to cultivate the image of a good corporate citizen by firms with a pervasive presence in American life. Partly it will be self-interest: "Having the confidence of the public is worth something," Leibner said. If you can get the public's attention with good news programming, you can sell them other things too. He speculated that someday, network owners would realize that it was valuable to them to have great news coverage.

The overwhelming public response to network coverage of the terrorist attacks in 2001 affirmed Leibner's theory, he thought. Perhaps it would mark the beginning of a "renaissance" for network news, he said in October 2001. The fact that the overwhelming majority of Americans turned to the three major networks for coverage of those events showed, Leibner said, that "the broadcast networks cannot go out of the news business. If they ever gave it up, then they'd be telling a big piece of their audience, you don't have any reason to be loyal to us anymore."

Leibner's most famous client, Rather, is ready for an enlightened new approach with his idea for a daily, prime-time, one-hour CBS news broadcast. But his attempts to sell the idea to CBS executives have been unsuccessful.

Rather is unabashedly old-fashioned; he talks all the time about journalism as a public service. But as his own CBS News demonstrates, modern corporations generally haven't found this idea very enticing. And in our day there haven't been many public-spirited tycoons who have chosen to launch or rescue a news organization with their millions, as Eugene Meyer did when he decided to buy the *Washington Post*. This might happen again; there certainly are vast new fortunes that could finance journalistic enterprises. Bill Gates of Microsoft toyed with the idea of trying to make his company an information provider; he settled instead for one online magazine, Slate.com, and partnerships with NBC for Internet and cable television news organizations. But Gates or another like him might someday take the plunge.

Because it's true that really fine news organizations can thrive as businesses, there will always be a basis for risking serious money to try to create one. But publicly traded companies that worry about their results quarter by quarter and must explain their decisions to Wall Street analysts are not going to be in the forefront of the risk takers.

The fate of the news will inevitably be decided by the citizens of America, and by what they do with their country. This is a society that can change quickly and profoundly, as demonstrated by the experiences of some of today's Americans, whose lives span an extraordinary slice of historical time: from the Great Depression through the Grateful Dead to the greatest horror of modern times, the crumbling towers of the World Trade Center.

In the quarter century before that cataclysmic event Americans had passed through two successive postwar eras, which have traditionally been times of frivolity and self-preoccupation. First came the post–Vietnam War era, which arguably continued right through the 1980s, when the country was given time to recover from the traumas of the sixties and seventies. Then, at the end of the eighties, the organizing principle of America's public policies for nearly half a century, the Soviet-American Cold War, disappeared. So the nineties became a post–Cold War era, another period of rest and relaxation after a long period of stress and anxiety.

In the fall of 2001 stress and anxiety returned; those postwar eras were over. It's never possible to see the shape of the future, but it seems destined to differ profoundly from the immediate past. We've entered something new and different now. Americans have been jolted into international action, forced to abandon their comfortable perch above the global fray. Whatever else is coming, we can confidently predict that it will be a compelling story, and a great time for good journalism.

But will it also be a great time for the news business? It certainly should be. Modern technology has shrunk the world, created huge new national and global audiences for American journalism, and given journalists great new tools with which to do their jobs. In the last several decades, smarter, better-trained journalists have taken their profession to new levels of insight, sophistication and revelation. Journalists have learned how to cover the world around us better than ever before, and, after September 11, 2001, Americans seemed more interested in that world than they had been in decades. This truly is an information age, and good journalists are among society's most reliable and helpful guides through it.

Nevertheless, the future is uncertain. The trends have been running in the wrong direction. Too many owners of news organizations have sacrificed good journalism in the pursuit of greater profits and popularity—despite the economic successes of the country's highest-quality media companies. Too many once-distinguished news organizations have lost their luster; too few new ones have materialized.

The fate of good journalism in the new century will be a leading indicator of the health of American society. If new generations of Americans are indifferent to good journalism, it cannot thrive. If economic pressures and unenlightened managements continue to depress the quality of the news, the country will suffer. If those with power in society are not held accountable for the way they use their power, they will misuse it. If communities cannot learn what they need to know about themselves, they will be less vibrant and successful than those with good news organizations to help them confront their needs and their failings and recognize their successes.

The benefits of good journalism are not hypothetical, but obvious and palpable. News is an important part of the American culture. The United States will be a better place if its citizens can get from the news what they need to know to govern themselves effectively and improve their lives.

But they'll only get that news if they demand it. In the end, the most important people shaping tomorrow's news won't be the owners or the journalists, but the readers and viewers. As long as they create a market for good journalism, there will be good journalism. That's the good news.

NOTES

ACKNOWLEDGMENTS

INDEX

# Notes

*Chapter One:* News Matters

6 **Citizens cannot function:** Michael Schudson, an insightful academic commentator on American news media, has described what's in the news as "public knowledge," the shared body of facts, impressions, public personalities and so on that constitute the American culture at any given time. "When the media offer the public an item of news, they confer upon it public legitimacy. They bring it into a common public forum where it can be discussed by a general audience," Schudson wrote in *The Power of News* (Cambridge, Mass.: Harvard University Press, 1995), p. 19. A professor of communication and sociology at the University of California, San Diego, Schudson has written several excellent books about the news. He has helped us understand what we do in a new way, and his thinking has influenced this book. See also *Discovering the News: A Social History of American Newspapers* (New York: Basic Books, 1978).

13 **he wrote a friend:** Merlo Pusey, *Eugene Meyer* (New York: Alfred A. Knopf, 1974), p. 256.

*Chapter Two:* Americans and Their News

15 **"The Penny Press":** Michael Schudson, *Discovering the News,* pp. 22–23.

19 **And according to press historian:** Michael C. Emery and Edwin Emery, *The Press and America: An Interpretive History of the Mass Media,* 7th ed. (Englewood Cliffs, N.J.: Prentice Hall, 1992), p. 276.
   **During what Northwestern University:** David Abrahamson, "Magazines," *Media Studies Journal,* Spring–Summer 1999.

22 **The Roper Survey:** Schudson, *The Power of News,* p. 172.

25 **"The media world was invaded":** Henry Johnson Fisher award speech to the Magazine Publishers of America, January 29, 1992.

27 **Surveys showed a steady decline:** Pew Research Center for the People and the Press, Biennial Media Consumption Survey, "Internet Sapping Broadcast News Audience," June 11, 2000.
   **Even before:** May 1998 survey by Pew Research Center for the People and the Press; 1996 survey by Princeton Survey Research Associates for the Radio and Television News Directors Foundation's News in the Next Century project.
   **In another Pew survey:** Pew Research Center for the People and the Press, "Internet Sapping Broadcast News Audience," June 11, 2000.

28 **"Moreover, if one expands the definition":** "Changing Definitions of News," Proj-

ect for Excellence in Journalism, the Medill News Service Washington Bureau and the Committee of Concerned Journalists, 1999. The study, posted on the Project for Excellence in Journalism Web site at www.journalism.org, examined 6,020 stories in sixteen news outlets ranging over a span of twenty years.

## *Chapter Three:* News That Makes a Difference

35   **One Scientology lawyer:** Feffer's quotation and all the details from Frantz's findings that appear in this chapter are taken from Frantz's original story, which ran in the *New York Times* on March 9, 1997.

## *Chapter Four:* Newspapers: Where the News (Mostly) Comes From

72   **The *News & Observer* newsroom:** Some metropolitan newspapers have staffs of fewer than 100; the *Los Angeles Times* and the *New York Times* each have more than 1,100 in their newsrooms. The *News & Observer* staff is relatively large for a paper with its circulation.

81   **Ashley Halsey, then the national editor:** Like nearly all papers, the *Inquirer*'s space for news rises and falls depending on the amount of advertising sold, so the minimum news hole would grow toward the end of the week, as the paper got fatter with ads for weekend shopping. The *New York Times* and the *Washington Post* have fixed news holes every day, regardless of the advertising.

83   **The prevailing ethos:** The quotation comes from an article by Charles Layton, "What Do Readers Really Want?," *American Journalism Review,* March 1999. The article was part of the Project on the State of the American Newspaper, an ambitious effort sponsored by the Pew Charitable Trusts and run by the University of Maryland's journalism school, which publishes *American Journalism Review.* Gene Roberts, the former Philadelphia editor and now a University of Maryland professor, was its leader. Roberts commissioned some of the country's best journalists to study various aspects of newspapering. We have drawn again and again on their good work.

93   **Geneva Overholser, the former:** Overholser, "Editor, Inc.," *American Journalism Review,* December 1998.

95   **In 1964:** Figures from the Newspaper Association of America available at www.naa.org/marketscope/databank/tdnpr1299.htm on the Internet.

97   **Gene Roberts saw this problem:** Roberts in *American Journalism Review,* December 1993. It's also true that market research can be plain wrong. We discovered this in the mid-1990s, when we asked our market researcher to poll *Post* readers on their favorite columnists in the paper. The answers were frustrating: According to the findings, readers liked the columnists pretty much identically. There were no big favorites and no unpopular ones. But then we noticed an oddity: One of the columnists who enjoyed pretty much the same regard as all the others was the late Carl Rowan, a well-known figure from his television appearances but not a columnist for the *Post.* The researcher had included his name by mistake, and our readers had responded to it mistakenly.
     **A particularly horrific example:** Quoted by Alicia C. Shepard in *American Journalism Review,* September 1996.

98   **When asked why:** The quotations are taken from a 1995 publication of the American Society of Newspaper Editors.

99 **The newspaper industry's share:** Figures from the Newspaper Association of America available at www.naa.org/marketscope/databank/ADExp9897.htm on the Internet.

104 **In 1998, one of the leading market researchers:** The quotation comes from Charles Layton, "What Do Readers Really Want?," *American Journalism Review,* March 1999.

108 **Later, Stephen Engelberg:** Engelberg in *American Journalism Review,* March 1999.

*Chapter Five:* The Network News

113 **We watched the 2000 version:** Our interview with Rather took place on June 16, 2000.

118 **We watched the *Nightly News:*** The Brokaw interview took place on May 18, 2000.

122 **The *ABC World News Tonight* on the night:** The interview was on April 24, 2000.

124 **By 2000, 281 million Americans owned:** According to the *Statistical Abstract of the United States* (1999), the average viewership was 4.3 hours a day in 1997. But the Television Bureau of Advertising, using Nielsen data, said it was nearly 7.5 hours daily.

**Later everyone could hear:** Americans have always been attracted to news sources that brought the news, effortlessly, to their ears and eyes. Radio—itself a new medium that spread through the society only in the 1930s—supplanted newspapers as the public's principal source of news during World War II, according to public opinion polls.

125 **Cronkite, perhaps the most influential personality:** Walter Cronkite, *A Reporter's Life* (New York: Alfred A. Knopf, 1996), p. 358.

**The text of Cronkite's evening news:** Our researcher, Douglas Steinke, made this interesting calculation: In a typical ninety-minute broadcast of the most substantive news program on radio, National Public Radio's *All Things Considered,* listeners hear about 13,000 words. The daily *Washington Post* contains about 110,000 words; the *New York Times* about 105,000.

**A news piece lasting:** Interview with the authors, October 1999.

127 **Broadcasters made elaborate promises:** See Newton N. Minow and Craig L. Lamay, *Abandoned in the Wasteland: Children, Television, and the First Amendment* (New York: Hill & Wang, 1995), pp. 58–104.

128 **In those days network executives:** Blair Clark, general manager of CBS News in the early 1960s, and Sandy Socolow, a CBS executive from the 1950s to the 1980s, in interviews.

132 **Salant wrote a preface for this rule book:** The quote is from Susan and Bill Buzenberg, eds., *Salant, CBS and the Battle for the Soul of Broadcast Journalism: The Memoirs of Richard S. Salant* (Boulder, Colo.: Westview Press, 1999), p. 192.

133 **But corporate headquarters didn't increase:** Interview, May 2000.

**By 1983 the number:** Edward Bliss Jr., *Now the News: The Story of Broadcast Journalism* (New York: Columbia University Press, 1991), p. 435.

134 **Gordon Manning, a charming and hard-driving:** Peter J. Boyer, *Who Killed CBS?: The Undoing of America's Number One News Network* (New York: Random House, 1988), p. 89.

**By 1982 the CBS News budget:** Boyer, Ibid., p. 90.

136 **Rather's blast didn't cause:** CBS News itself chose to ignore the substance of Rather's speech. On the *CBS Morning News* the next morning, host Harry Smith

noted only that Rather had given a speech to the convention on the occasion of the U.S. Postal Service issuing a stamp in honor of Murrow. This was Smith's entire report, including a snippet of film from Rather's speech:

> *And a man who was a legend here at CBS News has been given the stamp of approval by the U.S. Postal Service. The late Edward R. Murrow is being honored with his own postage stamp. In Miami yesterday, Dan Rather unveiled the new stamp at the Annual Convention of Radio and Television News Directors.*
> Dan Rather: *Ed Murrow was the best. Almost sixty years after he started, almost thirty years after his death and still the best.*
> Smith: *The Murrow stamp will be available starting in January.*

138   **In fact, in 2000, the only network news division:** "NBC to Report Record Revenue," *Broadcasting & Cable*, December 4, 2000.

141   **Amazingly, the humiliation of that reversal:** Fox's call was made by John Ellis, a journalist who is also George W. Bush's first cousin. Ellis later acknowledged that he had talked on the phone during election night with Bush and his brother Jeb, governor of Florida.

        **This didn't deter the networks:** According to Edelman, the VNS model at 2:10 a.m. was projecting that there were just under 180,000 Florida votes still uncounted, with Bush then ahead by 51,433. But both numbers were wildly wrong. At that moment there were nearly 360,000 outstanding votes, and Bush's real lead (misunderstood at that hour because of an error in the vote reported by Brevard County that the VNS computers could not catch) was just 27,085.

146   **Jeff Greenfield:** *Los Angeles Times*, September 1, 2000.

148   **Lack's news division:** "NBC to Report Record Revenue," *Broadcasting & Cable*, December 4, 2000.

        **"I am America's news leader":** Interview with Bill Carter, *New York Times*, November 26, 1997.

153   **One prominent television executive:** quoted in "Networks Move to Revive Foreign News," by Jim Rutenberg, *New York Times*, September 24, 2001.

## *Chapter Six:* Local Television News: Live at 4, 5, 6 and 11

159   **Unlike newspaper reporters:** John H. McManus of the University of California has done an original study of four local television news operations in California. He found that reporters typically spent half as much time reporting and preparing their stories as they spent traveling. See John H. McManus, *Market-Driven Journalism: Let the Citizen Beware?* (Thousand Oaks, Calif.: Sage Publications, 1994).

168   **Crime and disaster:** This figure represents more annual profit than is made by all but a handful of America's biggest newspapers.

169   **And it means making the story:** McManus, *Market-Driven Journalism*, pp. 162–63.

170   **An exhaustive 1999 study:** Tom Rosenstiel, Carl Gottlieb and Lee Ann Brady, "Quality Brings Higher Ratings, But Enterprise Is Disappearing," *Columbia Journalism Review*, November–December 1999.

171   **But the top-rated stations:** "Awash in Revenue from Thousands of Political Ads, TV Stations Offer Mere Seconds of Candidate Discourse," June 13, 2000, report by Alliance for Better Campaigns, which is seeking free airtime for candidates during election campaigns. The study was part of "Dollars vs. Discourse," a research project funded by the Alliance in conjunction with the Norman Lear Center at the Annenberg School for Communication at the University of Southern California

and the Annenberg Public Policy Center at the University of Pennsylvania. More results of the project can be seen at www.bettercampaigns.org.

**A University of Southern California study:** Martin Kaplan and Matthew L. Hale, "Where Was the Television News?," in *The 1998 Governor's Race: An Inside Look at the Candidates and Their Campaign by the People Who Managed Them,* ed. Gerald C. Lubenow (Berkeley: Institute of Governmental Studies Press, 1999).

**A similar national study of coverage:** "Local TV Coverage of the 2000 General Election," Norman Lear Center Campaign Media Monitoring Project, University of Southern California, Annenberg School for Communication, February 2001.

174  **General Electric's NBC:** Other big owners of local television stations include many of the big newspaper companies. For example: Tribune Company owned 23 local television stations in 2001. Gannett owned 22 TV stations. Belo Corporation, owner of the *Dallas Morning News,* controlled 19 stations. Cox, owner of the *Atlanta Journal-Constitution,* had 15 stations. Media General, owner of 25 newspapers, including the *Tampa Tribune* and the *Richmond Times-Dispatch,* owned 26 TV stations. The New York Times Company owned 8 local television stations, and the Washington Post Company had 6. Two Spanish-language television networks, Univision, with 25 local U.S. stations, and Telemundo, with 10 stations, were among the fastest-growing station owners. See "The Top 25 Television Groups," *Broadcasting & Cable,* April 23, 2001.

175  **In annual surveys:** Radio and Television News Directors Association Web site, www.rtnda.com/research/staff.shtml.

**When asked in these other surveys:** Rosenstiel, Gottlieb and Brady, "Quality Brings Higher Ratings."

**"Perhaps the best explanation":** Ibid.

176  **"The business of television":** Lansing delivered the remarks at a Poynter Institute for Media Studies seminar in New York titled "Journalism Values in an Era of Change," February 15, 1996. The transcript of the session is available online at http://www.poynter.org/dj/projects/jrnvalues/jv96a.htm.

**When a participant mentioned:** Freedom Forum panel, "As Good as It Can Get: The Best Local Newscast of Them All," Arlington, Virginia, November 8, 1999.

177  **New York's WCBS broadcast a news story:** *Electronic Media,* April 17, 2000.

178  **" 'If it bleeds, it leads' ":** *Not in the Public Interest: Local TV News in America,* Rocky Mountain Media Watch, Denver, March 11, 1998.

**The turning point came:** Pete Noyes, "L.A.'s Twisted Pursuit of the News," *Christian Science Monitor,* May 8, 1998.

181  **Frank Magid, founder of Frank Magid Associates:** Joseph Lelyveld, "Consultant Helps TV Decide What's News," *New York Times,* December 25, 1975.

184  **Frank Magid, who for three decades:** Remarks made at "What Is Journalism? Who Is a Journalist?" forum held at Northwestern University's Medill School of Journalism, Evanston, Illinois, November 6, 1997.

**Nevertheless, all local stations':** Rosenstiel, Gottlieb and Brady, "Quality Brings Higher Ratings." The study team graded newscasts on, among other things, the subjects and focus of their stories, the originality of their reporting, the number of sources, their expertise and viewpoints on each story and the relevance of their coverage to their communities and their needs.

190  **This study concluded that:** *Columbia Journalism Review,* November–December 2000.

193  **"Local television journalists":** McManus, *Market-Driven Journalism.*

*Chapter Seven:* The New News

206 **"Like reporters, he disseminates":** Tom Goldstein, "Journalist or Kangaroo," *Columbia Journalism Review,* February 2001.

**Even the editor of the supermarket tabloid:** Howard Kurtz, "Out There; It's 10 Past Monica, America. Do You Know Where Matt Drudge Is?" *Washington Post,* March 28, 1999.

**Drudge brushes off such criticism:** Address before the National Press Club, June 2, 1998.

208 **According to one survey:** Pew Research Center for the People and the Press, "Internet Sapping Broadcast News Audience," June 11, 2000.

215 **Research by the Pew Center:** Pew Research Center for the People and the Press, "Internet Election News Audience Seeks Convenience, Familiar Names," January 2001.

217 **The Pew Research Center's 2000 study:** Pew Research Center for the People and the Press, "Internet Sapping Broadcast News Audience," June 11, 2000.


*Chapter Eight:* News Values

225 **By contrast, "John Jr.'s accident":** "JFK to JFK Jr.: The Age of the Media Unbound," speech delivered by Robert MacNeil, Princeton University, Princeton, N.J., November 22, 1999.

226 **An interesting poll taken soon afterward:** Pew Research Center for the People and the Press, "JFK Jr. Tragedy Attracts Huge Audience," July 27, 1999.

229 **Michael Oreskes, who was then:** William Powers, *National Journal,* May 15, 1999.

232 **A study of media coverage:** Bill Kovach and Tom Rosenstiel, *Warp Speed: America in the Age of Mixed Media* (New York: Century Foundation Press, 1999), p. 17.

233 **Right from the start, Coulter:** Howard Kurtz, *Washington Post,* October 16, 1998.

234 **What were the thirty-year-old's:** Paul Farhi, *Washington Post,* May 25, 2000.

235 **When a *New York Times* reporter:** Bill Carter, *New York Times,* June 26, 2000.

**An extensive survey of voters:** Pew Research Center for the People and the Press, "Tough Job Communicating with Voters," February 2000.

236 **In an exhaustive study of their content:** Matthew C. Ehrlich, "Not Ready for Prime Time: Tabloid and Investigative TV Journalism," in *The Big Chill: Investigative Reporting in the Current Media Environment,* eds. Marilyn Greenwald and Joseph Brent (Ames: Iowa State University Press, 2000), p. 115.

239 **By one careful count:** Finding of the Tyndall Report, a service that keeps track of the content of television news, reported in the *New York Times,* September 24, 2001.

**At many times during the day:** Lisa De Moraes, *Washington Post,* November 15, 2000.

241 **Like Cunningham's readers in Rockford:** "The Power to Grow Readership," research from the Impact Study of Newspaper Readership, conducted by the Readership Institute, Media Management Center, at Northwestern University, sponsored by the Newspaper Association of America and the American Society of Newspaper Editors, April 2001.

241 **When in 1999 the Associated Press asked:** "The Future of Newspapers," report prepared for the Associated Press by Clark, Martire & Bartolomeo, June 1999.

**A number of newspapers reduced or eliminated:** See "Newspapers Overseas Press Corps," *American Journalism Review,* June 2000, and "Goodbye, World," *American Journalism Review,* November 1998.

242 **No newspaper at the time:** "The State of the American Newspaper," *American Jour-*

*nalism Review,* April 1999. The *Washington Post* again assigned a reporter to Interior in 2001.

**The federal government is covered rigorously:** *Statistical Abstract of the United States,* 1999 edition.

243 **Even good papers often send only:** *American Journalism Review,* July–August 1998. The project revisited the issue a year later (*American Journalism Review,* July–August 1999) and found a small increase in the number of reporters assigned to state capitals since the original study—a heartening sign, if a modest one.

244 **Consider the arrangement between Mercy Hospital and WBAL:** For accounts of the arrangement see *Business Week,* February 28, 2000; NPR's *Morning Edition,* March 28, 2000; *Baltimore Sun,* April 5, 2000.

245 **A 1998 poll conducted for:** "Local Television News Ethics Study of News Directors and the American Public for the Radio and Television News Directors Association Foundation," booklet published by the RTNDA in 1998.

**Worse were the results of a survey:** "Two-way Street," *Editor & Publisher,* December 4, 1999.

247 **Surveys showed a steadily declining number:** Pew Research Center for the People and the Press, "Internet Sapping Broadcast News Audience," June 11, 2000.

**Comparative surveys showed that Americans were:** "Mixed Messages About Press Freedom on Both Sides of Atlantic," Times Mirror Center for the People and the Press, March 16, 1994.

249 **In 1988 there were 13,541 magazines:** Figures provided by the Magazine Publishers of America.

250 **Douglas Bailey, a prophetic voice:** Quoted in the *Washington Post,* January 17, 1989.

## *Chapter Nine:* The Future of News

252 **In the summer of 1997 a group:** The full "Statement of Concern" can be found online at http://www.journalism.org/ccj/about/statement.html.

253 **More than 70 percent agreed that:** Survey conducted by the Committee for Concerned Journalists and the Pew Research Center for the People and the Press, "Striking the Balance: Audience Interests, Business Pressures and Journalists' Values," March 30, 1999.

**Three prominent social scientists:** Howard Gardner, Mihaly Csikszentmihalyi and William Damon, *Good Work: When Excellence and Ethics Meet* (New York: Basic Books, 2001).

257 **And as the Internet grows more popular:** Pew Research Center for the People and the Press, "Internet Sapping Broadcast News Audience," June 11, 2000.

# Acknowledgments

A great many people in the news business made this book possible by sharing their experiences and insights. Most of them did so without knowing how they might look in the final product, a form of courage we would like to acknowledge and salute. One of the reasons we love our business is that so many engaging, smart people populate it. Most of our sources are named somewhere in the book or its chapter notes, so we will not print another long list here. We thank them all.

Several individuals and organizations were helpful beyond the call of duty or politeness. Among them were the three network anchors, Tom Brokaw, Peter Jennings and Dan Rather; Andy Lack, now the president of NBC; Merrill Brown and his team at MSNBC; editors Joe Lelyveld and Dean Baquet and reporter Doug Frantz at the *New York Times* (Baquet has since moved to the *Los Angeles Times*); news director Bob Long and his colleagues at WRC television in Washington; Alan Frank and the news directors of Post-Newsweek stations; *Tampa Tribune* editor Gil Thelan; WFLA-TV news director Dan Bradley; managing editor Melanie Sill and her colleagues at the *Raleigh News & Observer;* and Jay Harris, former publisher of the *San Jose Mercury News.* Obviously, no one who helped deserves any blame for the way it turned out. That belongs to us.

We're especially grateful to our extraordinary agent, Binky Urban, who encouraged us throughout our labors; to Jon Segal of Knopf, our editor, who knocked some sense into us early on about how best to present our material, then sharpened and improved every chapter; to Professor Michael Schudson of the University of California in San Diego, who educated us and then gave our manuscript a critical, careful reading; and to six colleagues and friends who also scrubbed the first draft for us: Steve Coll, Bo Jones, David Maraniss, Tom Powers, Gene Robinson and Mary Ann Werner. Toni Rachiele was a helpful, careful copy editor. Douglas Steinke, a new graduate of the Columbia University School of Journalism when we met him, and now a reporter for the *Providence Journal,* was our resourceful and systematic researcher.

Financial support from the Pew Charitable Trusts allowed us to hire a researcher and financed our travel around the country to interview and observe. Tom Rosenstiel, director of the Project for Excellence in Journalism, and Don Kimelman of the Pew Charitable Trusts made this possible, and we thank them.

Most profoundly, we are grateful to all of our colleagues, past and present, at the *Washington Post*, from Katharine and Don Graham and Bo Jones in the executive suite to the hundreds of talented journalists in the newsroom. Don and Bo indulged our determination to write this book, and to use in it examples from our own experiences at the *Post*. But this book is our personal effort; the Post Company bears no responsibility for it.

The two of us have spent our adult lives at the *Post*, giving it our best energies and taking from it the most extraordinary education imaginable. The people of the *Post* are our extended family, and there is no way adequately to describe the gifts of friendship, humor and wisdom they have given us over the years. The creator of the modern *Post* was Benjamin Crowninshield Bradlee, the greatest editor of his time, who showed us the way.

Janice Downie and Hannah Jopling lost their husbands for a lot of weekends to this project, yet still agreed to be helpful critics and advisers. We both know we couldn't have done it without them.

# Index

## A Note About the Authors

LEONARD DOWNIE JR. and ROBERT G. KAISER have been colleagues on the *Washington Post* since 1964. From 1991 to 1998 they ran the paper together, Downie as executive editor and Kaiser as managing editor. Downie still holds that job; Kaiser has become associate editor of the paper.

Having begun his newspaper career as a reporter, Downie became an editor early on and helped guide the *Post*'s Watergate coverage. He was the paper's metropolitan editor, London correspondent, national editor and managing editor before becoming executive editor in 1991. This is his fourth book. He has four children and lives in Washington with his wife, Janice.

Kaiser spent nearly twenty years as a reporter for the *Post,* based at different times in Washington, London, Saigon and Moscow. He was the editor of the *Post*'s Sunday Outlook section and assistant managing editor for national news before becoming managing editor in 1991. Since 1998 he has been a roving correspondent. This is his sixth book. He has two daughters and lives in Washington with his wife, Hannah.

*A Note on the Type*

This book was set in Minion, a typeface produced by the
Adobe Corporation specifically for the Macintosh personal
computer, and released in 1990. Designed by Robert Slim-
bach, Minion combines the classic characteristics of old-
style faces with the full complement of weights required for
modern typesetting.

Composed by Creative Graphics,
Allentown, Pennsylvania
Printed and bound by Berryville Graphics,
Berryville, Virginia
Designed by Anthea Lingeman